Mastering Spring Cloud

Build self-healing, microservices-based, distributed systems using Spring Cloud

Piotr Mińkowski

BIRMINGHAM - MUMBAI

Mastering Spring Cloud

Commissioning Editor: Richa Tripathi
Acquisition Editor: Karan Sadawana
Content Development Editor: Lawrence Veigas
Technical Editor: Adhithya Haridas
Copy Editor: Safis Editing
Project Coordinator: Prajakta Naik
Proofreader: Safis Editing
Indexer: Rekha Nair
Graphics: Jisha Chirayil
Production Coordinator: Arvindkumar Gupta

First published: April 2018

Production reference: 1250418

Published by Packt Publishing Ltd.
Livery Place
35 Livery Street
Birmingham
B3 2PB, UK.

ISBN 978-1-78847-543-3

www.packtpub.com

`mapt.io`

Mapt is an online digital library that gives you full access to over 5,000 books and videos, as well as industry leading tools to help you plan your personal development and advance your career. For more information, please visit our website.

Why subscribe?

- Spend less time learning and more time coding with practical eBooks and Videos from over 4,000 industry professionals

- Improve your learning with Skill Plans built especially for you

- Get a free eBook or video every month

- Mapt is fully searchable

- Copy and paste, print, and bookmark content

PacktPub.com

Did you know that Packt offers eBook versions of every book published, with PDF and ePub files available? You can upgrade to the eBook version at `www.PacktPub.com` and as a print book customer, you are entitled to a discount on the eBook copy. Get in touch with us at `service@packtpub.com` for more details.

At `www.PacktPub.com`, you can also read a collection of free technical articles, sign up for a range of free newsletters, and receive exclusive discounts and offers on Packt books and eBooks.

Contributors

About the author

Piotr Mińkowski has more than 10 years of experience working as a developer and an architect in the banking and telecommunications sectors. He specializes in Java as well as in technologies, tools, and frameworks associated with it. Now, he is working at Play, a mobile operator in Poland, where he is responsible for the IT systems architecture. Here, he helps the organization migrate from monoliths/SOA to a microservices-based architecture, and also helps set up full Continuous Integration and Delivery environments.

About the reviewer

Samer ABDELKAFI has over 13 years of experience as a software architect and engineer, with a major focus on open source technologies. He has contributed to numerous and diverse projects in different sectors, such as banking, insurance, education, public services, and utility billing. In the end of 2016, he created DEVACT, a company specializing in information technology consulting. He also reviewed a book titled *Spring MVC Blueprints*. In addition to his day job, Samer shares his experience in his blog, writing articles related to Java and web technologies.

Packt is searching for authors like you

If you're interested in becoming an author for Packt, please visit `authors.packtpub.com` and apply today. We have worked with thousands of developers and tech professionals, just like you, to help them share their insight with the global tech community. You can make a general application, apply for a specific hot topic that we are recruiting an author for, or submit your own idea.

Table of Contents

Preface

Developing, deploying, and operating cloud applications should be as easy as local applications. This should be the governing principle behind any cloud platform, library, or tool. Spring Cloud makes it easy to develop JVM applications for the cloud. In this book, we introduce you to Spring Cloud and help you master its features.

You will learn to configure the Spring Cloud server and run the Eureka server to enable service registration and discovery. Then you will learn about techniques related to load balancing and circuit breaking and utilize all the features of the Feign client. We then dive into advanced topics where you will learn to implement distributed tracing solutions for Spring Cloud and build message-driven microservice architectures.

Who this book is for

This book appeals to developers keen to take advantage of Spring Cloud, an open source library which helps developers quickly build distributed systems. Knowledge of Java and Spring Framework will be helpful, but no prior exposure to Spring Cloud is required.

What this book covers

Chapter 1, *Introduction to Microservices*, will introduce you to the microservices architecture, cloud environment, etc. You will learn the difference between a microservice based application and a monolith application while also learning how to migrate to a microservices application.

Chapter 2, *Spring for Microservices*, will introduce you Spring Boot framework. You will learn how to effectively use it to create microservice application. We will cover such topics like creating REST API using Spring MVC annotations, providing API documentation using Swagger2, and exposing health checks and metrics using Spring Boot Actuator endpoints.

Chapter 3, *Spring Cloud Overview*, will provide a short description of the main projects being a part of Spring Cloud. It will focus on describing the main patterns implemented by Spring Cloud and assigning them to the particular projects.

Chapter 4, *Service Discovery*, will describe a service discovery pattern with Spring Cloud Netflix Eureka. You will learn how to run Eureka server in standalone mode and how to run multiple server instances with peer-to-peer replication. You will also learn how to enable discovery on the client side and register these clients in different zones.

Chapter 5, *Distributed Configuration with Spring Cloud Config*, will describe how use distributed configuration with Spring Cloud Config in your applications. You will learn how to enable different backend repositories of property sources and push change notifications using Spring Cloud Bus. We will compare discovery first bootstrap and config first bootstrap approaches to illustrate integration between discovery service and configuration server.

Chapter 6, *Communication Between Microservices*, will describe the most important elements taking a part in an inter-service communication: HTTP clients and load balancers. You will learn how to use Spring RestTemplate, Ribbon, and Feign clients with or without service discovery.

Chapter 7, *Advanced Load Balancing and Circuit Breakers*, will described more advanced topics related to inter-service communication between microservices. You will learn how to implement different load balancing algorithms with Ribbon client, enabling circuit breaker pattern using Hystrix and using Hystrix dashboard to monitor communication statistics.

Chapter 8, *Routing and Filtering with API Gateway*, will compare two projects used as an API gateway and proxy for Spring Cloud applications: Spring Cloud Netlix Zuul and Spring Cloud Gateway. You will learn how to integrate them with service discovery and create simple and more advanced routing and filtering rules.

Chapter 9, *Distributed Logging and Tracing*, will introduce some popular tools for collecting and analizing logging and tracing information generated by microservices. You will learn how to use Spring Cloud Sleuth to append tracing information and correlating messages. We will run sample applications that integrates with Elastic Stack in order to sent there log messages, and Zipkin to collect traces.

Chapter 10, *Additional Configuration and Discovery Features*, will introduce two popular products used for service discovery and distributed configuration: Consul and ZooKeeper. You will learn how to run these tools locally, and intergrate your Spring Cloud applications with them.

Chapter 11, *Message-Driven Microservices*, will guide you how to provide asynchronous, message-driven communication between your microservices. You will learn how to integrate RabbitMQ and Apache Kafka message brokers with your Spring Cloud application to enable asynchronous one-to-one and publish/subscribe communication styles.

Chapter 12, *Securing an API*, will describe varius ways of securing your microservices. We will implement a system consisting of all previously introduced elements, that communicates with each other over SSL. You will also learn how to use OAuth2 and JWT token to authorize requests coming to your API.

Chapter 13, *Testing Java Microservices*, will describe different strategies of microservices testing. It will focus on showing consumer-driven contract tests, especially useful in microservice-based environment. You will how to use such frameworks like Hoverfly, Pact, Spring Cloud Contract, Gatling for implemnting different types of automated tests.

Chapter 14, *Docker Support*, will provide a short introduction to Docker. It will focus on describing most commonly used Docker commands, which are used for running and monitoring microservices in containerized environment. You will also learn how to build and run containers using popular continuous integration server - Jenkins, and deploy them on Kubernetes platform.

Chapter 15, *Spring Microservices on Cloud Platforms*, will introduce two popular cloud platforms that support Java applications: Pivotal Cloud Foundry and Heroku. You will learn how to deploy, start, scale and monitor your applications on these platforms using command-line tools or web console.

To get the most out of this book

In order to successfully read through this book and work out all the code samples, we expect readers to fulfill the following requirements:

- An active internet connection
- Java 8+
- Docker
- Maven
- Git client

Download the example code files

You can download the example code files for this book from your account at `www.packtpub.com`. If you purchased this book elsewhere, you can visit `www.packtpub.com/support` and register to have the files emailed directly to you.

You can download the code files by following these steps:

1. Log in or register at `www.packtpub.com`.
2. Select the **SUPPORT** tab.
3. Click on **Code Downloads & Errata**.
4. Enter the name of the book in the **Search** box and follow the onscreen instructions.

Once the file is downloaded, please make sure that you unzip or extract the folder using the latest version of:

- WinRAR/7-Zip for Windows
- Zipeg/iZip/UnRarX for Mac
- 7-Zip/PeaZip for Linux

The code bundle for the book is also hosted on GitHub at `https://github.com/PacktPublishing/Mastering-Spring-Cloud`. We also have other code bundles from our rich catalog of books and videos available at `https://github.com/PacktPublishing/`. Check them out!

Conventions used

There are a number of text conventions used throughout this book.

`CodeInText`: Indicates code words in text, database table names, folder names, filenames, file extensions, pathnames, dummy URLs, user input, and Twitter handles. Here is an example: "The last available version of the HTTP API endpoint, `http://localhost:8889/client-service-zone3.yml`, returns data identical to the input file."

A block of code is set as follows:

```
<dependency>
  <groupId>org.springframework.cloud</groupId>
  <artifactId>spring-cloud-config-server</artifactId>
</dependency>
```

When we wish to draw your attention to a particular part of a code block, the relevant lines or items are set in bold:

```
spring:
 rabbitmq:
  host: 192.168.99.100
  port: 5672
```

Any command-line input or output is written as follows:

```
$ curl -H "X-Vault-Token: client" -X GET
http://192.168.99.100:8200/v1/secret/client-service
```

Bold: Indicates a new term, an important word, or words that you see onscreen. For example, words in menus or dialog boxes appear in the text like this. Here is an example: "In Google Chrome, you can import a PKCS12 keystore by going to section **Settings | Show advanced settings... | HTTPS/SSL | Manage certificates**."

Warnings or important notes appear like this.

Tips and tricks appear like this.

Get in touch

Feedback from our readers is always welcome.

General feedback: Email `feedback@packtpub.com` and mention the book title in the subject of your message. If you have questions about any aspect of this book, please email us at `questions@packtpub.com`.

Errata: Although we have taken every care to ensure the accuracy of our content, mistakes do happen. If you have found a mistake in this book, we would be grateful if you would report this to us. Please visit `www.packtpub.com/submit-errata`, selecting your book, clicking on the Errata Submission Form link, and entering the details.

Piracy: If you come across any illegal copies of our works in any form on the Internet, we would be grateful if you would provide us with the location address or website name. Please contact us at `copyright@packtpub.com` with a link to the material.

If you are interested in becoming an author: If there is a topic that you have expertise in and you are interested in either writing or contributing to a book, please visit `authors.packtpub.com`.

Reviews

Please leave a review. Once you have read and used this book, why not leave a review on the site that you purchased it from? Potential readers can then see and use your unbiased opinion to make purchase decisions, we at Packt can understand what you think about our products, and our authors can see your feedback on their book. Thank you!

For more information about Packt, please visit `packtpub.com`.

Introduction to Microservices

Microservices are one of the hottest trends to emerge in the IT world during the last few years. It is relatively easy to identify the most important reasons for their growing popularity. Both their advantages and disadvantages are well known, although what we describe as disadvantages can be easily solved using the right tools. The advantages that they offer include scalability, flexibility, and independent delivery; these are the reasons for its rapidly growing popularity. There are a few earlier IT trends that had some influence over this growth in the popularity of microservices. I'm referring to trends such as the usage of common cloud-based environments and the migration from relational databases to NoSQL.

Before discussing this at length, let's see the topics we will cover in this chapter:

- Cloud-native development with Spring Cloud
- The most important elements in microservices-based architecture
- Models of interservice communication
- Introduction to circuit breakers and fallback patterns

The blessings of microservices

The concept of microservices defines an approach to the architecture of IT systems that divides an application into a collection of loosely coupled services that implement business requirements. In fact, this is a variant of the concept of **service-oriented architecture** (**SOA**). One of the most important benefits of a migration to microservices-based architecture is an ability to perform continuous delivery of large and complex applications.

By now, you have probably had an opportunity to read some books or articles about microservices. I think that most of them would have given you a detailed description of their advantages and drawbacks. There are many advantages to using microservices. The first is that microservices are relatively small and easy to understand for a new developer in a project. We usually want to make sure that the change in the code performed in one place would not have an unwanted effect on all the other modules of our application. With microservices, we can have more certainty about this because we implement only a single business area, unlike monolithic applications where sometimes even seemingly unrelated functionalities are put in the same boat. That is not all. I have noticed that, usually, it is easier to maintain expected code quality in small microservices than in a large monolith where many developers have introduced their changes.

The second thing I like about microservices architecture concerns division. Until now, when I had to deal with complex enterprise systems, I always saw that dividing the system into subsystems was done according to other subsystems. For example, telecommunication organizations always have a billing subsystem. Then you create a subsystem that hides the billing complexity and provides an API. Then you find out that you need data that can't be stored in the billing system because it is not easily customizable. So you create another subsystem. This leads in effect to you building a complicated subsystem mesh, which is not easy to understand, especially if you are a new employee in the organization. With microservices, you do not have problems such as this. If they are well-designed, every microservice should be responsible for an entire selected area. In some cases, those areas are similar regardless of the sector in which an organization is active.

Building microservices with Spring Framework

Although the concept of microservices has been an important topic for some years, there are still not many stable frameworks that support all the features needed to run full microservices environments. Since the beginning of my adventure with microservices, I have been trying to keep up with the latest frameworks and find out the features developed towards the needs of microservices. There are some other interesting solutions, such as Vert.x or Apache Camel, but none of them is a match for Spring Framework.

Spring Cloud implements all proven patterns that are used in microservice-based architecture, such as service registries, the configuration server, circuit breakers, cloud buses, OAuth2 patterns, and API gateways. It has a strong community, therefore new features are released at a high frequency. It is based on Spring's open programming model used by millions of Java developers worldwide. It is also well-documented. You won't have any problems in finding many available examples of Spring Framework usage online.

Cloud-native development

Microservices are intrinsically linked to cloud-computing platforms, but the actual concept of microservices is nothing new. This approach has been applied in the IT development world for many years, but now, through the popularity of cloud solutions, it has evolved to a higher level. It is not hard to point out the reasons for this popularity. The use of a cloud offers you scalability, reliability, and low maintenance costs in comparison with on-premises solutions inside the organization. This has led to the rise of cloud-native application development approaches that are intended to give you the benefits from all of the advantages offered by cloud-like elastic scaling, immutable deployments, and disposable instances. It all comes down to one thing—decreasing the time and cost that is needed to meet new requirements. Today, software systems and applications are being improved continuously. If you have a traditional approach to development, based on monoliths, a code base grows and becomes too complex for modifications and maintenance. Introducing new features, frameworks, and technologies becomes hard, which in turn impacts innovations and inhibits new ideas. We can't argue with that.

There is also another side to this coin. Today, practically everyone thinks about migration to the cloud, partly because it's trendy. Does everyone need this? Certainly not. Those who are not absolutely sure about migrating their applications to a remote cloud provider, such as AWS, Azure, or Google, would like to at least have an on-premises private cloud or Docker containers. But will it really bring them the benefits that compensate for expenses incurred? It is worth answering that question before looking at cloud-native development and cloud platforms.

I'm not trying to dissuade you from using Spring Cloud—quite the opposite. We have to thoroughly understand what cloud-native development is. Here is a really fine definition:

> *"A native cloud application is a program that is specifically designed for a cloud computing environment as opposed to simply being migrated to the cloud."*

Spring is designed to accelerate your cloud-native development. Building an application with Spring Boot is very quick; I'll show you how to do this in detail in the next chapter. Spring Cloud implements microservice architecture patterns and helps us in using the most popular solutions from that field. Applications developed using these frameworks can easily be adapted to be deployed on Pivotal Cloud Foundry or Docker containers, but they might as well be launched in the traditional way as separated processes on one or more machines, and you would have the advantage of a microservices approach. Let's now dive into the microservices architecture.

Learning the microservices architecture

Let's imagine that a client approaches you, wanting you to design a solution for them. They need some kind of banking application that has to guarantee data consistency within the whole system. Our client had been using an Oracle database until now and has also purchased support from their side. Without thinking too much, we decide to design a monolithic application based on a relational data model. You can see a simplified diagram of the system's design here:

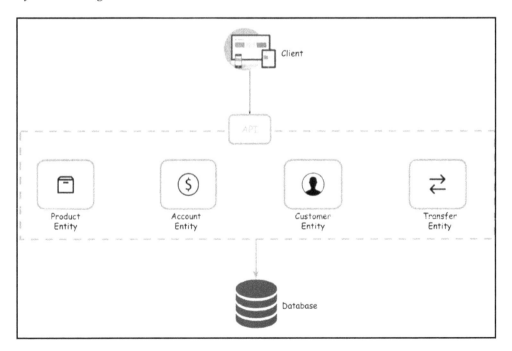

There are four entities that are mapped into the tables in the database:

- The first of them, **Customer**, stores and retrieves the list of active clients
- Every customer could have one or more accounts, which are operated by the **Account** entity
- The **Transfer** entity is responsible for performing all transfers of funds between accounts within the system
- There is also the **Product** entity that is created to store information such as the deposits and credits assigned to the clients

Without going into further details, the application exposes the API that provides all the necessary operations for realizing actions on the designed database. Of course, the implementation is in compliance with the three-layer model.

Consistency is not the most important requirement anymore; it is not even obligatory. The client expects a solution, but does not want the development to require the redeployment of the whole application. It should be scalable and should easily be able to extend new modules and functionalities. Additionally, the client does not put pressure on the developer to use Oracle or another relational database—not only that, but he would be happy to avoid using it. Are these sufficient reasons to decide on migrating to microservices? Let's just assume that they are. We divide our monolithic application into four independent microservices, each one of them with a dedicated database. In some cases, it can still be a relational database, while in others it can be a NoSQL database. Now, our system consists of many services that are independently built and run in our environment. Along with an increase in the number of microservices, there is a rising level of system complexity. We would like to hide that complexity from the external API client, which should not be aware that it talks to service *X* but not *Y*. The gateway is responsible for dynamically routing all requests to different endpoints. For example, the word *dynamically* means that it should be based on entries in the service discovery, which I'll talk about later in the section *Understanding the need for service discovery*.

Hiding invocations of specific services or dynamic routing is not the only function of an API gateway. Since it is the entry point to our system, it can be a great place to track important data, collect metrics of requests, and count other statistics. It can enrich requests or response headers in order to include some additional information that is usable by the applications inside the system. It should perform some security actions, such as authentication and authorization, and should be able to detect the requirements for each resource and reject requests that do not satisfy them. Here's a diagram that illustrates the sample system, consisting of four independent microservices, which is hidden from an external client behind an API gateway:

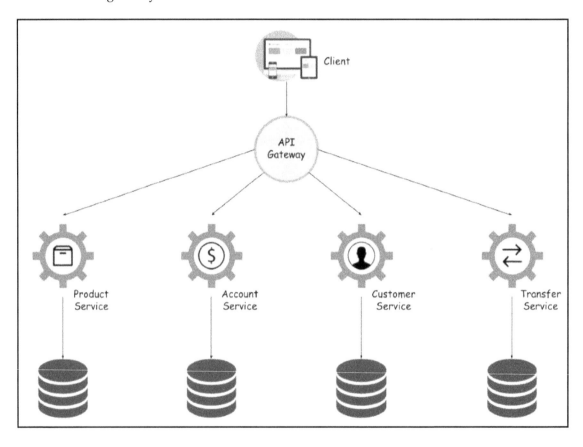

Understanding the need for service discovery

Let's imagine that we have already divided our monolithic application into smaller, independent services. From the outside, our system still looks the same as before, because its complexity is hidden behind the API gateway. Actually, there are not many microservices, but, there may well be many more. Additionally, each of them can interact with the others. That means that every microservice has to keep information about the others' network addresses. Maintaining such a configuration could be very troublesome, especially when it comes down to manually overwriting every configuration. And what if those addresses are changing dynamically after restart? The following diagram shows the calling routes between our example microservices:

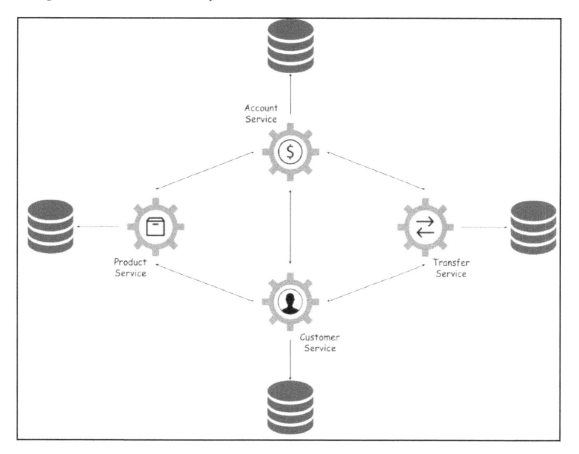

Service discovery is the automatic detection of devices and services offered by these devices on a computer network. In the case of microservice-based architecture, this is the necessary mechanism. Every service after startup should register itself in one central place that is accessible by all other services. The registration key should be the name of a service or an identificator, which has to be unique within the whole system in order to enable others to find and call the service using that name. Every single key with the given name has some values assigned to it. In the most common cases, these attributes indicate the network location of the service. To be more accurate, they indicate one of the instances of the microservice because it can be multiplied as independent applications running on different machines or ports. Sometimes it is possible to send some additional information, but it depends on the concrete service discovery provider. However, the important thing here is that under the one key, more than one instance of the same service may be registered. In addition to registration, each service gets a full list of the other services registered on the particular discovery server. Not only that, every microservice must be aware of any changes in the registration list. This may be achieved by periodically renewing the configuration earlier collected from the remote server.

Some solutions combine the usage of service discovery with the server configuration feature. When it comes right down to it, both approaches are pretty similar. The configuration of the server lets you centralize the management of all configuration files in your system. Usually, such a configuration is then a server as a REST web service. Before startup, every microservice tries to connect to the server and get the parameters prepared especially for it. One of the approaches stores such a configuration in the version control system—for example, Git. Then the configuration server updates its Git working copy and serves all properties as a JSON. In another approach, we can use solutions that store key-value pairs and fulfill the role of providers during the service discovery procedure. The most popular tools for this are Consul and Zookeeper. The following diagram illustrates an architecture of a system that consists of some microservices with a database backend that are registered in one central service known as a **discovery service**:

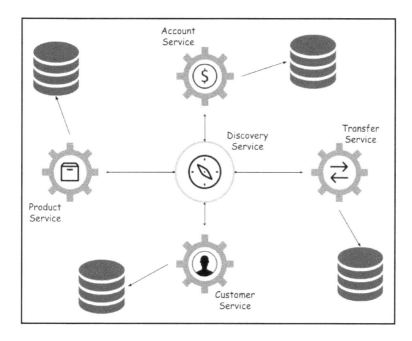

Communication between services

In order to guarantee the system's reliability, we cannot allow a situation where each service would have only one instance running. We usually aim to have a minimum of two running instances in case one of them experiences a failure. Of course, there could be more, but we'll keep it low for performance reasons. Anyway, multiple instances of the same service make it necessary to use load balancing for incoming requests. Firstly, the **load balancer** is usually built into an API gateway. This load balancer should get the list of registered instances from the discovery server. If there is no reason not to, then we usually use a round-robin rule that balances incoming traffic 50/50 between all running instances. The same rule also applies to load balancers on the microservices side.

The following diagram illustrates the most important components that are involved in interservice communication between multiple instances of two sample microservices:

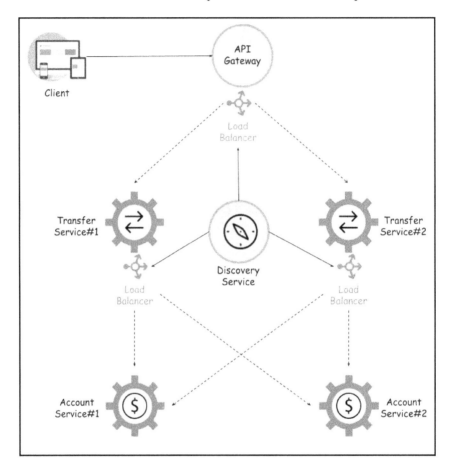

Most people, when they hear about microservices, consider it to consist of RESTful web services with JSON notation, but that's just one of the possibilities. We can use some other interaction styles, which, of course, apply not only to microservices-based architecture. The first categorization that should be performed is one-to-one or one-to-many communication. In one-to-one interaction, every incoming request is processed by exactly one service instance while, in one-to-many, it is processed by multiple service instances. But the most popular division criterion is whether the call is synchronous or asynchronous. Additionally, asynchronous communication can be divided into notifications. When a client sends a request to a service, but a reply is not expected, it can just perform a simple asynchronous call, which does not block a thread and replies asynchronously.

Furthermore, it is worth mentioning reactive microservices. Now, from version 5, Spring also supports this type of programming. There are also libraries with Reactive support for interaction with NoSQL databases, such as MongoDB or Cassandra. The last well-known communication type is publish-subscribe. This is a one-to-many interaction type where a client publishes a message that is then consumed by all listening services. Typically, this model is realized using message brokers, such as Apache Kafka, RabbitMQ, and ActiveMQ.

Failures and circuit breakers

We have discussed most of the important concepts related to the microservices architecture. Such mechanisms, such as service discovery, API gateways, and configuration servers, are useful elements that help us to create a reliable and efficient system. Even if you have considered many aspects of these while designing your system's architecture, you should always be prepared for failures. In many cases, the reasons for failures are totally beyond the control of the holder, such as network or database problems. Such errors can be particularly severe for microservice-based systems, where one input request is processed in many subsequent calls. The first good practice is to always use network timeouts when waiting for a response. If a single service has a performance problem, we should try to minimize the impact on the rest. It is better to send an error response than to wait on a reply for a long time, blocking other threads.

An interesting solution for the network timeout problems might be the **circuit breaker pattern**. It is a concept closely related to the microservice approach. A circuit breaker is responsible for counting successful and failed requests. If the error rate exceeds an assumed threshold, it trips and causes all further attempts to fail immediately. After a specific period of time, the API client should get back to sending requests, and if they succeed, it closes the circuit breaker. If there are many instances of each service available and one of them works slower than others, the result is that it is overlooked during the load balancing process. The second often-used mechanism for dealing with partial network failures is **fallback**. This is a logic that has to be performed when a request fails. For example, a service can return cached data, a default value, or an empty list of results. Personally, I'm not a big fan of this solution. I would prefer to propagate error code to other systems than return cached data or default values.

Summary

The big advantage of Spring Cloud is that it supports all the patterns and mechanisms we have looked at. These are also stable implementations, unlike some other frameworks. I'll describe in detail which of the patterns are supported by which Spring Cloud project in Chapter 3, *Spring Cloud Overview*.

In this chapter, we have discussed the most important concepts related to microservices architecture, such as cloud-native development, service discovery, distributed configuration, API gateways, and the circuit breaker pattern. I have attempted to present my point of view about the advantages and drawbacks of this approach in the development of enterprise applications. Then, I described the main patterns and solutions related to microservices. Some of these are well-known patterns that have been around for years and are treated as something new in the IT world. In this summary, I would like to turn your attention to some things. Microservices are cloud-native by their nature. Frameworks such as Spring Boot and Spring Cloud help you to accelerate your cloud-native development. The main motivation of migrating to cloud-native development is the ability to implement and deliver applications faster while maintaining high quality. In many cases, microservices help us to achieve this, but sometimes the monolithic approach is not a bad choice.

Although microservices are small and independent units, they are managed centrally. Information such as network location, configuration, logging files, and metrics should be stored in one central place. There are various types of tools and solutions that provide all these features. We will talk about them in detail in almost all of the chapters in this book. The Spring Cloud project is designed to help us in integrating with all that stuff. I hope to efficiently guide you through the most important integrations it offers.

Spring for Microservices

2

I don't know many Java developers who have never touched Spring Framework. Actually, it consists of so many projects and can be used with many other frameworks that sooner or later you will be forced to try it. Although experiences with Spring Boot are rather less common, it has quickly gained a lot of popularity. In comparison with Spring Framework, Spring Boot is a relatively new solution. Its actual version is 2, instead of 5 for Spring Framework. What was the purpose of its creation? What is the difference between a running application with Spring Boot instead of the standard Spring Framework way?

Topics we will cover in this chapter include:

- Using starters in order to enable additional features for the project
- Using Spring Web library for implementing services that expose REST API methods
- Customizing service configuration using properties and YAML files
- Documenting and providing the specification for exposed REST endpoints
- Configuring health checks and monitoring features
- Using Spring Boot profiles to adapt the application to run in different modes
- Using ORM features for interacting with embedded and remote NoSQL databases

Introducing Spring Boot

Spring Boot is dedicated to running standalone Spring applications, the same as simple Java applications, with the `java -jar` command. The basic thing that makes Spring Boot different than standard Spring configuration is simplicity. This simplicity is closely related to the first important term we need to know about, which is a starter. A **starter** is an artifact that can be included in the project dependencies. It does nothing more than provide a set of dependencies to other artifacts that have to be included in your application in order to achieve the desired functionality. A package delivered in that way is ready for use, which means that we don't have to configure anything to make it work. And that brings us to the second important term related to Spring Boot, auto-configuration. All artifacts included by the starters have default settings set, which can be easily overridden using properties or other types of starters. For example, if you include `spring-boot-starter-web` in your application dependencies it embeds a default web container and starts it on the default port during application startup. Looking forward, the default web container in Spring Boot is Tomcat, which starts on port `8080`. We can easily change this port by declaring the specified field in the application properties file and even change the web container by including `spring-boot-starter-jetty` or `spring-boot-starter-undertow` in our project dependencies.

Let me say a few words more about starters. Their official naming pattern is `spring-boot-starter-*`, where `*` is the particular type of starter. There are plenty of starters available within Spring Boot, but I would like to give you a short briefing on the most popular of them, which have also been used in the examples provided in the following chapters of this book:

Name	Description
`spring-boot-starter`	Core starter, including auto-configuration support, logging, and YAML.
`spring-boot-starter-web`	Allows us to build web applications, including RESTful and Spring MVC. Uses Tomcat as the default embedded container.
`spring-boot-starter-jetty`	Includes Jetty in the project and sets it as the default embedded servlet container.
`spring-boot-starter-undertow`	Includes Undertow in the project and sets it as the default embedded servlet container.

`spring-boot-starter-tomcat`	Includes Tomcat as the embedded servlet container. The default servlet container starter used by `spring-boot-starter-web`.
`spring-boot-starter-actuator`	Includes Spring Boot Actuator in the project, which provides features for monitoring and managing applications.
`spring-boot-starter-jdbc`	Includes Spring JBDC with the Tomcat connection pool. The driver for the specific database should be provided by yourself.
`spring-boot-starter-data-jpa`	Includes all artifacts needed for interaction with relational databases using JPA/Hibernate.
`spring-boot-starter-data-mongodb`	Includes all artifacts needed for interaction with MongoDB and initializing a client connection to Mongo on localhost.
`spring-boot-starter-security`	Includes Spring Security in the project and enables basic security for applications by default.
`spring-boot-starter-test`	Allows the creation of unit tests using such libraries as JUnit, Hamcrest, and Mockito.
`spring-boot-starter-amqp`	Includes Spring AMQP to the project and starts RabbitMQ as the default AMQP broker.

If you are interested in the full list of available starters, refer to the Spring Boot specification. Now, let's get back to the main differences between Spring Boot and standard configuration with Spring Framework. Like I mentioned before we can include `spring-boot-starter-web`, which embeds a web container into our application. With standard Spring configuration, we do not embed a web container into the application, but deploy it as a WAR file on the web container. This is a key difference and one of the most important reasons that Spring Boot is used for creating applications deployed inside microservice architecture. One of the main features of microservices is independence from other microservices. In this case, it is clear that they should not share common resources, such as databases or web containers. Deploying many WAR files on one web container is an anti-pattern for microservices. Spring Boot is, therefore, the obvious choice.

Personally, I have used Spring Boot while developing many applications, not only when working in a microservice environment. If you try it instead of standard Spring Framework configuration, you will not want to go back. In support of that conclusion you can find an interesting diagram that illustrates the popularity of Java frameworks repositories on GitHub: `http://redmonk.com/fryan/files/2017/06/java-tier1-relbar-20170622-logo.png`. Let's take a closer look at how to develop applications with Spring Boot.

Developing applications with Spring Boot

The recommended way to enable Spring Boot in your project is by using a dependency management system. Here, you can see a short snippet of how to include appropriate artifacts in your Maven and Gradle projects. Here is a sample fragment from the Maven `pom.xml`:

```
<parent>
    <groupId>org.springframework.boot</groupId>
    <artifactId>spring-boot-starter-parent</artifactId>
    <version>1.5.7.RELEASE</version>
</parent>
<dependencies>
    <dependency>
        <groupId>org.springframework.boot</groupId>
        <artifactId>spring-boot-starter-web</artifactId>
    </dependency>
</dependencies>
```

With Gradle, we do not need to define parent dependency. Here's a fragment from `build.gradle`:

```
plugins {
    id 'org.springframework.boot' version '1.5.7.RELEASE'
}
dependencies {
    compile("org.springframework.boot:spring-boot-starter-web:1.5.7.RELEASE")
}
```

When using Maven, it is not necessary to inherit from the `spring-boot-starter-parent` POM. Alternatively, we can use the dependency management mechanism:

```
<dependencyManagement>
    <dependencies>
        <dependency>
            <groupId>org.springframework.boot</groupId>
            <artifactId>spring-boot-dependencies</artifactId>
            <version>1.5.7.RELEASE</version>
            <type>pom</type>
            <scope>import</scope>
        </dependency>
    </dependencies>
</dependencyManagement>
```

Now, all we need is to create the main application class and annotate it with `@SpringBootApplication`, which is an equivalent to three other annotations used together—`@Configuration`, `@EnableAutoConfiguration`, and `@ComponentScan`:

```
@SpringBootApplication
public class Application {

    public static void main(String[] args) {
        SpringApplication.run(Application.class, args);
    }

}
```

Once we have the main class declared and `spring-boot-starter-web` included, we only need to run our first application. If you use a development IDE, such as Eclipse or IntelliJ, you should just run your main class. Otherwise, the application has to be built and run like a standard Java application with the `java -jar` command. First, we should provide the configuration that is responsible for packaging all dependencies into an executable JAR (sometimes called **fat JARs**) during application build. This action would be performed by `spring-boot-maven-plugin` if it is defined in the Maven `pom.xml`:

```
<build>
    <plugins>
        <plugin>
            <groupId>org.springframework.boot</groupId>
            <artifactId>spring-boot-maven-plugin</artifactId>
        </plugin>
    </plugins>
</build>
```

The sample application does nothing more than start a Spring context on the Tomcat container, which is available on port `8080`. The fat JAR is about 14 MB in size. You can easily, using an IDE, check out which libraries are included in the project. These are all basic Spring libraries, such as `spring-core`, `spring-aop`, `spring-context`; Spring Boot; Tomcat embedded; libraries for logging including Logback, Log4j, and Slf4j; and Jackson libraries used for JSON serialization or deserialization. A good idea is to set the default Java version for the project. You can easily set it up in `pom.xml` by declaring the `java.version` property:

```
<properties>
    <java.version>1.8</java.version>
</properties>
```

We can change the default web container just by adding a new dependency, for example, to the Jetty server:

```
<dependency>
    <groupId>org.springframework.boot</groupId>
    <artifactId>spring-boot-starter-jetty</artifactId>
</dependency>
```

Customizing configuration files

It's one thing to have the ability to create applications quickly and without a huge volume of work, but no less important is the ability to easily customize and override default settings. Spring Boot comes in handy and provides mechanisms that enable configuration management. The simplest way to do that is using configuration files, which are appended to the application fat JAR. Spring Boot automatically detects configuration files whose name start with the `application` prefix. Supported file types are `.properties` and `.yml`. Therefore, we can create configuration files, such as `application.properties` or `application.yml`, and even including profile-specific files such as, `application-prod.properties` or `application-dev.yml`. Moreover, we can use OS environment variables and command-line arguments to externalize configuration. When using properties or YAML files, they should be placed in one of the following locations:

- A `/config` subdirectory of the current application directory
- The current application directory
- A classpath `/config` package (for example, inside your JAR)
- The classpath root

If you would like to give a specific name to your configuration file, other than application or application-{profile}, you need to provide a spring.config.name environment property during startup. You can also use the spring.config.location property, which contains a comma-separated list of directory locations or file paths:

```
java -jar sample-spring-boot-web.jar --spring.config.name=example
java -jar sample-spring-boot-web.jar --
spring.config.location=classpath:/example.properties
```

Inside configuration files, we can define two types of properties. First, there is a group of common, predefined Spring Boot properties consumed by the underlying classes mostly from the spring-boot-autoconfigure library. We can also define our own custom configuration properties, which are then injected into the application using the @Value or @ConfigurationProperties annotations.

Let's begin with the predefined properties. The full list of supported by the Spring Boot project is available in their documentation in *Appendix A,* in the *Common application properties* section. Most of them are specific to certain Spring modules, such as databases, web servers, security, and some other solutions, but there is also a group of core properties. Personally, I prefer using YAML instead of properties files because it is easily readable by humans, but the decision is yours. Most commonly, I override such properties as application name, which is used for service discovery and distributed configuration management; web server port; logging; or database connection settings.
Usually, application.yml file is placed in the src/main/resources directory, which is then located in the JAR root directory after the Maven build. Here's a sample configuration file, which overrides default server port, application name, and logging properties:

```
server:
    port: ${port:2222}

spring:
    application:
        name: first-service

logging:
    pattern:
        console: "%d{HH:mm:ss.SSS} %-5level %logger{36} - %msg%n"
        file: "%d{HH:mm:ss.SSS} [%thread] %-5level %logger{36} - %msg%n"
    level:
        org.springframework.web: DEBUG
    file: app.log
```

The one really cool thing here is that you don't have to define any other external configuration files, for example, `log4j.xml` or `logback.xml`, for logging configuration. In the previous fragment, you can see that I changed the default log level for `org.springframework.web` to `DEBUG` and log patterns, and created a log file, `app.log`, placed in the current application directory. Now, the default application name is `first-service` and the default HTTP port is `2222`.

Our custom configuration settings should also be placed in the same properties or YAML files. Here's a sample `application.yml` with custom properties:

```
name: first-service
my:
  servers:
    - dev.bar.com
    - foo.bar.com
```

A simple property can be injected using the `@Value` annotation:

```
@Component
public class CustomBean {

    @Value("${name}")
    private String name;

    // ...
}
```

There is also the ability to inject more complex configuration properties using the `@ConfigurationProperties` annotation. The list of values defined in the `my.servers` property inside the YAML file was injected to the target bean of type `java.util.List`:

```
@ConfigurationProperties(prefix="my")
public class Config {

    private List<String> servers = new ArrayList<String>();

    public List<String> getServers() {
        return this.servers;
    }
}
```

So far, we have managed to create a simple application that does nothing more than start Spring on a web container such as Tomcat or Jetty. In this part of the chapter, I wanted to show you how simple it is to start application development using Spring Boot. Apart from that, I have described how to customize configuration using YAML or properties files. For those people who prefer clicking to typing, I recommend the Spring Initializr website (`https://start.spring.io/`), where you can generate the project stub based on options you choose. In the simple site view, you can choose build tools (Maven/Gradle), language (Java/Kotlin/Groovy), and Spring Boot version. Then, you should provide all necessary dependencies using the search engine following the **Search for dependencies** label. I included `spring-boot-starter-web`, which is just labeled as `Web` on Spring Initializr as you see in the following screenshot. After clicking on **Generate project**, the ZIP file with the generated source code gets downloaded onto your computer. You might also be interested in knowing that by clicking **Switch to the full version**, you are able to see almost all available Spring Boot and Spring Cloud libraries, which can be included in the generated project:

I think that, since we have been going over the basics about building projects using Spring Boot, this is the right time to add some new features to our sample application.

Creating RESTful Web Services

As a first step, let's create RESTful Web Services exposing some data to the calling clients. As mentioned before, the Jackson library, which is responsible for the serialization and deserialization of JSON messages, is automatically included in our classpath together with `spring-boot-starter-web`. Thanks to that, we don't have to do anything more than declare a model class, which is then returned or taken as a parameter by REST methods. Here's our sample model class, `Person`:

```
public class Person {

    private Long id;
    private String firstName;
    private String lastName;
    private int age;
    private Gender gender;

    public Long getId() {
        return id;
    }

    public void setId(Long id) {
        this.id = id;
    }

    //...
}
```

Spring Web provides some annotations for creating RESTful Web Services. The first of them is the `@RestController` annotation, which should be set on your controller bean class that is responsible for handling incoming HTTP requests. There is also the `@RequestMapping` annotation, which is usually used for mapping controller methods to HTTP. As you see in the following code fragment, it can be used on the whole controller class to set the request path for all methods inside it. We can use more specific annotations for the concrete HTTP methods such as `@GetMapping` or `@PostMapping`. `@GetMapping` is the same as `@RequestMapping` with the parameter `method=RequestMethod.GET`. Two other commonly used annotations are `@RequestParam` and `@RequestBody`. The first binds path and query params to objects; the second maps input JSON to objects using the Jackson library:

```
@RestController
@RequestMapping("/person")
public class PersonController {
```

```
    private List<Person> persons = new ArrayList<>();

    @GetMapping
    public List<Person> findAll() {
        return persons;
     }

    @GetMapping("/{id}")
    public Person findById(@RequestParam("id") Long id) {
        return persons.stream().filter(it ->
  it.getId().equals(id)).findFirst().get();
     }

    @PostMapping
    public Person add(@RequestBody Person p) {
        p.setId((long) (persons.size()+1));
        persons.add(p);
        return p;
     }

    // ...
}
```

To be compatible with REST API standards, we should handle PUT and DELETE methods. After their implementation, our service performs all CRUD operations:

Method	Path	Description
GET	/person	Returns all existing persons
GET	/person/{id}	Returns person with the given *id*
POST	/person	Adds new person
PUT	/person	Updates existing person
DELETE	/person/{id}	Removes person from list using given *id*

Here's a fragment of a sample @RestController implementation with the DELETE and PUT methods:

```
@DeleteMapping("/{id}")
public void delete(@RequestParam("id") Long id) {
    List<Person> p = persons.stream().filter(it ->
it.getId().equals(id)).collect(Collectors.toList());
    persons.removeAll(p);
}
```

```
@PutMapping
public void update(@RequestBody Person p) {
    Person person = persons.stream().filter(it ->
it.getId().equals(p.getId())).findFirst().get();
    persons.set(persons.indexOf(person), p);
}
```

The controller code is really simple. It stores all data in the local `java.util.List`, which is obviously not a good programming practice. However, treat that as a simplification adopted for the purposes of the basic example. In the section *Integrating application with database*, in this chapter, I'll cover more advanced sample application that integrates with the NoSQL database.

Probably some of you have experience with SOAP Web Services. If we had created a similar service using SOAP instead of REST, we would provide a WSDL file for the client with all service definitions described. Unfortunately, REST doesn't support such standard notation as WSDL. In the initial stage of RESTful Web Services, it was said that **Web Application Description Language (WADL)** would perform that role. But the reality is that many providers, including Spring Web, do not generate WADL files after application startup. Why am I mentioning this? Well, we have already finished our first microservice, which exposes some REST operations over HTTP. You have probably run this microservice from your IDE or using the `java -jar` command after building the fat JAR. If you didn't change the configuration properties inside the `application.yml` file, or did not set the `-Dport` option while running the application, it is available under `http://localhost:2222`. In order to enable others to call our API, we have two choices. We can share a document describing its usage or mechanisms for automatic API client generation. Or both of them. That's where Swagger comes in.

API Documentation

Swagger is the most popular tool for designing, building, and documenting RESTful APIs. It has been created by SmartBear, the designers of a very popular tool for SOAP Web Services, SoapUI. I think that might be sufficient recommendation for those who have long experience with SOAP. Anyway, with Swagger, we can design APIs using notation and then generate source code from it, or the other way around, where we start with the source code and then generate a Swagger file. With Spring Boot, we use the second option.

Using Swagger 2 together with Spring Boot

The integration between Spring Boot and Swagger 2 is realized by the Springfox project. It examines application at runtime to infer API semantics based on Spring configurations, class structure, and Java annotations. To use Swagger in conjunction with Spring, we need to add the following two dependencies to the Maven `pom.xml` and annotate the main application class with `@EnableSwagger2`:

```
<dependency>
    <groupId>io.springfox</groupId>
    <artifactId>springfox-swagger2</artifactId>
    <version>2.7.0</version>
</dependency>
<dependency>
    <groupId>io.springfox</groupId>
    <artifactId>springfox-swagger-ui</artifactId>
    <version>2.7.0</version>
</dependency>
```

The API documentation will be automatically generated from the source code by the Swagger library during application startup. The process is controlled by the `Docket` bean, which is also declared in the main class. A nice idea might be to get the API version from the Maven `pom.xml` file. We can get it by including the `maven-model` library in the classpath and using the `MavenXpp3Reader` class. We also set some other properties, such as title, author, and description using the `apiInfo` method. By default, Swagger generates documentation for all REST services, including those created by Spring Boot. We would like to limit this documentation only to our `@RestController` located inside the `pl.piomin.services.boot.controller` package:

```
@Bean
public Docket api() throws IOException, XmlPullParserException {
  MavenXpp3Reader reader = new MavenXpp3Reader();
  Model model = reader.read(new FileReader("pom.xml"));
  ApiInfoBuilder builder = new ApiInfoBuilder()
      .title("Person Service Api Documentation")
      .description("Documentation automatically generated")
      .version(model.getVersion())
      .contact(new Contact("Piotr Mińkowski",
"piotrminkowski.wordpress.com", "piotr.minkowski@gmail.com"));
    return new Docket(DocumentationType.SWAGGER_2).select()
.apis(RequestHandlerSelectors.basePackage("pl.piomin.services.boot.controll
er"))
      .paths(PathSelectors.any()).build()
      .apiInfo(builder.build());
  }
```

Testing API with Swagger UI

An API documentation dashboard is available at
`http://localhost:2222/swagger-ui.html` after application startup. This is a more
user-friendly version of the Swagger JSON definition file, which is also automatically
generated and available at `http://localhost:2222/v2/api-docs`. That file can be
imported by any other REST tools, for example, SoapUI:

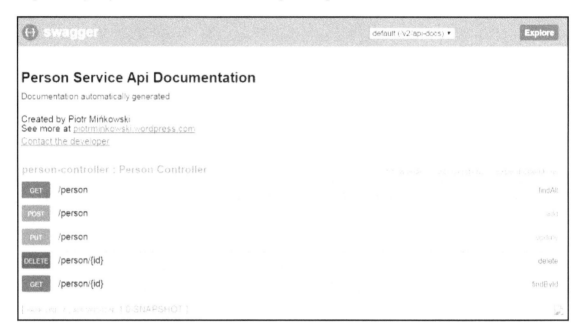

If you prefer SoapUI instead of Swagger UI, you can easily import the Swagger definition
file by selecting **Project** | **Import Swagger**. Then, you need to provide a file address, as you
can see in this screenshot:

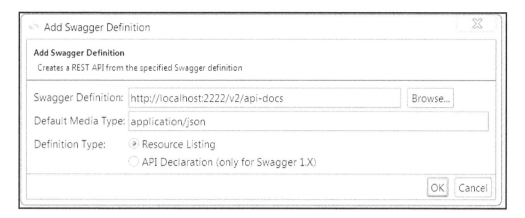

Personally, I prefer Swagger UI. You can expand every API method to see their details. Every operation can be tested by providing the required parameters or JSON input, and clicking the **Try it out!** button. Here's a screenshot illustrating sending a POST /person test request:

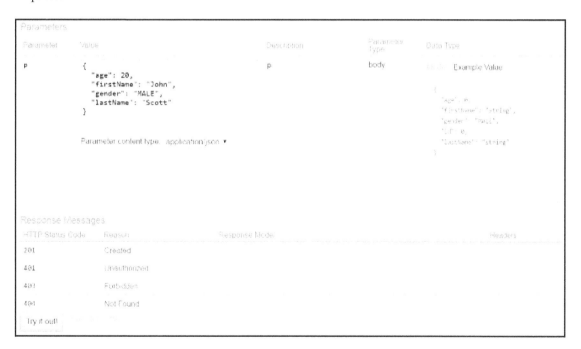

Here's the response screen:

```
Response Body


  {
    "id": 1,
    "firstName": "John",
    "lastName": "Scott",
    "age": 20,
    "gender": "MALE"
  }


Response Code

 200

Response Headers

 {
   "date": "Wed, 04 Oct 2017 08:41:24 GMT",
   "transfer-encoding": "chunked",
   "content-type": "application/json;charset=UTF-8"
 }
```

Spring Boot Actuator features

Just creating the working application and sharing standardized API documentation is not everything, especially if we are talking about microservices, where there are plenty of independent entities structuring one managed environment. The next important thing that needs to be mentioned is monitoring and gathering metrics from applications. In that aspect, Spring Boot also comes through. Project Spring Boot Actuator provides a number of built-in endpoints, which allow us to monitor and interact with the application. To enable it in our project, we should include `spring-boot-starter-actuator` in the dependencies. Here's a list of the most important Actuator endpoints:

Path	Description
`/beans`	Displays a full list of all the Spring beans initialized in the application.
`/env`	Exposes properties from Spring's Configurable Environment, which means, for example, OS environment variables and properties from configuration files.

`/health`	Shows application health information.
`/info`	Displays arbitrary application information. It can be taken, for example, from the `build-info.properties` or `git.properties` files.
`/loggers`	Shows and modifies the configuration of loggers in the application.
`/metrics`	Shows metrics information for the current application, such as memory usage, number of running threads, or REST method response time.
`/trace`	Displays trace information (by default the last 100 HTTP requests).

Endpoints can be easily customized using Spring configuration properties. For example, we can disable one of the enabled by default endpoints. By default, all endpoints except for `shutdown` are enabled. Most of these endpoints are secured. If you would like to call them from your web browser, you should provide security credentials in the request header or disable security for the whole project. To do the latter, you have to include the following statement in your `application.yml` file:

```
management:
  security:
    enabled: false
```

Application information

The full list of endpoints available for the project is visible in application logs during startup. After disabling security, you can test all of them in your web browser. It's interesting that the `/info` endpoint does not provide any information by default. If you would like to change this, you might use one of the three available auto-configured `InfoContributor` beans or write your own. The first of them, `EnvironmentInfoContributor`, exposes environment keys in the endpoint. The second, `GitInfoContributor`, detects the `git.properties` file in the classpath and then displays all necessary information about commits, such as branch name or commit ID. The last one, named `BuildInfoContributor`, gathers information from the `META-INF/build-info.properties` file and also displays it in the endpoint. These two properties files for Git and build information can be automatically generated during application build. To achieve this, you should include `git-commit-id-plugin` in your `pom.xml` and customize `spring-boot-maven-plugin` to generate `build-info.properties` in the way visible in this code fragment:

```
<plugin>
    <groupId>org.springframework.boot</groupId>
```

```xml
<artifactId>spring-boot-maven-plugin</artifactId>
<executions>
    <execution>
        <goals>
            <goal>build-info</goal>
            <goal>repackage</goal>
        </goals>
        <configuration>
            <additionalProperties>
                <java.target>${maven.compiler.target}</java.target>
                <time>${maven.build.timestamp}</time>
            </additionalProperties>
        </configuration>
    </execution>
</executions>
</plugin>
<plugin>
    <groupId>pl.project13.maven</groupId>
    <artifactId>git-commit-id-plugin</artifactId>
    <configuration>
    <failOnNoGitDirectory>false</failOnNoGitDirectory>
    </configuration>
</plugin>
```

With the `build-info.properties` file available, your `/info` would be a little different than before:

```json
{
    "build": {
        "version":"1.0-SNAPSHOT",
        "java": {
            "target":"1.8"
        },
        "artifact":"sample-spring-boot-web",
        "name":"sample-spring-boot-web",
        "group":"pl.piomin.services",
        "time":"2017-10-04T10:23:22Z"
    }
}
```

Health information

As with the `/info` endpoint, there are also some auto-configured indicators for the `/health` endpoint. We can monitor the status of disk usage, mail service, JMS, data sources, and NoSQL databases, such as MongoDB or Cassandra. If you check out that endpoint from our sample application, you only get the information about disk usage. Let's add MongoDB to the project to test one of the available health indicators, `MongoHealthIndicator`. MongoDB is not a random selection. It will be useful for us in the future for a more advanced example of the `Person` microservice. To enable MongoDB use, we need to add the following dependencies to `pom.xml`. The `de.flapdoodle.embed.mongo` artifact is responsible for starting the embedded database instance during application startup:

```xml
<dependency>
    <groupId>org.springframework.boot</groupId>
    <artifactId>spring-boot-starter-data-mongodb</artifactId>
</dependency>
<dependency>
    <groupId>de.flapdoodle.embed</groupId>
    <artifactId>de.flapdoodle.embed.mongo</artifactId>
</dependency>
```

Now, the `/health` endpoint returns information about disk usage and MongoDB status:

```json
{
    "status":"UP",
    "diskSpace":{
        "status":"UP",
        "total":499808989184,
        "free":193956904960,
        "threshold":10485760
    },
    "mongo":{
        "status":"UP",
        "version":"3.2.2"
    }
}
```

In this example, we can see the power of Spring Boot auto-configuration. We didn't have to do anything more than include two dependencies to the project to enable embedded MongoDB. Its status has been automatically added to the `/health` endpoint. It also has a ready-to-use client connection to Mongo, which can be further used by the repository bean.

Metrics

As we usually say, there is no such thing as a free lunch. Development is fast and easy, but after including some additional libraries in the project, the fat JAR file now has about 30 MB. Using one of the auto-configured actuator endpoints, /metrics, we can easily check out our microservice heap and non-heap memory usage. After sending some test requests, heap usage was about 140 MB and non-heap was 65 MB. Total memory usage for the application was about 320 MB. Of course, these values can be reduced a little even just by using the -Xmx parameter during startup with the java -jar command. However, we should not reduce this limit too much if we care about reliable working in production mode. Apart from memory usage, the /metrics endpoint displays information about the number of loaded classes, the number of active threads, the average duration of each API method, and a lot more. Here's a fragment of the endpoint response for our sample microservice:

```
{
    "mem":325484,
    "mem.free":121745,
    "processors":4,
    "instance.uptime":765785,
    "uptime":775049,
    "heap.committed":260608,
    "heap.init":131072,
    "heap.used":138862,
    "heap":1846272,
    "nonheap.committed":75264,
    "nonheap.init":2496,
    "nonheap.used":64876,
    "threads.peak":28,
    "threads.totalStarted":33,
    "threads":28,
    "classes":9535,
    "classes.loaded":9535,
    "gauge.response.person":7.0,
    "counter.status.200.person":4,
    // ...
}
```

There is the possibility to create our own custom metrics. Spring Boot Actuator provides two classes in case we would like to do that—CounterService and GaugeService. CounterService, as its name indicates, exposes methods for value incrementation, decrementation, and reset. By contrast, GaugeService is intended to just submit the current value. Default metrics for the API method calling statistics are a little imperfect because they are based only on the invoking path. There is no distinguishing between method types if they are available on the same path. In our sample endpoint, this applies to GET /person, POST /person, and PUT /person. Anyway, I created the PersonCounterService bean, which counts the number of add and delete method calls:

```
@Service
public class PersonCounterService {
    private final CounterService counterService;

    @Autowired
    public PersonCounterService(CounterService counterService) {
        this.counterService = counterService;
    }

    public void countNewPersons() {
        this.counterService.increment("services.person.add");
    }

    public void countDeletedPersons() {
        this.counterService.increment("services.person.deleted");
    }
}
```

This bean needs to be injected into our REST controller bean, and the methods incrementing the counter value can be invoked when a person is added or removed:

```
public class PersonController {

    @Autowired
    PersonCounterService counterService;

    // ...

    @PostMapping
    public Person add(@RequestBody Person p) {
        p.setId((long) (persons.size()+1));
        persons.add(p);
        counterService.countNewPersons();
        return p;
    }
```

```
    @DeleteMapping("/{id}")
    public void delete(@RequestParam("id") Long id) {
        List<Person> p = persons.stream().filter(it ->
it.getId().equals(id)).collect(Collectors.toList());
        persons.removeAll(p);
        counterService.countDeletedPersons();
    }
}
```

Now, if you display application metrics again, you will see the following two new fields in the JSON response:

```
{
    // ...
    "counter.services.person.add":4,
    "counter.services.person.deleted":3
}
```

All metrics generated by the Spring Boot application may be exported from the in-memory buffers to a place where they can be analyzed and displayed. We can store them, for example, in Redis, Open TSDB, Statsd, or even InfluxDB.

I think that's about all the details about built-in monitor endpoints I wanted to give you. I had designated a relatively large amount of space to such topics as documentation, metrics, and health checks, but in my opinion, these are the important aspects of microservice development and maintenance. Developers often do not care if these mechanisms are well implemented, but others often see our application just through the prism of those metrics, health checks and application's logs quality. Spring Boot provides such an implementation out of the box, and therefore developers do not have to spend much time enabling them.

Developer tools

Spring Boot offers some other useful tools for developers. The really cool thing for me is that the application is automatically restarted whenever files on the project classpath change. If you use Eclipse as your IDE, the only thing you have to do to enable it is to add the `spring-boot-devtools` dependency to the Maven `pom.xml`. Then, try to change something in one of your classes and save it. The application automatically restarts, and it takes much less than stopping and starting in the standard way. When I start our sample application, it takes about 9 seconds, and automatic restart takes only 3 seconds:

```
<dependency>
    <groupId>org.springframework.boot</groupId>
    <artifactId>spring-boot-devtools</artifactId>
```

```
      <optional>true</optional>
   </dependency>
```

We can exclude some resources if there is no need to trigger a restart when they are changed. By default, any file available on the classpath that points to a folder will be monitored for changes, even static assets or view templates, which do not need restarting. For example, if they are placed in the static folder, you can exclude them by adding the following property to the `application.yml` configuration file:

```
spring:
  devtools:
    restart:
      exclude: static/**
```

Integrating application with database

You can find more interesting features described in the Spring Boot specification. I would like to spend more time describing other cool functionalities provided by that framework, but we should not go too far away from the main topic—Spring for microservices. As you may recall, through including embedded MongoDB in the project, I promised you a more advanced microservice example. Before starting to work on it, let's go back for a moment to the current version of our application. Its source code is available on my public GitHub account. Clone the following Git repository to your local machine: `https://github.com/piomin/sample-spring-boot-web.git`.

Building a sample application

The basic example is available in the `master` branch. The more advanced sample, with embedded MongoDB, is committed to the `mongo` branch. In case you would like to try running more advanced sample, you need to switch to that branch using `git checkout mongo`. Now, we need to perform some changes in the model class to enable object mapping to MongoDB. The model class has to be annotated with `@Document` and the primary key field with `@Id`. I also changed the ID field type from `Long` to `String` because MongoDB generates primary keys in UUID format, for example, `59d63385206b6d14b854a45c`:

```
@Document(collection = "person")
public class Person {

    @Id
    private String id;
```

```
    private String firstName;
    private String lastName;
    private int age;
    private Gender gender;

    public String getId() {
        return id;
    }

    public void setId(String id) {
        this.id = id;
    }
    // ...
}
```

The next step is to create a repository interface that extends `MongoRepository`. MongoRepository provides basic methods for searching and storing data, such as `findAll`, `findOne`, `save`, and `delete`. Spring Data has a very smart mechanism for performing queries using repository objects. We don't have to implement queries by ourselves, but only define an interface method with the right name. The method name should have the prefix `findBy` and then the searched field name. It may end with a standard search keyword suffix, such as `GreaterThan`, `LassThan`, `Between`, `Like`, and many more. A MongoDB query is automatically generated by Spring Data classes based on the full method name. The same keywords may be used in conjunction with `delete...By` or `remove...By` to create remove queries. In the `PersonRepository` interface, I decided to define two find methods. The first of them, `findByLastName`, selects all `Person` entities with the given `lastName` value. The second, `findByAgeGreaterThan`, is designed to retrieve all `Person` entities with an age greater than a given value:

```
public interface PersonRepository extends MongoRepository<Person, String> {

    public List<Person> findByLastName(String lastName);
    public List<Person> findByAgeGreaterThan(int age);

}
```

The repository should be injected into the REST controller class. Then, we can finally call all the required CRUD methods provided by `PersonRepository`:

```
@Autowired
private PersonRepository repository;
@Autowired
private PersonCounterService counterService;

@GetMapping
```

```
public List<Person> findAll() {
    return repository.findAll();
}

@GetMapping("/{id}")
public Person findById(@RequestParam("id") String id) {
    return repository.findOne(id);
}

@PostMapping
public Person add(@RequestBody Person p) {
    p = repository.save(p);
    counterService.countNewPersons();
    return p;
}

@DeleteMapping("/{id}")
public void delete(@RequestParam("id") String id) {
    repository.delete(id);
    counterService.countDeletedPersons();
}
```

We have also added two API methods for custom find operations from the
`PersonRepository` bean:

```
@GetMapping("/lastname/{lastName}")
public List<Person> findByLastName(@RequestParam("lastName") String
lastName) {
    return repository.findByLastName(lastName);
}

@GetMapping("/age/{age}")
public List<Person> findByAgeGreaterThan(@RequestParam("age") int age) {
    return repository.findByAgeGreaterThan(age);
}
```

That's all that had to be done. Our microservice that exposes basic API methods implementing CRUD operations on an embedded Mongo database is ready to launch. You have probably noticed that it didn't require us to create a lot of source code. Implementation of any interaction with databases, whether relational or NoSQL, using Spring Data is fast and relatively easy. Anyway, there is still one more challenge facing us. An embedded database is a good choice, but only in development mode or for unit testing, not in production. If you have to run your microservice in production mode, you would probably launch one standalone instance or some instances of Mongo deployed as a sharded cluster, and connect the application to them. For our example purposes, I'll run a single instance of MongoDB using Docker.

 If you are not familiar with Docker, you can always just install Mongo on your local or remote machine. For more information about Docker, you can also refer to Chapter 14, *Docker Support* where I will give you a short briefing about it. There, you will find all you need to begin, for example, how to install it on Windows and use basic commands. I will also use Docker in the examples implemented for the purposes of the next chapters and topics, so I think it would be useful if you have basic knowledge about it.

Running the application

Let's start MongoDB using the Docker run command:

```
docker run -d --name mongo -p 27017:27017 mongo
```

Something that may be useful for us is the Mongo database client. Using this, it is possible to create a new database and add some users with credentials. If you have Docker installed on Windows, the default virtual machine address is 192.168.99.100. The Mongo container has port 27017 exposed as a result of setting the -p parameter inside the run command. Well, in fact, we do not have to create the database because, when we provide the name while defining the client connection, it will automatically be created if it doesn't exist:

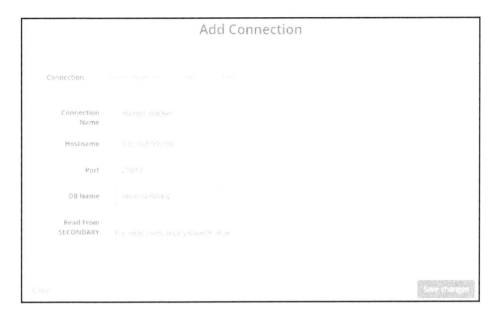

Next, we should create a user for the application with sufficient authority:

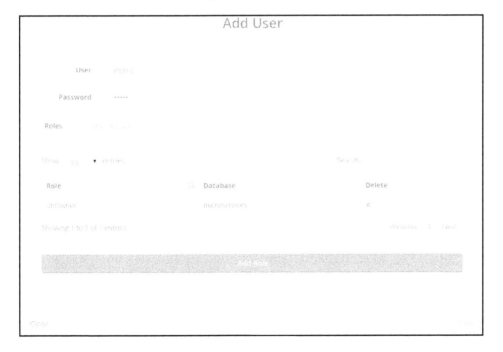

Finally, we should set the Mongo database connection settings and credentials in the `application.yml` configuration file:

```
server:
  port: ${port:2222}
spring:
  application:
  name: first-service

// ...

---

spring:
  profiles: production
  application:
    name: first-service
  data:
    mongodb:
      host: 192.168.99.100
      port: 27017
      database: microservices
      username: micro
      password: micro
```

Spring Boot has good support for multi-profile configuration. A YAML file can be separated into a sequence of documents using `---` lines, and each section of the document is parsed independently to a flattened map. The preceding example does exactly the same as a separated configuration file with `application-production.yml`. If you run the application without any additional options, it uses the default settings, which have no profile name set. If you would like to run it using production properties, you should set the VM argument `spring.profiles.active`:

```
java -jar -Dspring.profiles.active=production sample-spring-boot-web-1.0-
SNAPSHOT.jar
```

That's not all. Now, the application with the active production profile failed to start because it tried to initialize the `embeddedMongoServer` bean. As you might already know, almost all of the additional solutions have auto configuration set in Spring Boot. It is no different in this case. We need to exclude the `EmbeddedMongoAutoConfiguration` class from auto configuration in the production profile:

```
spring:
  profiles: production
  // ...
  autoconfigure:
```

```
    exclude:
org.springframework.boot.autoconfigure.mongo.embedded.EmbeddedMongoAutoConf
iguration
```

We might as well use the configuration class to exclude that artifact:

```
@Configuration
@Profile("production")
@EnableAutoConfiguration(exclude = EmbeddedMongoAutoConfiguration.class)
public class ApplicationConfig {
    // ...
}
```

Of course, we could have used a more elegant solution, such as Maven profiles, and excluded the whole de.flapdoodle.embed.mongo artifact from the target build package. The presented solution is just one of several possibilities to solve the problem, but it shows the auto configuration and profile mechanisms in Spring Boot. Now, you can run our sample application and perform some tests using, for example, Swagger UI. You can also connect to the database using the Mongo client and check out the changes in the database. Here's our sample project's final file structure:

```
pl
  +- piomin
    +- services
      +- boot
        +- Application.java
        |
        +- controller
        |   +- PersonController.java
        |
        +- data
        |   +- PersonRepository.java
        |
        +- model
        |   +- Person.java
        |   +- Gender.java
        |
        +- service
        |   +- PersonCounterService.java
```

The example application is complete. These are all Spring Boot features I would like to show you in this chapter. I have focused on those that are especially useful for creating REST-based services.

Summary

I have guided you through the process of single-microservice development, from a really basic example to a more advanced, production-ready Spring Boot application. I have described how to use starters to enable additional features for the project; use the Spring Web library to implement services that expose REST API methods; and then we moved on to customizing the service configuration using properties and YAML files. We also saw how to document and provide specifications for exposed REST endpoints. Next, we configured health checks and monitoring features. We used Spring Boot profiles to adapt the application to run in different modes and, finally, we used ORM features for interacting with embedded and remote NoSQL databases.

It's not an accident that I have not mentioned anything about Spring Cloud in this chapter. You just can't start using Spring Cloud projects without basic knowledge and experience in working with Spring Boot. Spring Cloud provides many different features that allow you to place your service inside a full microservice-based ecosystem. We will be discussing these functionalities one by one in the following chapters.

Spring Cloud Overview

3

In `Chapter 1`, *Introduction to Microservices*, I mentioned the cloud-native development style and also that Spring Cloud helps you in the easy adoption of the best practices associated with this concept. The most commonly used best practices have been collected together in an interesting initiative called **The Twelve-Factor App**. As you might read on their website (`https://12factor.net/`), this is a methodology for building **Software as a Service** (**SaaS**) modern applications, which must be scalable, easily deployable on cloud platforms, and delivered in the continuous deployment process. It is worth being familiar with these principles, especially if you are a developer who builds applications running as a service. Spring Boot and Spring Cloud provide features and components that make your application compliant with *Twelve-Factor rules*. We can distinguish some typical features that the most modern distributed systems usually use. Every opinionated framework should provide them and there is no difference for Spring Cloud. Those features are as follows:

- Distributed/versioned configuration
- Service registration and discovery
- Routing
- Service-to-service calls
- Load balancing
- Circuit breakers
- Distributed messaging

Beginning with the basics

Let's go back to the previous chapter for a moment. There I have already described in detail the structure of a Spring Boot project. Configuration should be provided in YAML or a properties file with the application or the `application-{profile}` name. In contrast to a standard Spring Boot application, Spring Cloud is based on the configuration taken from a remote server. However, minimal settings are needed inside the application; for example, its name and config server address. That's why a Spring Cloud application creates a bootstrap context, which is responsible for loading properties from the external sources. Bootstrap properties are added with the highest priority and they cannot be overridden by local configuration. Bootstrap context, which is a parent for the main application context, uses `bootstrap.yml` instead of `application.yml`. Usually, we put the application name and Spring Cloud Config settings, as follows:

```
spring:
  application:
    name: person-service
  cloud:
    config:
      uri: http://192.168.99.100:8888
```

Bootstrap context startup can be easily disabled by setting the `spring.cloud.bootstrap.enabled` property to `false`. We can also change the name of the bootstrap configuration file using the `spring.cloud.bootstrap.name` property or even changing the location by setting `spring.cloud.bootstrap.location`. The profile mechanisms are also available here, so we are allowed to create, for example, `bootstrap-development.yml`, which is loaded on an active development profile. This and some other features are available in the Spring Cloud Context library, which is added as a parent dependency to the project classpath together with any other Spring Cloud library. One of these features is some additional management endpoints included with the Spring Boot Actuator:

- `env`: A new `POST` method for `Environment`, log levels update, and `@ConfigurationProperties` rebind
- `refresh`: This reloads bootstrap context and refreshes all beans annotated with `@RefreshScope`
- `restart`: This restarts Spring `ApplicationContext`
- `pause`: This stops Spring `ApplicationContext`
- `resume`: This starts Spring `ApplicationContext`

The next library together with Spring Cloud Context, which is included as a parent dependency with Spring Cloud projects, is Spring Cloud Commons. It provides a common abstraction layer for mechanisms such as service discovery, load balancing, and circuit breakers. These include, among other things, frequently used annotations such as `@EnableDiscoveryClient` or `@LoadBalanced`. I'll present more details about them in the following chapters.

Netflix OSS

On reading the first two chapters, you have probably noticed the appearance of many keywords related to microservice architecture. For some of you, it might be a new term, for others, it is well known. But so far, one important word to the microservices community has not been mentioned yet. It is definitely known by most of you, this word is *Netflix*. Well, I also like their TV shows and other productions, but for developers, they are famous for another reason. This reason is microservices. Netflix is one of the earliest pioneers of migration from a traditional development model where we created monolithic applications for a cloud-native microservices development approach. This company shares their expertise with the community by pushing a great part of the source code into the public repository, speaking in conference presentations, and publishing blog posts. Netflix has been so successful with its architecture concept that they became a role model for other large organizations and their IT architects such as Adrian Cockcroft are now prominent evangelists for microservices. In turn, many open source frameworks based their libraries on the solutions available under the code shared by Netflix. It is no different for Spring Cloud, which provides integrations with the most popular Netflix OSS features such as Eureka, Hystrix, Ribbon, or Zuul.

By the way, I don't know if you have been following Netflix, but they shed some light on the reasons why they decided to open source much of their code. I think it is worth quoting because that partly explains the success and unwaning popularity of their solutions in the IT world:

> *"When we said we were going to move all of Netflix to the cloud everyone said we were completely crazy. They didn't believe we were actually doing that, they thought we were just making stuff up."*

Service discovery with Eureka

The first pattern provided by Spring Cloud Netflix is the service discovery with Eureka. This package is divided into client and server.

To include a Eureka Client in your project you should use the `spring-cloud-starter-eureka` starter. The client is always a part of an application and is responsible for connecting to a remote discovery server. Once the connection is established it should send a registration message with a service name and network location. In case the current microservice has to call an endpoint from another microservice, the client should retrieve the newest configuration with a list of registered services from the server. The server can be configured and run as an independent Spring Boot application and it is supposed to be highly available with each server replicating its state to other nodes. To include a Eureka Server in your project you need to use the `spring-cloud-starter-eureka-server` starter.

Routing with Zuul

The next popular pattern available under the Spring Cloud Netflix project is intelligent routing with Zuul. It is not only a JVM-based router but it also acts as a server-side load balancer and/or performs some filtering. It can also have a wide variety of applications. Netflix uses it for cases such as authentication, load shedding, static response handling, or stress testing. It is the same as Eureka Server in that it can be configured and run as an independent Spring Boot application.

To include Zuul in your project use the `spring-cloud-starter-zuul` starter. In the microservices architecture, Zuul has a vital role of the API gateway, which is an entry point to the whole system. It needs to have knowledge of the network location of each service, so it is able to interact with the Eureka Server by including the discovery client to the classpath.

Load balancing with Ribbon

We cannot ignore the next Spring Cloud Netflix feature used for client-side load balancing—Ribbon. It supports the most popular protocols such as TCP, UDP, and HTTP. It can be used not only for synchronous REST calls, but also in asynchronous and reactive models. In addition to load balancing, it provides integration with service discovery, caching, batching, and fault tolerance. Ribbon is the next abstraction level over basic HTTP and TCP clients.

To include it in your project use the `spring-cloud-starter-ribbon` starter. Ribbon supports round robin, availability filtering, and weighted response time load balancing rules out-of-the-box and can be easily extended with custom defined rules. It is based on the *named client* concept, where servers included for the load balancing should be provided with a name.

Writing Java HTTP clients

Feign is a slightly less popular Netflix OSS package. It is a declarative REST client, which helps us in writing web service clients more easily. With Feign, a developer only needs to declare and annotate an interface while the actual implementation will be generated at runtime.

To include Feign in your project you need to use the `spring-cloud-starter-feign` starter. It integrates with the Ribbon client, so it supports, by default, load balancing and other Ribbon features including communication with the discovery service.

Latency and fault tolerance with Hystrix

I have already mentioned the circuit breaker pattern in `Chapter 1`, *Introduction to Microservices*, and Spring Cloud provides a library that implements this pattern. It is based on the Hystrix package created by Netflix as a circuit breaker implementation. Hystrix is by default integrated with the Ribbon and Feign clients. Fallback is closely related to the circuit breaker concept. With Spring Cloud libraries you can easily configure fallback logic, which should be performed if there is a read or circuit breaker timeout. To include Hystrix in your project you should use the `spring-cloud-starter-hystrix` starter.

Configuration management with Archaius

The last important feature provided under the Spring Cloud Netflix project is Archaius. Personally, I haven't touched this library, but it might be useful in some cases. The Spring Cloud reference Archaius is an extension of the Apache Commons Configuration project. It allows updating the configuration by either polling a source for changes or pushing changes to the client.

Discovery and distributed configuration

Service discovery and distributed configuration management are vital parts of the microservices architecture. The technical implementation of these two different mechanisms is pretty similar. It comes down to storing parameters under specific keys in a flexible key-value storage. Actually, there are several interesting solutions available on the market which provide both of these functionalities. Spring Cloud integrates with the most popular of them. But there is also one exception where Spring Cloud has its own implementation created only for distributed configuration. This feature is available under the Spring Cloud Config project. In contrast, Spring Cloud does not provide its own implementation for service registration and discovery.

As usual, we can divide this project into the server and client-side support. The server is the one, central place where all of the external properties for applications are managed across all of the environments. Configuration can be maintained simultaneously in several versions and profiles. This is achieved by using Git as a storage backend. The mechanism is really smart and we will discuss it in detail in `Chapter 5`, *Distributed Configuration with Spring Cloud Config*. The Git backend is not the only one option for storing properties. The config files could also be located on a file system or server classpath. The next option is to use Vault as a backend. Vault is an open source tool for managing secrets such as tokens, passwords, or certificates released by HashiCorp. I know that many organizations pay particular attention to security issues such as storing credentials in a secure place, so it could be the right solution for them. Generally, we can also manage security on the configuration server access level. No matter which backend is used for storing properties, Spring Cloud Config Server exposes an HTTP, resource-based API which provides easy access to them. By default, this API is secured with basic authentication, but it is also available to set an SSL connection with private/public key authentication.

A server can be run as an independent Spring Boot application with properties exposed over the REST API. To enable it for our project we should add the `spring-cloud-config-server` dependency. There is also support on the client-side. Every microservice that uses a configuration server as a properties source needs to connect to it just after startup, before creating any Spring beans. Interestingly, the Spring Cloud Config Server can be used by non Spring applications. There are some popular microservice frameworks that integrate with it on the client side. To enable Spring Cloud Config Client for your application you need to include the `spring-cloud-config-starter` dependency.

An alternative – Consul

An interesting alternative for Netflix discovery and Spring distributed configuration seems to be Consul created by Hashicorp. Spring Cloud provides integrations with this popular tool for discovering and configuring services in your infrastructure. As usual, this integration can be enabled using a few simple common annotations and the only difference in comparison with an earlier presented solution is in configuration settings. In order to establish communication with a Consul server, its agent needs to be available for the application. It has to be able to run as a separated process, which is available by default at the `http://localhost:8500` address. Consul also provides REST API, which can be directly used for registration, collecting a list of services, or configuration of properties.

To activate Consul Service Discovery we need to use the `spring-cloud-starter-consul-discovery` starter. After application startup and registration, a client would query Consul in order to locate other services. It supports both the client-side load balancer with Netflix Ribbon and dynamic router and filter with Netflix Zuul.

Apache Zookeeper

The next popular solution within this area supported by Spring Cloud is Apache Zookeeper. Following its documentation, it is a centralized service for maintaining configuration, naming, which also provides distributed synchronization, and is able to group services. Everything that has previously applied to Consul regarding support in Spring Cloud is also true for Zookeeper. I'm thinking here about simple common annotations, which have to be used to enable integration, configuration though properties inside settings files and auto-configuration for interacting with Ribbon or Zuul. To enable service discovery with Zookeeper on the client side we need not only include `spring-cloud-starter-zookeeper-discovery`, but also Apache Curator. It provides an API framework and utilities to make integration easy and more reliable. It is not needed for distributed configuration clients where we only have to include the `spring-cloud-starter-zookeeper-config` for our project dependencies.

Miscellaneous projects

It is worth mentioning two other projects, which are now in the incubation stage. All such projects are available in the GitHub repository, `https://github.com/spring-cloud-incubator`. Some of them will probably be officially attached to the Spring Cloud package in the short term. The first of them is Spring Cloud Kubernetes, which provides integration with this very popular tool. We could talk about it for a long time, but let's try to introduce it in a few words. It is a system for automating deployment, scaling, and management of containerized applications originally designed by Google. It is used for container orchestration and has many interesting features including service discovery, configuration management, and load balancing. In some cases, it might be treated as Spring Cloud's competition. The configuration is provided with the usage of YAML files.

Important features from the Spring Cloud point of view are service discovery and distributed configuration mechanisms, which are available on the Kubernetes platform. To use them in your application you should include `spring-cloud-starter-kubernetes` starter.

The second interesting project at the incubation stage is Spring Cloud Etcd. Exactly the same as before, its main features are distributed configuration, service registration, and discovery. Etcd is not a powerful tool like Kubernetes. It just provides a distributed key-value store with a reliable way to store data in a clustered environment. And a little trivia—Etcd is the backend for service discovery, cluster state, and configuration management in Kubernetes.

Distributed tracing with Sleuth

Another one of Spring Cloud's essential functionalities is distributed tracing. It is implemented in the Spring Cloud Sleuth library. Its primary purpose is to associate subsequent requests dispatched between different microservices under processing single input request. As in most cases, these are HTTP requests that implement tracing mechanisms based on HTTP headers. The implementation is built over Slf4j and MDC. Slf4j provides facade and abstraction for specific logging frameworks such as logback, log4j, or `java.util.logging`. **MDC** or **mapped diagnostic context** in full, is a solution for distinguishing log output from different sources and enriching them with additional information that could be not available in the actual scope.

Spring Cloud Sleuth adds trace and span IDs to the Slf4J MDC, so that we are able to extract all of the logs with a given trace or span. It also adds some other entries such as application name or exportable flag. It integrates with the most popular messaging solutions such as Spring REST template, Feign client, Zuul filters, Hystrix, or Spring Integration message channels. It can also be used together with RxJava or scheduled tasks. To enable it in your project you should add the `spring-cloud-starter-sleuth` dependency. The usage of basic span and trace IDs mechanisms is completely transparent for a developer.

Adding tracing headers is not the only feature of Spring Cloud Sleuth. It is also responsible for recording timing information, which is useful in latency analysis. Such statistics can be exported to Zipkin, a tool that can be used for querying and visualization timing data.

 Zipkin is a distributing tracing system specially designed for analyzing latency problems inside microservices architecture. It exposes HTTP endpoints used for collecting input data. To enable generating and sending traces to Zipkin we should include the `spring-cloud-starter-zipkin` dependency to the project.

Frequently, there is no need to analyze everything; the input traffic volume is so high that we would need to collect only a certain percentage of data. For that purpose, Spring Cloud Sleuth provides a sampling policy, where we can decide how much input traffic is sent to Zipkin. The second smart solution to the big data problem is to send statistics using the message broker instead of the default HTTP endpoint. To enable this feature we have to include the `spring-cloud-sleuth-stream` dependency, which allows your application to become a producer of messages sent to Apache Kafka or RabbitMQ.

Messaging and integration

I have already mentioned messaging brokers and their usage for communication between your application and Zipkin server. Generally, Spring Cloud supports two types of communications via synchronous/asynchronous HTTP and with messaging brokers. The first project from this area is Spring Cloud Bus. It allows you to send broadcast events to applications informing them about state changes such as configuration property updates or other management commands. Actually, we might want to use starters for AMQP with a RabbitMQ broker or for Apache Kafka. As usual, we only need to include `spring-cloud-starter-bus-amqp` or `spring-cloud-starter-bus-kafka` to the dependency management and all other necessary operations are performed through auto-configuration.

Spring Cloud Bus is a rather small project allowing you to use distributed messaging features for common operations such as broadcasting configuration change events. The right framework for building a system consisting of message-driven microservices is the Spring Cloud Stream. This is a really powerful framework and one of the biggest Spring Cloud projects, to which I have dedicated an entire chapter, Chapter 11, *Message Driven Microservices*, of the book. The same as for Spring Cloud Bus, there are two binders available, first for AMQP with RabbitMQ, and second for Apache Kafka. Spring Cloud Stream is based on Spring Integration, which is another large project part of Spring. It provides a programming model, supporting most Enterprise Integration Patterns such as endpoint, channel, aggregator, or transformer. The applications included in the whole microservice system communicate with each other through the Spring Cloud Stream input and output channels. The main communication model between them is Publish/Subscribe, where messages are broadcast through shared topics. Additionally, it is important to support multi instances of every microservice. In most cases, a message should be processed only by a single instance, which is not supported in a Publish/Subscribe model. That's why Spring Cloud Stream introduces grouping mechanisms where only one member of the group receives a message from a destination. The same as earlier, these are two starters that can include a project depending on the binder type `spring-cloud-starter-stream-kafka` or `spring-cloud-starter-stream-rabbit`.

There are two more projects related to Spring Cloud Stream. First, Spring Cloud Stream App Starters defines a set of Spring Cloud Stream applications that can be run independently or using the second project, Spring Cloud Data Flow. Among these applications, we can distinguish connectors, adapters for network protocols, and generic protocols. Spring Cloud Data Flow is another extensive and powerful Spring Cloud toolkit. It simplifies development and deployment by providing a smart solution for building data integration and real-time data processing pipelines. The orchestration of microservice-based data pipelines is achieved with simple DSL, a drag-and-drop UI dashboard, and REST APIs together.

Cloud platform support

Pivotal Cloud Foundry is a cloud-native platform for deploying and managing modern applications. Pivotal Software, as some of you probably already know, is an owner of the Spring framework trademark. The patronage of a large, commercial platform is one of the important reasons for Spring's growing popularity. What is obvious is that PCF fully supports both Spring Boot's executable JAR files, and all of Spring Cloud microservices patterns such as Config Server, service registry, and circuit breaker. These types of tools can be easily run and configured using the marketplace available on the UI dashboard or client command line. Development for PCF is even simpler than with standard Spring Cloud application. The only thing we have to do is to include the right starters to project dependencies:

- `spring-cloud-services-starter-circuit-breaker`
- `spring-cloud-services-starter-config-client`
- `spring-cloud-services-starter-service-registry`

It's difficult to find an opinionated cloud framework that does not have support for AWS. The same is true for Spring Cloud. Spring Cloud for Amazon Web Services provides integration with the most popular web tools available there. This includes modules for communication with **Simple Queueing Service** (**SQS**), **Simple Notification Service** (**SNS**), **ElasticCache**, and **Relational Database Service** (**RDS**) that offer engines such as Aurora, MySQL, or Oracle. The remote resources can be accessed using their name defined in the CloudFormation stack. Everything is opaque in well-known Spring convention and patterns. There are four main modules available:

- **Spring Cloud AWS Core**: Included using the `spring-cloud-starter-aws` starter, provides core components enabling direct access to the EC2 instance
- **Spring Cloud AWS Context**: Delivers access to the Simple Storage Service, Simple E-mail Service, and caching service
- **Spring Cloud AWS JDBC**: Included using starter `spring-cloud-starter-aws-jdbc` starter, provides data source lookup and configuration, which can be used with any data access technology supported by Spring
- **Spring Cloud AWS Messaging**: Included using `starter spring-cloud-starter-aws-messaging` starter, allows an application to send and receive messages with SQS (point-to-point) or SNS (Publish/Subscribe)

There is another project that is worth mentioning although it is still at an early stage of development. That is Spring Cloud Function, which offers support for serverless architecture. Serverless is also known as **FaaS** (**Function-as-a-Service**), where a developer creates only very small modules that are deployed on containers fully managed by a third-party provider. Actually, Spring Cloud Functions implemented adapters for AWS Lambda and Apache OpenWhisk, the most popular FaaS providers. I will be following the development of this project designed for supporting a serverless approach.

In this section, we should not forget about the Spring Cloud Connectors project, formerly known as **Spring Cloud**. It provides an abstraction for JVM-based applications deployed on a cloud platform. Actually, it has support for Heroku and Cloud Foundry, where our application could connect SMTP, RabbitMQ, Redis, or one of the available relational databases using one of the Spring Cloud Heroku Connectors and Spring Cloud Foundry Connector modules.

Other useful libraries

There are some important aspects surrounding microservices architecture, which can't be considered its core features, but are also very important. The first of them is security.

Security

The big part of standard implementation for securing APIs with mechanisms such as OAuth2, JWT, or basic authentication is available in Spring Security and Spring Web projects. Spring Cloud Security uses those libraries to allow us to easily create systems that implement common patterns such as single sign-on and token relay. To enable security management for our application we should include the `spring-cloud-starter-security` starter.

Automated testing

The next important area in microservices development is automated testing. For microservices architecture, contact tests are growing in importance. Martin Fowler gave the following definition:

> *"An integration contract test is a test at the boundary of an external service verifying that it meets the contract expected by a consuming service."*

Spring Cloud has a very interesting implementation for that approach to unit testing, Spring Cloud Contract. It uses WireMock for traffic recording and Maven plugin for generating stubs.

It is also possible that you get the opportunity to use Spring Cloud Task. It helps a developer to create short lived microservices using Spring Cloud, and run them locally or in the cloud environment. To enable it in the project we should include the `spring-cloud-starter-task` starter.

Cluster features

Finally, the last project, Spring Cloud Cluster. It provides a solution for the leadership election and common stateful patterns with an abstraction and implementation for Zookeeper, Redis, Hazelcast, and Consul.

Projects overview

As you can see, Spring Cloud contains many subprojects providing integration with lots of different tools and solutions. I think it is easy to lose track, especially if you are using Spring Cloud for the first time. In accordance with the principle that one diagram might express things better than a thousand words, I'm presenting the most important projects divided into categories as shown in the following diagram:

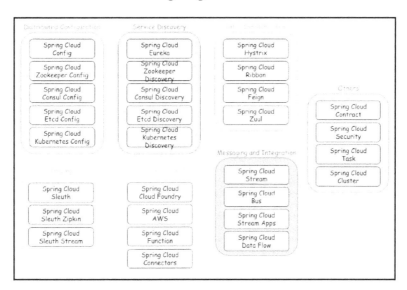

Release trains

As we can see in the preceding diagram, there are many projects inside Spring Cloud and there are many relationships between them. By definition, these are all independent projects with different release cascades and version numbers. In a situation like this, dependency management in our application might be problematic and that will require knowledge about relationships between versions of all projects. To help make it easier, Spring Cloud introduced the starter mechanism, which we have already discussed, and release trains. The release trains are identified by names, not versions, to avoid confusion with the subprojects. What is interesting is that they are named after London tube stations and they are alphabetically ordered. The first release was Angel, the second was Brixton, and so on. The whole mechanism of dependency management is based on **BOM (bill of materials)**, which is a standard Maven concept for managing artifacts versioned independently. Here's an actual table with Spring Cloud project versions assigned to release trains. Names with the suffix M[X], where [X] is the version number, means **milestone**, SR[X] means **service release**, which refers to changes that fix critical bugs. As you can see in the following table, Spring Cloud Stream has it own release trains, which groups its subprojects using the same rules as Spring Cloud project:

Component	Camden.SR7	Dalston.SR4	Edgware.M1	Finchley.M2	Finchley.BUILD-SNAPSHOT
spring-cloud-aws	1.1.4.RELEASE	1.2.1.RELEASE	1.2.1.RELEASE	2.0.0.M1	2.0.0.BUILD-SNAPSHOT
spring-cloud-bus	1.2.2.RELEASE	1.3.1.RELEASE	1.3.1.RELEASE	2.0.0.M1	2.0.0.BUILD-SNAPSHOT
spring-cloud-cli	1.2.4.RELEASE	1.3.4.RELEASE	1.4.0.M1	2.0.0.M1	2.0.0.BUILD-SNAPSHOT
spring-cloud-commons	1.1.9.RELEASE	1.2.4.RELEASE	1.3.0.M1	2.0.0.M2	2.0.0.BUILD-SNAPSHOT
spring-cloud-contract	1.0.5.RELEASE	1.1.4.RELEASE	1.2.0.M1	2.0.0.M2	2.0.0.BUILD-SNAPSHOT
spring-cloud-config	1.2.3.RELEASE	1.3.3.RELEASE	1.4.0.M1	2.0.0.M2	2.0.0.BUILD-SNAPSHOT
spring-cloud-netflix	1.2.7.RELEASE	1.3.5.RELEASE	1.4.0.M1	2.0.0.M2	2.0.0.BUILD-SNAPSHOT
spring-cloud-security	1.1.4.RELEASE	1.2.1.RELEASE	1.2.1.RELEASE	2.0.0.M1	2.0.0.BUILD-SNAPSHOT
spring-cloud-cloudfoundry	1.0.1.RELEASE	1.1.0.RELEASE	1.1.0.RELEASE	2.0.0.M1	2.0.0.BUILD-SNAPSHOT
spring-cloud-consul	1.1.4.RELEASE	1.2.1.RELEASE	1.2.1.RELEASE	2.0.0.M1	2.0.0.BUILD-SNAPSHOT
spring-cloud-sleuth	1.1.3.RELEASE	1.2.5.RELEASE	1.3.0.M1	2.0.0.M2	2.0.0.BUILD-SNAPSHOT
spring-cloud-stream	Brooklyn.SR3	Chelsea.SR2	Ditmars.M2	Elmhurst.M1	Elmhurst.BUILD-SNAPSHOT
spring-cloud-zookeeper	1.0.4.RELEASE	1.1.2.RELEASE	1.2.0.M1	2.0.0.M1	2.0.0.BUILD-SNAPSHOT
spring-boot	1.4.5.RELEASE	1.5.4.RELEASE	1.5.6.RELEASE	2.0.0.M3	2.0.0.M3
spring-cloud-task	1.0.3.RELEASE	1.1.2.RELEASE	1.2.0.RELEASE	2.0.0.M1	2.0.0.RELEASE

Now, all we need to do is provide the right release train name in the dependency management section in the Maven `pom.xml` and then include projects using starters:

```xml
<dependencyManagement>
    <dependencies>
        <dependency>
            <groupId>org.springframework.cloud</groupId>
            <artifactId>spring-cloud-dependencies</artifactId>
            <version>Finchley.M2</version>
            <type>pom</type>
            <scope>import</scope>
        </dependency>
    </dependencies>
</dependencyManagement>
<dependencies>
    <dependency>
        <groupId>org.springframework.cloud</groupId>
        <artifactId>spring-cloud-starter-config</artifactId>
    </dependency>
    ...
</dependencies>
```

Here's the same sample for Gradle:

```
dependencyManagement {
    imports {
        mavenBom ':spring-cloud-dependencies:Finchley.M2'
    }
}
dependencies {
    compile ':spring-cloud-starter-config'
    ...
}
```

Summary

In this chapter, I have introduced the most important projects that are part of Spring Cloud. I have pointed out several areas to which I assigned each of those projects. After reading this chapter, you should be able to recognize which library has to be included in your application to able to implement patterns such as service discovery, distributed configuration, circuit breaker, or load balancer. You should also recognize the differences between application context, and bootstrap context and understand how to include dependencies in the project using dependency management based on the release trains concept. The last thing I wanted to draw your attention to in this chapter were some tools integrated with Spring Cloud such as Consul, Zookeeper, RabbitMQ, or Zipkin. I described all of them in some details. I also pointed out the projects responsible for interaction with those tools.

This chapter completes the first part of the book. In this part, the main goal was to get you into the basics related to Spring Cloud project. After reading it you should be able to recognize the most important elements of microservices-based architecture, effectively use Spring Boot to create simple and more advanced microservices, and finally, you should also be able to list all of the most popular subprojects being that are a part of Spring Cloud. Now, we may proceed to the next part of the book and discuss in detail those subprojects, which are responsible for implementing common patterns of distributed systems in Spring Cloud. Most of them are based on Netflix OSS libraries. We will begin with the solution providing service registry, Eureka discovery server.

4
Service Discovery

Before we got to this point, we had discussed service discovery many times in previous chapters. In fact, it is one of the most popular technical aspects of microservice architecture. Such a subject could not have been omitted from the Netflix OSS implementation. They did not decide to use any existing tool with similar features, but designed and developed a discovery server especially for their own needs. Then, it had been open sourced along with several other tools. The Netflix OSS discovery server is known as **Eureka**.

The Spring Cloud library for integration with Eureka consists of two parts, the client side and the server side. The server is launched as a separate Spring Boot application and exposes an API that allows for the collection of a list of registered services and adding a new service with a location address. The server can be configured and deployed to be highly available, with each server replicating its state with the others. The client is included in the microservice application as a dependency. It is responsible for the registration after startup, the deregistration before shutdown, and for keeping the registration list up to date by polling the Eureka Server.

Here's a list of topics we will cover in this chapter:

- Developing an application that runs embedded Eureka Server
- Connecting to the Eureka Server from the client-side application
- Advanced discovery client configuration
- Enabling secure communication between client and server
- Configuring failover and peer-to-peer replication mechanisms
- Registering instances of a client-side application in different zones

Running Eureka on the server side

Running the Eureka Server within a Spring Boot application is not a difficult task. Let's take a look at how this can be done:

1. First, the right dependency has to be included to our project. Obviously, we will use a starter for that:

```
<dependency>
    <groupId>org.springframework.cloud</groupId>
    <artifactId>spring-cloud-starter-eureka-server</artifactId>
</dependency>
```

2. Eureka Server should also be enabled on the main application class:

```
@SpringBootApplication
@EnableEurekaServer
public class DiscoveryApplication {

    public static void main(String[] args) {
        new
SpringApplicationBuilder(DiscoveryApplication.class).web(true).run(
args);
    }

}
```

3. It is interesting that together with the server starter, client's dependencies are also included. They can be useful for us, but only when launching Eureka in high availability mode with peer-to-peer communication between discovery instances. When running a standalone instance, it doesn't really get us anywhere except printing some errors in the logs during startup. We can either exclude `spring-cloud-netflix-eureka-client` from the starter dependencies or disable discovery client using configuration properties. I prefer the second choice, and also on this occasion, I changed the default server port to something other than `8080`. Here's the fragment of the `application.yml` file:

```
server:
 port: ${PORT:8761}
eureka:
 client:
   registerWithEureka: false
   fetchRegistry: false
```

4. After completing the preceding steps, we can finally launch our first Spring Cloud application. Just run the main class from your IDE or build project with Maven; run it using the `java -jar` command and wait for the log line, `Started Eureka Server`. It's up. A simple UI dashboard is available as a home page at `http://localhost:8761` and HTTP API methods may be called with the `/eureka/*` path. The Eureka dashboard does not provide many features; in fact, it is mostly used for checking out the list of registered services. This could be found out by calling the REST API `http://localhost:8761/eureka/apps` endpoint.

So, to conclude, we know how to run a Eureka standalone server with Spring Boot and how to check the list of registered microservices using the UI console and HTTP methods. But we still don't have any service that is able to register itself in discovery, and it's time to change that. An example application with a discovery server and client implementation is available on GitHub (`https://github.com/piomin/sample-spring-cloud-netflix.git`) in the `master` branch.

Enabling Eureka on the client side

As on the server side, there is only one dependency that has to be included to enable a Eureka Client for the application. So, first include the following starter to your project's dependencies:

```
<dependency>
    <groupId>org.springframework.cloud</groupId>
    <artifactId>spring-cloud-starter-eureka</artifactId>
</dependency>
```

The example application does nothing more than communicate with the Eureka Server. It has to register itself and send metadata information such as host, port, health indicator URL, and home page. Eureka receives heartbeat messages from each instance belonging to a service. If the heartbeat isn't received after a configured period of time, the instance is removed from the registry. The second responsibility of discovery client is fetching data from the server, then caching it and periodically asking for changes. It can be enabled by annotating the main class with `@EnableDiscoveryClient`. Surprisingly, there is another way to activate this feature. You may use an annotation `@EnableEurekaClient`, especially if there are multiple implementations of discovery client within the classpath (Consul, Eureka, ZooKeeper). While `@EnableDiscoveryClient` lives in `spring-cloud-commons`, `@EnableEurekaClient` lives in `spring-cloud-netflix` and only works for Eureka. Here's the main class of the discovery client's application:

```
@SpringBootApplication
@EnableDiscoveryClient
public class ClientApplication {

    public static void main(String[] args) {
        new
SpringApplicationBuilder(ClientApplication.class).web(true).run(args);
    }

}
```

The discovery server address doesn't have to be provided in the client's configuration, because it is available on the default host and port. However, we could easily imagine that Eureka is not listening on its default `8761` port. The fragment of configuration file is visible below. The discovery server network address can be overridden with the `EUREKA_URL` parameter, as can the client's listening port with the `PORT` property. The name under which the application is registered in the discovery server is taken from the `spring.application.name` property:

```
spring:
 application:
   name: client-service

server:
 port: ${PORT:8081}

eureka:
 client:
   serviceUrl:
     defaultZone: ${EUREKA_URL:http://localhost:8761/eureka/}
```

Let's run two independent instances of our sample client application on localhost. To achieve that, the number of the listening port should be overridden for the instance on startup like this:

```
java -jar -DPORT=8081 target/sample-client-service-1.0-SNAPSHOT.jar
java -jar -DPORT=8082 target/sample-client-service-1.0-SNAPSHOT.jar
```

As you can see in the following screenshot, there are two instances of `client-service` registered with the hostname `piomin` and ports `8081` and `8082`:

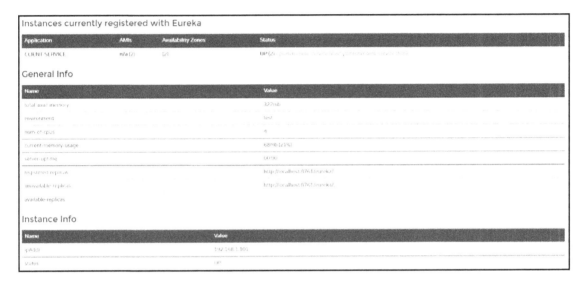

Deregistration on shutdown

Checking how a deregistration works with a Eureka Client is a bit more of a difficult task. Our application should be shut down gracefully in order to be able to intercept a stopped event and send an event to the server. The best way for a graceful shutdown is by using the Spring Actuator `/shutdown` endpoint. The actuator is a part of Spring Boot and it can be included in the project by declaring the `spring-boot-starter-actuator` dependency in `pom.xml`. It is disabled by default, so we have to enable it in the configuration properties. For the sake of simplicity, it is worth disabling user/password security for that endpoint:

```
endpoints:
  shutdown:
    enabled: true
    sensitive: false
```

To shut down the application, we have to call the `POST /shutdown` API method. If you receive the response `{"message": "Shutting down, bye..."}`, it means everything went well and the procedure has been started. Before the application is disabled, some logs starting from the line **Shutting down DiscoveryClient ...** will be printed out. After that, the service will be unregistered from the discovery server and it completely disappears from the list of registered services. I decided to shut down client instance #2 by calling `http://localhost:8082/shutdown` (you may call it using any REST client, for example, Postman), so only the instance running on port `8081` is still visible in the dashboard:

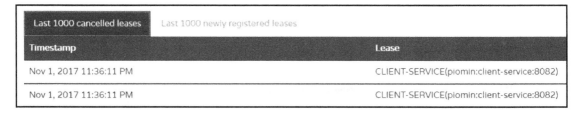

The Eureka Server dashboard also provides a convenient way to check out the history of newly created and canceled leases:

Last 1000 cancelled leases	Last 1000 newly registered leases	
Timestamp		**Lease**
Nov 1, 2017 11:36:11 PM		CLIENT-SERVICE(piomin:client-service:8082)
Nov 1, 2017 11:36:11 PM		CLIENT-SERVICE(piomin:client-service:8082)

Graceful shutdown is obviously the most suitable way of stopping an application, but in the real world, we are not always able to achieve it. Many unexpected things can happen, such as a server machine restart, application failure, or just network problems at the interface between client and server. Such a situation is the same from a discovery server point of view as stopping the client application from your IDE or killing the process from the command line. If you try to do that, you will see that the discovery client shutdown procedure won't be triggered and the service is still visible in the Eureka dashboard with the *UP* status. Moreover, the lease will never expire.

In order to avoid this situation, the default configuration on the server side should be changed. *Why does such a problem appear in the default settings?* Eureka provides a special mechanism by which the registry stops expiring entries when it detects that an certain number of services didn't renew their lease in time. This should protect the registry from clearing all entries when a part of a network failure occurs. That mechanism is called **self-preservation mode** and can be disabled using the `enableSelfPreservation` property in `application.yml`. Of course, it should not be disabled in production:

```
eureka:
  server:
    enableSelfPreservation: false
```

Using discovery client programmatically

After client application startup, the list of registered services is fetched from the Eureka Server automatically. However, it might turn out to be necessary to use Eureka's client API programmatically. We have two possibilities:

- `com.netflix.discovery.EurekaClient`: It implements all HTTP API methods exposed by the Eureka Server, which have been described in the Eureka API section.
- `org.springframework.cloud.client.discovery.DiscoveryClient`: It is a Spring Cloud alternative to the native Netflix `EurekaClient`. It provides a simple, generic API useful for all of the discovery clients. There are two methods available, `getServices` and `getInstances`:

  ```
  private static final Logger LOGGER =
  LoggerFactory.getLogger(ClientController.class);

  @Autowired
  private DiscoveryClient discoveryClient;

  @GetMapping("/ping")
  public List<ServiceInstance> ping() {
   List<ServiceInstance> instances =
  discoveryClient.getInstances("CLIENT-SERVICE");
   LOGGER.info("INSTANCES: count={}", instances.size());
   instances.stream().forEach(it -> LOGGER.info("INSTANCE: id={},
  port={}", it.getServiceId(), it.getPort()));
   return instances;
  }
  ```

There is one interesting thing related to the preceding implementation. If you call the `/ping` endpoint just after the service startup, it won't display any instances. This is related to the response caching mechanisms and it is described in detail in the next section.

Advanced configuration settings

Eureka's configuration settings may be divided into three parts:

- **Server**: It customizes the server behavior. It includes all of the properties with the prefix `eureka.server.*`. The full list of available fields may be found in the `EurekaServerConfigBean` class (`https://github.com/spring-cloud/spring-cloud-netflix/blob/master/spring-cloud-netflix-eureka-server/src/main/java/org/springframework/cloud/netflix/eureka/server/EurekaServerConfigBean.java`).

- **Client**: It is the first of two available property sections on the Eureka Client's side. It is responsible for the configuration of how the client can query the registry in order to locate other services. It includes all of the properties with the prefix `eureka.client.*`. For the full list of available fields, you may refer to the `EurekaClientConfigBean` class (`https://github.com/spring-cloud/spring-cloud-netflix/blob/master/spring-cloud-netflix-eureka-client/src/main/java/org/springframework/cloud/netflix/eureka/EurekaClientConfigBean.java`).

- **Instance**: It customizes the current instance of the Eureka Client's behavior, such as port or name. It includes all of the properties with the prefix `eureka.instance.*`. For the full list of available fields, you may refer to the `EurekaInstanceConfigBean` class (`https://github.com/spring-cloud/spring-cloud-netflix/blob/master/spring-cloud-netflix-eureka-client/src/main/java/org/springframework/cloud/netflix/eureka/EurekaInstanceConfigBean.java`).

I have already shown you how to use some of those properties in order to have the desired effect. I'm going to talk about some interesting scenarios related to configuration settings customization in the next part of this section. It is not needed to describe all of the properties. You may read about them in the comments included in the source code of all of those classes that were listed previously.

Refreshing the registry

Let's back up for a moment to the previous sample. Self-preservation mode has been disabled, but it still takes a long time to wait on the lease cancellation by the server. There are several reasons for this. The first is that every client service sends heartbeats to the server every 30 seconds (default value), which is configurable with the `eureka.instance.leaseRenewalIntervalInSeconds` property. If the server doesn't receive a heartbeat, it waits 90 seconds before removing the instance from the registry and thereby cutting off traffic sent to that instance. It is configurable with the `eureka.instance.leaseExpirationDurationInSeconds` property. Those two parameters are set on the client side. For testing purposes, we define small values in seconds:

```
eureka:
  instance:
    leaseRenewalIntervalInSeconds: 1
    leaseExpirationDurationInSeconds: 2
```

There is also one property that should be changed on the server side. Eureka runs the evict task in the background, which is responsible for checking whether heartbeats from the client are still being received. By default, it is fired every 60 seconds. So even if the interval of lease renewal and the duration of lease expiration are set to relatively low values, the service instance might be removed at worst after 60 seconds. The delay between the subsequent timer ticks can be configured using the `evictionIntervalTimerInMs` property, which is set, in contrast to properties discussed previously, in milliseconds:

```
eureka:
  server:
    enableSelfPreservation: false
    evictionIntervalTimerInMs: 3000
```

All of the required parameters have been defined on both the client and server side. Now, we can run the discovery server again and then three instances of the client application on ports 8081, 8082, and 8083 using the -DPORT VM argument. After that, we will shut down the instances on ports 8081 and 8082 one by one, just by killing their processes. What is the result? The disabled instances are almost immediately removed from Eureka registry. Here's the log fragment from the Eureka Server:

```
2017-11-02 21:44:56.533 INFO 40056 --- [a-EvictionTimer] c.n.e.registry.AbstractInstanceRegistry : Evicting 1 items (expired=1, evictionLimit=1)
2017-11-02 21:44:56.533 WARN 40056 --- [a-EvictionTimer] c.n.e.registry.AbstractInstanceRegistry : DS: Registry: expired lease for CLIENT-SERVICE/piomin:client-
service:8082
2017-11-02 21:44:56.538 INFO 40056 --- [a-EvictionTimer] c.n.e.registry.AbstractInstanceRegistry : Cancelled instance CLIENT-SERVICE/piomin:client-service:8082
(replication=false)
2017-11-02 21:44:59.533 INFO 40056 --- [a-EvictionTimer] c.n.e.registry.AbstractInstanceRegistry : Running the evict task with compensationTime 0ms
2017-11-02 21:44:59.533 INFO 40056 --- [a-EvictionTimer] c.n.e.registry.AbstractInstanceRegistry : Evicting 1 items (expired=1, evictionLimit=1)
2017-11-02 21:44:59.533 WARN 40056 --- [a-EvictionTimer] c.n.e.registry.AbstractInstanceRegistry : DS: Registry: expired lease for CLIENT-SERVICE/piomin:client-
service:8081
2017-11-02 21:44:59.534 INFO 40056 --- [a-EvictionTimer] c.n.e.registry.AbstractInstanceRegistry : Cancelled instance CLIENT-SERVICE/piomin:client-service:8081
(replication=false)
```

There is still one instance available running on port 8083. The appropriate warning related to the deactivation of the self-preservation mode will be printed out on the UI dashboard. Some additional information such as lease expiration status or the number of renews during the last minute may also be interesting. By manipulating all of those properties, we are able to customize the maintenance of the expired lease removal procedure. However, it is important to ensure that defined settings would not lack the performance of a system. There are some other elements sensitive to the changes of configuration, like load balancers, gateways, and circuit breakers. Eureka prints a warning message if you disable the self-preservation mode, you can see it in the following screenshot:

Changing the instance identificator

Instances registered on Eureka are grouped by name, but each of them must send a unique ID, on the basis of which, the server is able to recognize it. Maybe you have noticed that `instanceId` is displayed in the dashboard for every service's group in the **Status** column. Spring Cloud Eureka automatically generates that number and it is equal to the combination of the following fields:

```
${spring.cloud.client.hostname}:${spring.application.name}:${spring.applica
tion.instance_id:${server.port}}}.
```

This identificator may be easily overridden with the `eureka.instance.instanceId` property. For testing purposes, let's launch some instances of the client application with the following configuration settings and the `-DSEQUENCE_NO=[n]` VM argument, where `[n]` is a sequence number starting from `1`. Here's a sample configuration of a client's application that dynamically sets the listen port and discovery `instanceId` based on the `SEQUENCE_NO` parameter:

```
server:
  port: 808${SEQUENCE_NO}
eureka:
  instance:
    instanceId: ${spring.application.name}-${SEQUENCE_NO}
```

The results may be viewed in the Eureka dashboard:

Instances currently registered with Eureka			
Application	**AMIs**	**Availability Zones**	**Status**
CLIENT-SERVICE	n/a (3)	(3)	UP (3) - client-service-2 , client-service-3 , client-service-1

Preferring the IP address

By default, all instances are registered under their hostname. It is a very convenient approach, on the assumption that we have DNS enabled on our network. However, it is not uncommon that DNS is not available for a group of servers used as the microservice environment in the organization. I just had that kind of situation myself. There remains nothing else to do but to add host names and their IP addresses to the `/etc/hosts` file on all of the Linux machines. An alternative to this solution is to change the registration process configuration settings to advertise the IP addresses of services rather than the hostname. To achieve this, the `eureka.instance.preferIpAddress` property should be set to `true` on the client side. Every service instance in the registry will still be printed out to a Eureka dashboard with `instanceId` containing a hostname, but if you click this link the redirection will be performed based on the IP address. The Ribbon client that is responsible for calling other services via HTTP will also follow the same principle.

If you decide to use an IP address as a primary method of determining the network location of the service, you may have a problem. The problem may arise if you have more than one network interface assigned to your machine. For example, in one organization where I have been working, there were different networks for a management mode (a connection from my workstation to the server) and for a production mode (a connection between two servers). In consequence, each server machine had two network interfaces assigned with different IP prefixes. To select the right interface, you can define a list of ignored patterns in the `application.yml` configuration file. For example, we would like to ignore all interfaces where the name starts with `eth1`:

```
spring:
  cloud:
    inetutils:
      ignoredInterfaces:
        - eth1*
```

There is also another way to get that effect. We can define network addresses that should be preferred:

```
spring:
  cloud:
    inetutils:
      preferredNetworks:
        - 192.168
```

Response cache

The Eureka Server caches responses by default. The cache is invalidated every 30 seconds. It can be easily checked by calling the HTTP API endpoint /eureka/apps. If you call it just after the registration of the client application, you will figure out that it is still not returned in the response. Try again after 30 seconds, and you will see that the new instance appears. The response cache timeout may be overridden with the responseCacheUpdateIntervalMs property. Interestingly, there is no cache while displaying a list of registered instances using the Eureka dashboard. In contrast to the REST API, it bypasses the response cache:

```
eureka:
  server:
    responseCacheUpdateIntervalMs: 3000
```

We should remember that the Eureka registry is also cached on the client side. So, even if we changed the cache timeout on the server, it may still take some time until it would be refreshed by the client. The registry is periodically refreshed in an asynchronous, background task that is scheduled every 30 seconds by default. This setting may be overridden by declaring the registryFetchIntervalSeconds property. It only fetches the delta in comparison to the last fetch attempt. This option may be disabled using the shouldDisableDelta property. I defined 3 seconds timeouts on both the server and client sides. If you start the sample application with such settings, /eureka/apps will show the newly registered instance of the service, probably at your first attempt. Unless caching on the client side makes sense, I'm not sure about the sense of caching on the server side, especially since Eureka doesn't have any backend store. Personally, I have never had any need to change the values of those properties, but I guess it can be important, for example, if you develop unit tests with Eureka and you need an immediate response without caching:

```
eureka:
  client:
    registryFetchIntervalSeconds: 3
    shouldDisableDelta: true
```

Enabling secure communication between client and server

Until now, none of the client's connections were being authenticated by the Eureka Server. While in the development mode, security doesn't really matter as much as in the production mode. The lack of it may be a problem. We would like to have, as a bare minimum, the discovery server secured with basic authentication to prevent unauthorized access to any service that knows its network address. Although Spring Cloud reference material claims that *HTTP basic authentication will be automatically added to your Eureka Client*, I had to include a starter with security to the project dependencies:

```
<dependency>
    <groupId>org.springframework.boot</groupId>
    <artifactId>spring-boot-starter-security</artifactId>
</dependency>
```

Then, we should enable security and set the default credentials by changing the configuration settings in the `application.yml` file:

```
security:
 basic:
   enabled: true
 user:
   name: admin
   password: admin123
```

Now, all HTTP API endpoints and the Eureka dashboard are secured. To enable the basic authentication mode on the client side, the credentials should be provided within the URL connection address, as you can see in the following configuration settings. An example application that implements secure discovery is available in the same repository (`https://github.com/piomin/sample-spring-cloud-netflix.git`) as the basic example, but you need to switch to the `security` branch (`https://github.com/piomin/sample-spring-cloud-netflix/tree/security`). Here's the configuration that enabled HTTP basic authentication on the client side:

```
eureka:
 client:
   serviceUrl:
     defaultZone: http://admin:admin123@localhost:8761/eureka/
```

For more advanced use, such as secure SSL connection with certificate authentication between discovery client and server, we should provide a custom implementation of `DiscoveryClientOptionalArgs`. We will discuss such an example in `Chapter 12`, *Securing an API*, specifically dedicated to security for Spring Cloud applications.

Registering a secure service

Securing the server side is one thing; registering a secure application is something else. Let's look at how we can do this:

1. To enable SSL for a Spring Boot application, we need to start with generating a self-signed certificate. I recommend you use `keytool` for that, which is available under your JRE root in the `bin` catalog:

```
keytool -genkey -alias client -storetype PKCS12 -keyalg RSA -
keysize 2048 -keystore keystore.p12 -validity 3650
```

2. Enter the required data and copy the generated keystore file `keystore.p12` to your application's `src/main/resources` catalog. The next step is to enable HTTPS for Spring Boot using configuration properties in `application.yml`:

```yaml
server:
  port: ${PORT:8081}
  ssl:
    key-store: classpath:keystore.p12
    key-store-password: 123456
    keyStoreType: PKCS12
    keyAlias: client
```

3. After running the application, you should be able to call the secure endpoint `https://localhost:8761/info`. We also need to perform some changes in the Eureka client instance configuration:

```yaml
eureka:
  instance:
    securePortEnabled: true
    nonSecurePortEnabled: false
    statusPageUrl: https://${eureka.hostname}:${server.port}/info
    healthCheckUrl: https://${eureka.hostname}:${server.port}/health
    homePageUrl: https://${eureka.hostname}:${server.port}/
```

Eureka API

Spring Cloud Netflix provides a client written in Java that hides the Eureka HTTP API from the developer. In case we use other frameworks than Spring, Netflix OSS provides a vanilla Eureka client that can be included as a dependency. However, we may imagine a need to call the Eureka API directly, for example, if the application is written in another language than Java, or we need such information as a list of registered services in the Continuous Delivery process. Here's a table for quick reference:

HTTP endpoint	Description
POST /eureka/apps/appID	Add a new instance of the service to the registry
DELETE /eureka/apps/appID/instanceID	Remove the instance of the service from the registry
PUT /eureka/apps/appID/instanceID	Send a heartbeat to the server
GET /eureka/apps	Get details about the list of all registered instances of services
GET /eureka/apps/appID	Get details about the list of all registered instances of a specific service
GET /eureka/apps/appID/instanceID	Get details about a single instance of the service
PUT /eureka/apps/appID/instanceID/metadata?key=value	Update metadata parameters
GET /eureka/instances/instanceID	Get details about all registered instances with a specific ID
PUT /eureka/apps/appID/instanceID/status?value=DOWN	Update the status of the instance

Replication and high availability

We have already discussed some useful Eureka settings, but until now we have analyzed only a system with a single service discovery server. Such a configuration is valid, but only in development mode. For production mode, we would like to have at least two discovery servers running in case one of them fails or a network problem occurs. Eureka is by definition built for availability and resiliency, two primary pillars of development at Netflix. But it does not provide standard clustering mechanisms such as leadership election or automatically joining to the cluster. It is based on the peer-to-peer replication model. It means that all of the servers replicate data and send heartbeats to all of the peers, which are set in configuration for the current server node. Such an algorithm is simple and effective for containing data, but it also has some drawbacks. It limits scalability, because every node has to withstand the entire write load on the server.

Architecture of the sample solution

Interestingly, a replication mechanism was one of the major motivations to begin work on the new version of the Eureka Server. Eureka 2.0 is still under active development. Besides optimized replication, it will also provide some interesting features such as a push model from the server to clients for any changes in the registration list, auto-scaled servers, and a rich dashboard. This solution seems promising, but Spring Cloud Netflix still uses version 1 and to be honest I was not able to find any plans for the migration to version 2. The current Eureka version for Dalston.SR4 Release Train is 1.6.2. The configuration of the clustering mechanism on the server side comes down to one thing, the set URL of another discovery server using `eureka.client.*` properties section. The selected server would just register itself in the other servers, which were chosen to be a part of the created cluster. The best way to show how this solution works in practice is of course by example.

Let's begin with the architecture of the example system, which is shown in the following diagram. All of our applications will be run locally on different ports. At this stage, we have to introduce the example of the API gateway based on Netflix Zuul. It would be helpful for the purpose of load balancing tests between three instances of a service registered in different zones:

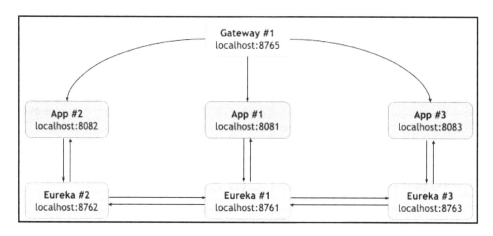

Building the example application

For the Eureka Server, all of the required changes may be defined in configuration properties. In the `application.yml` file, I defined three different profiles for each instance of the discovery service. Now, if you try to run Eureka Server embedded in the Spring Boot application, you need to activate the specific profile by providing the VM argument – `Dspring.profiles.active=peer[n]`, where `[n]` is the instance sequence number:

```
spring:
 profiles: peer1
eureka:
 instance:
   hostname: peer1
   metadataMap:
     zone: zone1
 client:
   serviceUrl:
     defaultZone:
http://localhost:8762/eureka/,http://localhost:8763/eureka/
 server:
 port: ${PORT:8761}
```

```
---
spring:
  profiles: peer2
eureka:
  instance:
    hostname: peer2
    metadataMap:
      zone: zone2
  client:
    serviceUrl:
      defaultZone:
http://localhost:8761/eureka/,http://localhost:8763/eureka/
  server:
    port: ${PORT:8762}

---
spring:
  profiles: peer3
eureka:
  instance:
    hostname: peer3
    metadataMap:
      zone: zone3
  client:
    serviceUrl:
      defaultZone:
http://localhost:8761/eureka/,http://localhost:8762/eureka/
  server:
    port: ${PORT:8763}
```

After running all three instances of Eureka using different profile names, we created a local discovery cluster. If you take a look at the Eureka dashboard for any instance just after startup, it always looks the same, we have three instances of **DISCOVERY-SERVICE** visible:

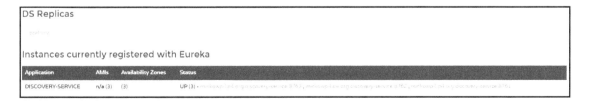

The next step is to run the client application. The configuration settings in the projects are very similar to those for the application with the Eureka Server. The order of addresses provided in the `defaultZone` field determines the sequence of connection attempts to different discovery services. If the connection to the first server cannot be established, it tries to connect with the second one from the list, and so on. The same as earlier, we should set the VM argument `-Dspring.profiles.active=zone[n]` to select the right profile. I also suggest you set the `-Xmx192m` parameter, keeping in mind that we test all of the services locally. If you do not provide any memory limits for the Spring Cloud application it consumes around 350 MB of heap after starting, and about 600 MB of total memory. Unless you have got a lot of RAM it may make it difficult to run multiple instances of microservices on your local machine:

```
spring:
 profiles: zone1
eureka:
 client:
   serviceUrl:
     defaultZone:
http://localhost:8761/eureka/,http://localhost:8762/eureka/,http://localhos
t:8763/eureka/
 server:
  port: ${PORT:8081}


---
spring:
 profiles: zone2
eureka:
 client:
   serviceUrl:
     defaultZone:
http://localhost:8762/eureka/,http://localhost:8761/eureka/,http://localhos
t:8763/eureka/
 server:
  port: ${PORT:8082}


---
spring:
 profiles: zone3
eureka:
 client:
   serviceUrl:
     defaultZone:
http://localhost:8763/eureka/,http://localhost:8761/eureka/,http://localhos
t:8762/eureka/
 server:
  port: ${PORT:8083}
```

Let's take a look at the Eureka dashboard again. We have three instances of `client-service` registered everywhere, although the application has been originally connected to only one instance of the discovery service. The result is the same no matter which discovery service instance's dashboard we go into to look at. It was the exact purpose of this exercise. Now, we create some additional implementation only to demonstrate that everything works in accordance with the assumptions:

The client application does nothing more than expose a REST endpoint that prints the selected profile name. The profile name points to the primary discovery service instance for the particular application instance. Here's a simple `@RestController` implementation that prints the name of the current zone:

```
@RestController
public class ClientController {
  @Value("${spring.profiles}")
  private String zone;

  @GetMapping("/ping")
  public String ping() {
    return "I'm in zone " + zone;
  }

}
```

Finally, we can proceed to the implementation of API gateway. It's out of the scope of this chapter to go into detail about features provided by Zuul, Netflix's API gateway, and router. We will discuss it in the next chapters. Zuul will now be helpful in testing our sample solution, because it is able to retrieve the list of services registered in the discovery server and perform load balancing between all of the running instances of the client application. As you can see in the following configuration fragment, we use a discovery server listening on port `8763`. All incoming requests with the `/api/client/**` path would be routed to `client-service`:

```
zuul:
 prefix: /api
 routes:
```

```
    client:
      path: /client/**
      serviceId: client-service

  eureka:
    client:
      serviceUrl:
        defaultZone: http://localhost:8763/eureka/
      registerWithEureka: false
```

Let's move on to the testing. Our application with the Zuul proxy should be launched using the `java -jar` command and unlike previous services, there is no need to set any additional parameters, including a profile name. It is connected by default with discovery service number #3. To invoke the client API via the Zuul proxy, you have to type the following address into your web browser, `http://localhost:8765/api/client/ping`. The result is visible in the following screenshot:

If you retry the request a few times in a row, it should be load balanced between all of the existing `client-service` instances in the proportions 1:1:1, although our gateway is connected only to discovery #3. This example fully demonstrates how to build service discovery with multiple Eureka instances.

The preceding example application is available on GitHub (`https://github.com/piomin/sample-spring-cloud-netflix.git`) in the `cluster` branch (`https://github.com/piomin/sample-spring-cloud-netflix/tree/cluster_no_zones`).

Failover

You probably wish to ask what's going to happen if one instance of service discovery breaks down? In order to check how the cluster would behave in case of failure, we are going to modify the earlier sample a little. Now, Zuul has a failover connection to the second service discovery available on port `8762` set in its configuration settings. For testing purposes, we shut down the third instance of the discovery service available on port `8763`:

```
eureka:
  client:
    serviceUrl:
      defaultZone:
http://localhost:8763/eureka/,http://localhost:8762/eureka/
    registerWithEureka: false
```

The current situation is illustrated in the following diagram. Testing is performed in the same way as earlier, by calling the gateway's endpoint available under the `http://localhost:8765/api/client/ping address`. And the result is also the same as for the previous test, load balancing is performed equally among all three `client-service` instances as expected. Although discovery service #3 has been disabled, two other instances are still able to communicate with each other and have information about the network location of the third client application instance replicated from instance #3 as long as it was active. Now, even if we restart our gateway, it is still able to connect the discovery cluster using the second address in order, set inside the `defaultZone` field `http://localhost:8762/eureka`. The same applies to the third instance of the client application, which in turn has discovery service #1 as a backup connection:

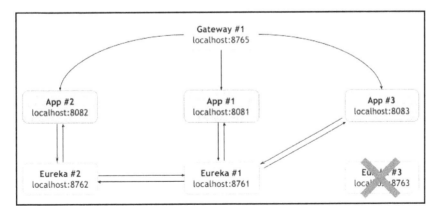

Zones

A cluster-based on a peer-to-peer replication model is a good way to go in most cases, but not always enough. Eureka has one more interesting feature that can be very useful in a clustered environment. A zone mechanism is, in fact, the default behavior. Even if we have a single standalone service discovery instance, every client's property has to be set to `eureka.client.serviceUrl.defaultZone` in the configuration settings. When will this be useful to us? To analyze it, we go back to the example from the previous section. Let's imagine that now we have our environment divided into three different physical networks, or we just have three different machines processing the incoming requests. Of course, discovery services are still grouped logically in the cluster, but each instance is placed in a separated zone. Every client application would be registered in the same zone as its main discovery server. Instead of one instance of the Zuul gateway, we are going to launch three instances, each one for a single zone. If the request comes into a gateway, it should prefer those clients that leverage services within the same zone before trying to call services registered in another zone. The current system architecture is visualized in the following diagram. Of course, for example purposes, the architecture was simplified to be able to run on a single local machine. In the real world, like I mentioned before, it would be launched on three different machines or even on three different groups of machines, physically separated into other networks:

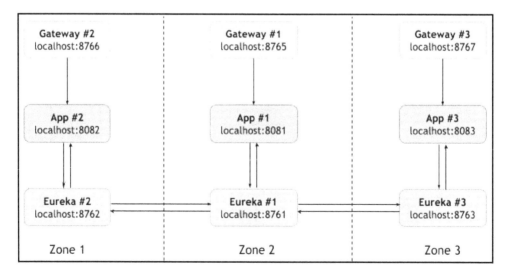

Zones with a standalone server

At this stage, we should emphasize one important thing, the zoning mechanism is realized only on the client side. This means that the service discovery instance is not assigned to any zone. So the preceding diagram may be slightly confusing, but it indicates which Eureka is the default service discovery for all client applications and gateways registered in the specific zone. Our purpose is to check out the mechanisms in the high availability mode, but we may as well build it only with a single discovery server. The following diagram illustrates a similar situation as the previous diagram, except that it assumes the existence of only a single discovery server for all of the applications:

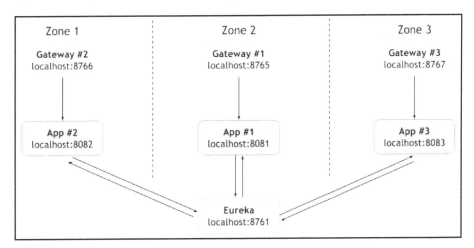

Building an example application

To enable zone handling, we need to perform some changes in the client's and gateway's configuration settings. Here's a modified `application.yml` file from the client application:

```
spring:
  profiles: zone1
eureka:
  instance:
    metadataMap:
      zone: zone1
  client:
    serviceUrl:
      defaultZone:
http://localhost:8761/eureka/,http://localhost:8762/eureka/,http://localhos
t:8763/eureka/
```

The only thing that had to be updated is
the `eureka.instance.metadataMap.zone` property, where we set the names of the zone
and our service had been registered.

More changes have to be made in the gateway configuration. First, we need to add three
profiles to be able to run an application registered in three different zones and three
different discovery servers. Now when launching the gateway application, we should set
the VM argument `-Dspring.profiles.active=zone[n]` to select the right profile.
Similar to `client-service`, we also had to add
the `eureka.instance.metadataMap.zone` property within the configuration
settings. There is also one property, `eureka.client.preferSameZoneEureka`, used for
the first time in the example, which had to be equal to `true` if the gateway should prefer
instances of the client application registered in the same zone:

```
spring:
 profiles: zone1
eureka:
 client:
   serviceUrl:
     defaultZone: http://localhost:8761/eureka/
     registerWithEureka: false
     preferSameZoneEureka: true
 instance:
   metadataMap:
     zone: zone1
server:
 port: ${PORT:8765}


---
spring:
 profiles: zone2
eureka:
 client:
   serviceUrl:
     defaultZone: http://localhost:8762/eureka/
     registerWithEureka: false
     preferSameZoneEureka: true
 instance:
   metadataMap:
     zone: zone2
server:
 port: ${PORT:8766}


---
spring:
```

```
    profiles: zone3
  eureka:
   client:
     serviceUrl:
       defaultZone: http://localhost:8763/eureka/
       registerWithEureka: false
       preferSameZoneEureka: true
   instance:
     metadataMap:
       zone: zone3
  server:
   port: ${PORT:8767}
```

After launching all of the instances of discovery, client, and gateway applications, we can try to call endpoints available under the `http://localhost:8765/api/client/ping`, `http://localhost:8766/api/client/ping`, and `http://localhost:8767/api/client/ping` addresses. Every one of them would always be communicating with the client instance registered in the same zone. So in contrast to tests without a preferred zone, for example, the first instance of gateway available under port 8765 always prints **I'm in zone zone1** while calling the ping endpoint:

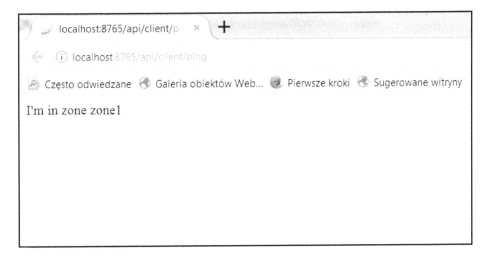

What will happen when client #1 is not available? The incoming requests would be load balanced 50/50 between two other instances of the client application, because they are both in different zones than gateway #1.

Summary

In this chapter, we had the opportunity to develop applications using Spring Cloud for the first time in this book. In my opinion, the best way to start an adventure with a framework for microservices is with trying to figure out how to implement service discovery properly. Starting with the simplest use cases and examples, we have been going through advanced and production-ready features provided by the Netflix OSS Eureka project. I have shown you how to create and run a basic client and a standalone discovery server in *five minutes*. Based on that implementation, I have introduced how to customize the Eureka client and server to meet our specific needs, placing the emphasis on negative scenarios such as network or application failure. Such features as the REST API or UI dashboard have been discussed in detail. Finally, I have shown you how to create a production-ready environment using Eureka's mechanisms such as replication, zones, and high availability. With that knowledge, you should be able to choose those features of Eureka through which you build a service discovery adapted to the specifics of your microservice-based architecture.

Once we have discussed service discovery, we may proceed to the next essential element in microservice-based architecture, a configuration server. Both discovery and configuration services are usually based on key/value stores, so they may be provided with the same products. However, since Eureka is dedicated only to discovery, Spring Cloud introduces their own framework for managing distributed configurations, Spring Cloud Config.

Distributed Configuration with Spring Cloud Config

5

It is the right time to introduce a new element in our architecture, a distributed configuration server. Similar to service discovery, this is one of the key concepts around microservices. In the previous chapter, we discussed in detail how to prepare discovery, both on the server and client sides. But so far, we have always provided a configuration for the application using properties placed inside a fat JAR file. That approach has one big disadvantage, it requires a recompilation and a redeployment of the microservice's instance. Another approach supported by Spring Boot assumes the use of an explicit configuration stored in a filesystem outside of the fat JAR. It can be easily configured for an application during startup with the `spring.config.location` property. That approach does not require a redeployment, but it is also not free from drawbacks. With a lot of microservices, a configuration management based on explicit files placed in a filesystem may be really troublesome. In addition, let's imagine that there are many instances of every microservice and each of them has a specific configuration. Well, with that approach it is better not to imagine it.

Anyway, a distributed configuration is a very popular standard in a cloud-native environment. Spring Cloud Config provides server-side and client-side support for externalized configuration in a distributed system. With that solution, we have one central place where we can manage external properties for applications across all environments. The concept is really simple and easy to implement. A server does nothing more than expose HTTP and resource-based API interfaces, which returns `property` files in JSON, YAML, or properties formats. Additionally, it performs decryption and encryption operations for returned property values. A client needs to fetch configuration settings from a server, and also decrypt them if such a feature has been enabled on the server side.

Configuration data may be stored in different repositories. The default implementation of `EnvironmentRepository` uses a Git backend. It is also possible to set up other VCS systems such as SVN. If you don't want to take advantage of features provided by VCS as a backend, you may use the filesystem or Vault. Vault is a tool for managing secrets, which stores and controls access to such resources as tokens, passwords, certificates, and API keys.

The topics we will cover in this chapter are:

- HTTP API exposed by Spring Cloud Config Server
- Different types of repository backend on the server side
- Integrating with service discovery
- Reloading the configuration automatically with Spring Cloud Bus and message broker

Introduction to HTTP API resources

The Config Server provides the HTTP API, which may be invoked in various ways. The following endpoints are available:

- `/{application}/{profile}[/{label}]`: This returns data in a JSON format; the label parameter is optional
- `/{application}-{profile}.yml`: This returns the YAML format
- `/{label}/{application}-{profile}.yml`: A variant of the previous endpoint, where we can pass an optional label parameter
- `/{application}-{profile}.properties`: This returns the simple key/value format used by properties files
- `/{label}/{application}-{profile}.properties`: A variant of the previous endpoint, where we can pass an optional label parameter

From a client point of view, the application parameter is the name of the application, which is taken from the `spring.application.name` or `spring.config.name` property, and profile is an active profile or comma-separated list of active profiles. The last available parameter `label` is an optional property, important only while working with Git as a backend store. It sets the name of the Git branch for configuration and defaults to `master`.

Native profile support

Let's begin with the simplest example, based on a filesystem backend. By default, Spring Cloud Config Server tries to fetch configuration data from a Git repository. To enable the native profile, we should launch the server with the `spring.profiles.active` option set to `native`. It searches for files stored in the following locations, `classpath:/`, `classpath:/config`, `file:./`, `file:./config`. It means that properties or YAML files may be also placed inside a JAR file. For test purposes, I created a config folder inside `src/main/resources`. Our configuration files will be stored in that location. Now, we need to go back for a moment to the example from the previous chapter. As you probably remember, I introduced the configuration for a clustered discovery environment, where each client service instance was launched in a different zone. There were three available zones and three client instances, each of them has its own profile in the `application.yml` file. The source code for that example is available in the `config` branch. Here's the link:

```
https://github.com/piomin/sample-spring-cloud-netflix/tree/config
```

Our current task is to migrate that configuration to the Spring Cloud Config Server. Let's remind ourselves the properties set for that example. Here are the profile settings used for the first instance of the client application. According to the selected profile, there are a changing instance running port, a default discovery server URL and a zone name:

```
---
spring:
  profiles: zone1

eureka:
  instance:
    metadataMap:
      zone: zone1
    client:
      serviceUrl:
        defaultZone: http://localhost:8761/eureka/

server:
  port: ${PORT:8081}
```

In the described example I placed all of the profiles settings in a single `application.yml` file for simplicity. That file might as well be divided into three different files with the names including the profiles, `application-zone1.yml`, `application-zone2.yml`, and `application-zone3.yml`. Of course, such names are unique to a single application, so if we decided to move the files into a remote configuration server, we should take care of their names. The client application name is injected from `spring.application.name` and in this case, it is `client-service`. So, to conclude, I created three configuration files with the name `client-service-zone[n].yml` in the `src/main/resources/config` catalog, where [n] is an instance's number. Now, when you call the `http://localhost:8888/client-service/zone1` endpoint, you will receive the following response in JSON format:

```
{
  "name":"client-service",
  "profiles":["zone1"],
  "label":null,
  "version":null,
  "state":null,
  "propertySources":[{
    "name":"classpath:/config/client-service-zone1.yml",
    "source":{
      "eureka.instance.metadataMap.zone":"zone1",
"eureka.client.serviceUrl.defaultZone":"http://localhost:8761/eureka/",
      "server.port":"${PORT:8081}"
    }
  }]
}
```

We can also call `http://localhost:8888/client-service-zone2.properties` for the second instance, which returns the following response as a list of properties:

```
eureka.client.serviceUrl.defaultZone: http://localhost:8762/eureka/
eureka.instance.metadataMap.zone: zone2
server.port: 8082
```

The last available version of the HTTP API endpoint, `http://localhost:8889/client-service-zone3.yml`, returns data identical to the input file. Here's the result for the third instance:

```
eureka:
  client:
    serviceUrl:
      defaultZone: http://localhost:8763/eureka/
  instance:
    metadataMap:
```

```
     zone: zone3
  server:
   port: 8083
```

Building a server-side application

We have started by discussing HTTP, a resource-based API provided by the Spring Cloud Config Server, and the way of creating and storing properties there. But now let's move back to the basics. The same as a discovery server, a Config Server may be run as a Spring Boot application. To enable it on the server side, we should include spring-cloud-config-server in our dependencies in the pom.xml file:

```
<dependency>
   <groupId>org.springframework.cloud</groupId>
   <artifactId>spring-cloud-config-server</artifactId>
</dependency>
```

In addition to this, we should enable the Config Server on the main application class. It would be a good idea to change the server port to 8888, because it is the default value of the spring.cloud.config.uri property on the client side. For example, it is auto configured on the client side. To switch the server to a different port, you should set the server.port property on 8888 or launch it with the spring.config.name=configserver property. There is a configserver.yml embedded in the spring-cloud-config-server library:

```
@SpringBootApplication
@EnableConfigServer
public class ConfigApplication {

 public static void main(String[] args) {
    new
SpringApplicationBuilder(ConfigApplication.class).web(true).run(args);
  }

}
```

Building a client-side application

If you set port 8888 as the default for the server, the configuration on the client side is really simple. All you need to do is to provide the bootstrap.yml file with the application name and include the following dependency in your pom.xml. Of course, that rule is applicable only on localhost, because the auto-configured Config Server address for a client is http://localhost:8888:

```
<dependency>
  <groupId>org.springframework.cloud</groupId>
  <artifactId>spring-cloud-starter-config</artifactId>
</dependency>
```

If you set a port different than 8888 for the server, or it is running on a different machine than the client application, you should also set its current address in bootstrap.yml. Here are the bootstrap context settings, which allow you to fetch properties for client-service from the server available on port 8889. When running the application with the --spring.profiles.active=zone1 argument, it automatically fetches the properties set for the zone1 profile in the configuration server:

```
spring:
 application:
   name: client-service
 cloud:
   config:
     uri: http://localhost:8889
```

Adding a Eureka Server

As you have probably noticed, there is the discovery service network location address in the client's properties. So, before launching the client service we should have a Eureka Server running. Of course, Eureka also has its own configuration, which has been stored in the application.yml file for the example from the previous chapter. That configuration, similar to client-service, has been divided into three profiles, where each of them differ from the others in such properties as the number of the server's HTTP port and the list of discovery peers to communicate with.

Now, we place those `property` files on the configuration server. Eureka fetches all of the settings assigned to the selected profile on startup. File naming is consistent with the already described standard, which means `discovery-service-zone[n].yml`. Before running the Eureka Server, we should include `spring-cloud-starter-config` in the dependencies to enable Spring Cloud Config Client, and replace `application.yml` with `bootstrap.yml`, which is shown here:

```
spring:
  application:
    name: discovery-service
  cloud:
    config:
      uri: http://localhost:8889
```

Now, we may run three instances of the Eureka Server in peer-to-peer communication mode by setting a different profile name in the `--spring.profiles.active` property. After launching three instances of `client-service`, our architecture looks like the following diagram. In comparison to the example from the previous chapter, both client and discovery services fetch the configuration from the Spring Cloud Config Server, instead of keeping it as a YML file inside a fat JAR:

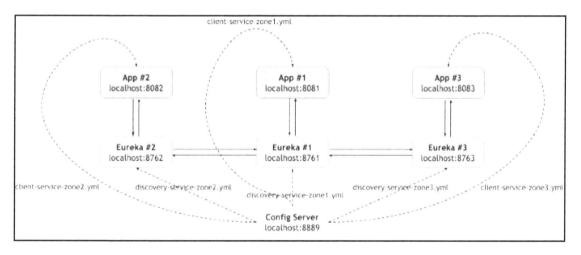

Client-side bootstrap approaches

In the example solution described previously, all of the applications must hold the network location of the configuration server. The network location of service discovery is stored there as a property. At this point, we are confronted with an interesting problem to discuss. We could ask whether our microservices should be aware of the Config Server's network address. In previous discussions, we have agreed that the main place all the service's network locations should be kept is the service discovery server. The configuration server is also a Spring Boot application like other microservices, so logically it should register itself with Eureka to enable the automated discovery mechanism for other services that have to fetch data from the Spring Cloud Config Server. This in turn requires placing the service discovery connection settings in `bootstrap.yml` instead of the `spring.cloud.config.uri` property.

Choosing between these two different approaches is one of the decisions you need to make while designing your system architecture. It's not that one solution is better than the other. The default behavior for any application that uses the `spring-cloud-config-client` artifact is called **Config First Bootstrap** in Spring Cloud nomenclature. When a config client starts up, it binds to the server and initializes the context with remote property sources. That approach has been presented in the first example in this chapter. In the second solution, the Config Server registers with the service discovery and all of the applications may use `DiscoveryClient` to locate it. That approach is called **Discovery First Bootstrap**. Let's implement an example that illustrates that concept.

Config Server discovery

To access that example on GitHub, you need to switch to the `config_with_discovery` branch. Here's the link:

`https://github.com/piomin/sample-spring-cloud-netflix/tree/config_with_discovery`.

The first change is related to the `sample-service-discovery` module. We don't need the `spring-cloud-starter-config` dependency there. The simple configuration is not fetched from remote property sources, but set in `bootstrap.yml`. In contrast to the previous example, we launch a single standalone Eureka instance in order to simplify the exercise:

```
spring:
  application:
    name: discovery-service
```

```
server:
 port: ${PORT:8761}

eureka:
 client:
    registerWithEureka: false
    fetchRegistry: false
```

By contrast, we should include the `spring-cloud-starter-eureka` dependency for the
Config Server. Now, the full list of dependencies is shown in the following code. Moreover,
a discovery client has to be enabled by declaring the `@EnableDiscoveryClient`
annotation on the main class, and the Eureka Server address should be provided by setting
the `eureka.client.serviceUrl.defaultZone` property to
`http://localhost:8761/eureka/` in the `application.yml` file:

```
<dependency>
   <groupId>org.springframework.cloud</groupId>
   <artifactId>spring-cloud-config-server</artifactId>
</dependency>
<dependency>
   <groupId>org.springframework.cloud</groupId>
   <artifactId>spring-cloud-starter-eureka</artifactId>
</dependency>
```

On the client application side, it is no longer needed to hold the address of the configuration
server. The only thing that has to be set is the service ID, in case it is different than
the Config Server. In accordance with the naming convention used for the services in the
presented examples, that ID is `config-server`. It should be overridden with the
`spring.cloud.config.discovery.serviceId` property. In order to allow discovery
mechanism enable the discovery mechanism to fetch remote property sources from
the configuration server, we should set
`spring.cloud.config.discovery.enabled=true`:

```
spring:
 application:
    name: client-service
 cloud:
    config:
      discovery:
        enabled: true
        serviceId: config-server
```

Here's the screen with the Eureka dashboard, with one instance of the Config Server and three instances of `client-service` registered. Every instance of the client's Spring Boot application is the same as for the previous example and was launched with the `--spring.profiles.active=zone[n]` parameter, where `n` is the number of the zone. The only difference is that all of the client's service configuration files served by the Spring Cloud Config Server have the same connection address as the Eureka Server:

Instances currently registered with Eureka			
Application	**AMIs**	**Availability Zones**	**Status**
CLIENT-SERVICE	n/a (3)	(3)	**UP** (3) - minkowp-l.p4.org:client-service:8082 , minkowp-l.p4.org:client-service:8081 , minkowp-l.p4.org:client-service:8083
CONFIG-SERVER	n/a (1)	(1)	**UP** (1) - minkowp-l.p4.org:config-server:8889

Repository backend types

All of the previous examples in this chapter have used the filesystem backend, which means that the config files were loaded from the local filesystem or classpath. This type of backend is very good for tutorial purposes or for testing. If you would like to use Spring Cloud Config in production, it is worth considering the other options. The first of them is a repository backend based on Git, which is also enabled by default. It is not the only one **version control system** (**VCS**) that can be used as a repository for configuration sources. The other option is SVN, or we can even decide to create a composite environment, which may consist of both Git and SVN repositories. The next supported backend type is based on a tool provided by HashiCorp, Vault. It is especially useful when managing security properties such as passwords or certificates. Let's take a closer look at each of the solutions listed here.

Filesystem backend

I won't write a lot about this topic, because it has already been discussed in the previous examples. All of them have shown how to store property sources in the classpath. There is also the ability to load them from disk. By default, the Spring Cloud Config Server tries to locate files inside an application's working directory or the config subdirectory at this location. We can override the default location with the `spring.cloud.config.server.native.searchLocations` property. The search location path may contain placeholders for `application`, `profile`, and `label`. If you don't use any placeholders in the location path, the repository automatically appends the label parameter as a suffix.

As a consequence, the configuration files are loaded from each search location and a subdirectory with the same name as the label. For example, `file:/home/example/config` is the same as `file:/home/example/config,file:/home/example/config/{label}`. This behavior may be disabled by setting `spring.cloud.config.server.native.addLabelLocations` to `false`.

As I have already mentioned, a filesystem backend is not a good choice for a production deployment. If you place property sources in a classpath inside a JAR file, every change requires a recompilation of the application. On the other hand, using a filesystem outside of a JAR does not need recompilation, but this approach may be troublesome if you have more than one instance of a config service working in a high availability mode. In that case, share the filesystem across all of the instances or hold a copy of all of the property sources per running instance. The Git backend is free from such disadvantages, and that's why it is recommended for production use.

Git backend

The Git version control system has some features that make it very useful as a repository for property sources. It allows you to easily manage and audit changes. By using well-known VCS mechanisms such as commit, revert, and branching, we can perform important operations a lot easier than in a filesystem approach. This type of backend also has another two key advantages. It forces a separation between the Config Server source code and the `property` files repository. If you take a look one more time at the previous examples, you will see that the `property` files were stored together with the application source code. Probably some of you would say that even if we used a filesystem backend, we can store the whole configuration as a separate project on Git and upload it to a remote server on demand. Of course, you would be right. But when using a Git backend with the Spring Cloud Config, you have those mechanisms available out of the box. In addition, it resolves the problems related to running multiple instances of the server. If you use a remote Git server, the changes may be easily shared across all of the running instances.

Different protocols

To set the location of the Git repository for the application, we should use the `spring.cloud.config.server.git.uri` property in `application.yml`. If you are familiar with Git, you well know that cloning may be realized using file, http/https, and ssh protocols. The local repository access allows you to get started quickly without a remote server. It is configured with file, prefix, for example, `spring.cloud.config.server.git.uri=file:/home/git/config-repo`. For more advanced usage when running Config Server in the high availability mode, you should use the remote protocols SSH or HTTPS. In this case, Spring Cloud Config clones a remote repository and then bases it on the local working copy as a cache.

Using placeholders in URIs

All the recently listed placeholders, `application`, `profile`, and `label`, are also supported here. We can create a single repository per application using a placeholder as in `https://github.com/piomin/{application}`, or even per profile, `https://github.com/piomin/{profile}`. This type of backend implementation maps the label parameter of the HTTP resource to a Git label, which may refer to commit ID, branch, or tag name. The most appropriate way to discover interesting features for us is obviously through an example. Let's begin by creating a Git repository dedicated to storing the application's property sources.

Building a server application

I created an example configuration repository, which is available on GitHub here:

`https://github.com/piomin/sample-spring-cloud-config-repo.git`.

I placed all of the property sources used in the first example in this chapter, which illustrated native profile support for client applications running in different discovery zones. Now, our repository holds the files visible in this list:

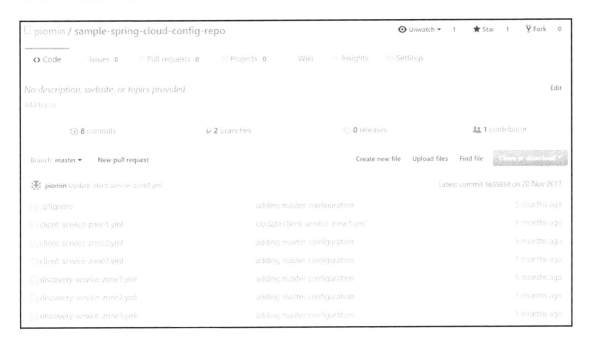

The Spring Cloud Config Server by default tries to clone a repository after the first HTTP resource call. If you would like to force cloning it after startup, you should set the cloneOnStart property to true. Beyond this, it is required to set the repository connection settings and the account authentication credentials:

```
spring:
  application:
    name: config-server
  cloud:
    config:
      server:
        git:
          uri: https://github.com/piomin/sample-spring-cloud-config-repo.git
          username: ${github.username}
          password: ${github.password}
          cloneOnStart: true
```

After running the server, we can call the endpoints known from the previous exercises, for example, `http://localhost:8889/client-service/zone1` or `http://localhost:8889/client-service-zone2.yml`. The result would be the same as for the earlier tests; the only difference is in the data source. Now, let's perform another exercise. As you probably remember, we had to change the client's properties a little when we created the example with discovery first bootstrap with the `native` profile enabled. Because right now we are using a Git backend, we can develop a smarter solution for that case. In the current approach, we would create `discovery` branch (`https://github.com/piomin/sample-spring-cloud-config-repo/tree/discovery`) at our configuration repository on GitHub, and we would place the files dedicated to the application illustrating the discovery first bootstrap mechanism. If you call the Config Server endpoints with the `label` parameter set to `discovery`, you will fetch data from our new branch. Try to call `http://localhost:8889/client-service/zone1/discovery` and/or `http://localhost:8889/discovery/client-service-zone2.yml` and check the result.

Let's consider another situation. I changed the server port for the third instance of `client-service`, but for some reason I would like to move back to the previous value. Do I have to change and commit `client-service-zone3.yml` with the previous port value? No, all I have to do is to pass the commit ID as a `label` parameter while calling the HTTP API resource. The change performed is illustrated in the following screenshot:

If I invoke the API endpoint with the parent commit ID instead of branch name, the older port number would be returned as a response. Here's the result of calling `http://localhost:8889/e546dd6/client-service-zone3.yml`, where `e546dd6` is the previous commit ID:

```
eureka:
  client:
    serviceUrl:
      defaultZone: http://localhost:8761/eureka/
  instance:
    metadataMap:
```

```
        zone: zone3
  server:
    port: 8083
```

Client-side configuration

While building the server side with a Git backend, I have only shown you examples of HTTP resource calls. Here's the example configuration for the client's application. Instead of setting the `profile` property inside `bootstrap.yml`, we may also pass it in the `spring.profiles.active` running parameter. This configuration makes the client fetch properties from the `discovery` branch. We may also decide to switch to a certain commit ID by setting it in the `label` property, as I have already mentioned:

```
spring:
 application:
   name: client-service
 cloud:
   config:
     uri: http://localhost:8889
     profile: zone1
     label: discovery
#    label: e546dd6 // uncomment for rollback
```

Multiple repositories

Sometimes, you may need to configure multiple repositories for a single Config Server. I can imagine the situation that you would have to separate the business configuration from a typical technical configuration. This is absolutely possible:

```
spring:
 cloud:
   config:
     server:
       git:
         uri:
https://github.com/piomin/spring-cloud-config-repo/config-repo
         repos:
           simple: https://github.com/simple/config-repo
           special:
             pattern: special*/dev*,*special*/dev*
             uri: https://github.com/special/config-repo
           local:
             pattern: local*
             uri: file:/home/config/config-repo
```

Vault backend

I have already mentioned Vault as a tool for securely accessing secrets through a unified interface. In order to enable the Config Server to use that type of backend, you must run it with the Vault profile `--spring.profiles.active=vault`. Of course, before running the Config Server you need to install and launch the Vault instance. I suggest you use Docker for this. I know that this is our first contact with Docker in this book, and not everyone has knowledge of that tool. I have provided a short introduction to Docker, its basic commands, and use cases in `Chapter 14`, *Docker Support*. So, if this is your first contact with that technology, please first take a look at that introduction. For those of you who are familiar with Docker, here's the command for running a Vault container in development mode. We may override the default listen address with the `VAULT_DEV_LISTEN_ADDRESS` parameter or the ID of the initial generated root token with the `VAULT_DEV_ROOT_TOKEN_ID` parameter:

```
docker run --cap-add=IPC_LOCK -d --name=vault -e
'VAULT_DEV_ROOT_TOKEN_ID=client' -p 8200:8200 vault
```

Getting started with Vault

Vault provides a command line interface, which may be used for adding new values to the server and reading them from the server. Examples of calling those commands are shown here. However, we have run Vault as a Docker container, so the most convenient way to manage the secrets is through the HTTP API:

```
$ vault write secret/hello value=world
$ vault read secret/hello
```

The HTTP API is available for our instance of Vault under the `http://192.168.99.100:8200/v1/secret` address. When calling every method of that API, you need to pass a token as the request header `X-Vault-Token`. Because we set that value in the `VAULT_DEV_ROOT_TOKEN_ID` environment parameter while launching a Docker container, it is equal to `client`. Otherwise, it would be automatically generated during startup and may be read from logs by invoking the command `docker logs vault`. To start working with Vault, we in fact need to be aware of two HTTP methods—`POST` and `GET`. When calling the `POST` method, we may define the list of secrets that should be added to the server. The parameters passed in the `curl` command shown here are created using the kv backend, which acts like a key/value store:

```
$ curl -H "X-Vault-Token: client" -H "Content-Type: application/json" -X
POST -d '{"server.port":8081,"sample.string.property": "Client
App","sample.int.property": 1}'
```

```
http://192.168.99.100:8200/v1/secret/client-service
```

The newly added values may be read from the server by using the GET method:

```
$ curl -H "X-Vault-Token: client" -X GET
http://192.168.99.100:8200/v1/secret/client-service
```

Integration with Spring Cloud Config

As I have mentioned before, we have to run the Spring Cloud Config Server with the --spring.profiles.active=vault parameter to enable Vault as a backend store. To override the default auto configured settings, we should define the properties under the spring.cloud.config.server.vault.* key. The current configuration for our example application is shown here. An example application is available on GitHub; you need to switch to the config_vault branch (https://github.com/piomin/sample-spring-cloud-netflix/tree/config_vault) to access it:

```
spring:
  application:
    name: config-server
  cloud:
    config:
      server:
        vault:
          host: 192.168.99.100
          port: 8200
```

Now, you may call the endpoint exposed by the Config Server. You have to pass the token in the request header, but this time its name is X-Config-Token:

```
$ curl -X "GET" "http://localhost:8889/client-service/default" -H "X-
Config-Token: client"
```

The response should be the same as what is shown next. These properties are the default for all of the profiles of the client application. You may also add specific settings for the selected profile by calling the Vault HTTP `API` method with the profile name after a comma character, like this, `http://192.168.99.100:8200/v1/secret/client-service,zone1`. If such a profile name is included in the calling path, the properties for both the `default` and `zone1` profiles are returned in the response:

```
{
    "name":"client-service",
    "profiles":["default"],
    "label":null,
    "version":null,
    "state":null,
    "propertySources":[{
        "name":"vault:client-service",
        "source":{
            "sample.int.property":1,
            "sample.string.property":"Client App",
            "server.port":8081
        }
    }]
}
```

Client-side configuration

When using Vault as a backend to your Config Server, the client will need to pass a token for the server to be able to retrieve values from Vault. This token should be provided in the client configuration settings with the `spring.cloud.config.token` property in the `bootstrap.yml` file:

```
spring:
  application:
    name: client-service
  cloud:
    config:
      uri: http://localhost:8889
      token: client
```

Additional features

Let's take a look at some other useful features of the Spring Cloud Config.

Fail on start and retry

Sometimes it doesn't make any sense to launch the application if the Config Server is unavailable. In this case, we would like to halt a client with an exception. To achieve this, we have to set the bootstrap configuration property `spring.cloud.config.failFast` to `true`. Such a radical solution is not always the desired behavior. If a Config Server is unreachable only occasionally, the better approach would be to keep trying to reconnect until it succeeds. The `spring.cloud.config.failFast` property still has to be equal to `true`, but we would also need to add the `spring-retry` library and `spring-boot-starter-aop` to the application classpath. The default behavior assumes to retry six times with an initial backoff interval of 1000 milliseconds. You may override these settings by using the `spring.cloud.config.retry.*` configuration properties.

Secure client

The same as for the service discovery, we may secure the Config Server with basic authentication. It can be easily enabled on the server side with Spring Security. In that case, all the client needs to set is the username and password in the `bootstrap.yml` file:

```
spring:
  cloud:
    config:
      uri: https://localhost:8889
      username: user
      password: secret
```

Reload configuration automatically

We have already discussed the most important features of Spring Cloud Config. At that point, we implemented examples illustrating how to use different backend storage as a repository. But no matter whether we decided to choose filesystem, Git, or Vault, our client-side application needed to restart to be able to fetch the newest configuration from the server. However, sometimes this is not an optimal solution, especially if we have many microservices running and some of them use the same generic configuration.

Solution architecture

Even if we created a dedicated `property` file per single application, an opportunity to dynamically reload it without restart could be very helpful. As you may have deduced, such a solution is available for Spring Boot and therefore for Spring Cloud. In `Chapter 4`, *Service Discovery* while describing deregistration from the service discovery server, I introduced an endpoint, `/shutdown`, which may be used for gracefully shutting down. There is also an endpoint available for Spring context restart, which works in a similar way to that for shutdown.

An endpoint on the client side is just one component of the much larger system that needs to be included to enable push notifications for the Spring Cloud Config. The most popular source code repository providers, such as GitHub, GitLab, and Bitbucket, are able to send notifications about changes in a repository by providing a WebHook mechanism. We may configure the WebHook using the provider's web dashboard as a URL and a list of selected event types. Such a provider will call the `POST` method defined in the WebHook with a body containing a list of commits. It is required to include a Spring Cloud Bus dependency in the project to enable the monitor endpoint on the Config Server side. When this endpoint is invoked as a result of the WebHook activation, a Config Server prepares and sends an event with a list of property sources that has been modified by the last commit. That event is sent to a message broker. The Spring Cloud Bus provides implementations for RabbitMQ and Apache Kafka. The first may be enabled for the project by including the `spring-cloud-starter-bus-amqp` dependency, and the second by including the `spring-cloud-starter-bus-kafka` dependency. Those dependencies should also be declared for a client application to enable receiving messages from a message broker. We should also enable the dynamic refresh mechanism on the client side by annotating the selected configuration class with `@RefreshScope`. An architecture of this solution is shown here:

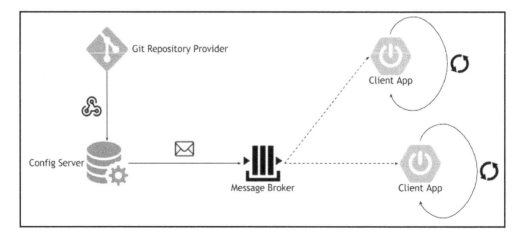

Reload configuration with @RefreshScope

This time we will start unusually from the client side. The example application is available on GitHub (`https://github.com/piomin/sample-spring-cloud-config-bus.git`). The same as the previous examples, it uses a Git repository as backend storage, which is also created on GitHub (`https://github.com/piomin/sample-spring-cloud-config-repo`). I added some new properties to the client's configuration file and committed changes to the repository. Here's the current version of the client's configuration:

```
eureka:
  instance:
    metadataMap:
      zone: zone1
  client:
    serviceUrl:
      defaultZone: http://localhost:8761/eureka/
server:
  port: ${PORT:8081}
management:
  security:
    enabled: false
sample:
  string:
    property: Client App
  int:
    property: 1
```

I disabled security for Spring Boot Actuator endpoints by setting `management.security.enabled` to `false`. It is required to be able to call those endpoints without passing security credentials. I also added two test parameters, `sample.string.property` and `sample.int.property`, to demonstrate bean refresh mechanisms based on their values in the example. Spring Cloud provides some additional HTTP management endpoints for the Spring Boot Actuator. One of them is `/refresh`, which is responsible for reloading the bootstrap context and refreshing beans annotated with `@RefreshScope`. This is an HTTP `POST` method, which may be called on our client's instance at `http://localhost:8081/refresh`. Before testing that functionality, we need to have the discovery and Config Servers running. The client application should be launched with the `--spring.profiles.active=zone1` parameter. Here's the class where the test properties `sample.string.property` and `sample.int.property` are injected into the fields:

```
@Component
@RefreshScope
public class ClientConfiguration {
```

```
@Value("${sample.string.property}")
private String sampleStringProperty;
@Value("${sample.int.property}")
private int sampleIntProperty;

public String showProperties() {
    return String.format("Hello from %s %d", sampleStringProperty,
sampleIntProperty);
  }

}
```

That bean is injected into the `ClientController` class and invoked inside the `ping` method, which is exposed at `http://localhost:8081/ping`:

```
@RestController
public class ClientController {

@Autowired
private ClientConfiguration conf;

@GetMapping("/ping")
public String ping() {
    return conf.showProperties();
  }

}
```

Now, let's change the values for test properties in `client-service-zone1.yml` and commit them. If you call the Config Server HTTP endpoint `/client-service/zone1`, you'll see the newest values returned as a response. But when you call the `/ping` method exposed on the client application, you will still see older values visible on the left side of the following screen. Why? Although the Config Server automatically detects repository changes, the client application is not able to automatically refresh without any trigger. It requires a restart to read the newest settings, or we may force a configuration reload by invoking the previously described `/refresh` method:

After calling the /refresh endpoint on the client application, you will see in the log files that the configuration has been reloaded. Now, if you invoke /ping one more time, the newest property values are returned in the response. That example illustrates how a hot reload works for a Spring Cloud application, but it is obviously not our target solution. The next step is to enable communication with the message broker:

Consuming events from a message broker

I have already mentioned that we may choose between two message brokers that are integrated with the Spring Cloud Bus. In this example, I'm going to show you how to run and use RabbitMQ. Let me just say a few words about that solution, because we are dealing with it for the first time in the book. RabbitMQ has grown into the most popular message broker software. It is written in Erlang and implements **Advanced Message Queueing Protocol** (**AMQP**). It is easy to use and configure, even if we are talking about such mechanisms as clustering or high availability.

The most convenient way to run RabbitMQ on your machine is through a Docker container. Two ports have been exposed outside the container. The first of them is used for client connections (`5672`) and the second is dedicated to the management dashboard (`15672`). I also ran the image with the management tag to enable the UI dashboard, which is not available in the default version:

```
docker run -d --name rabbit -p 5672:5672 -p 15672:15672 rabbitmq:management
```

To enable support for the RabbitMQ broker for our example client application, we should include the following dependency in `pom.xml`:

```
<dependency>
    <groupId>org.springframework.cloud</groupId>
    <artifactId>spring-cloud-starter-bus-amqp</artifactId>
</dependency>
```

That library contains auto-configuration settings. Because I run Docker on Windows, I need to override some default properties. The full service configuration is stored inside a Git repository, so the changes affect only remote files. We should add the following parameters to the previously used version of the client's property source:

```
spring:
  rabbitmq:
    host: 192.168.99.100
    port: 5672
    username: guest
    password: guest
```

If you run the client application, an exchange and a queue would be automatically created in RabbitMQ. You can easily check this out by logging in to the management dashboard available at `http://192.168.99.100:15672`. The default username and password are `guest/guest`. Here's the screen from my RabbitMQ instance. There is one exchange with the name `SpringCloudBus` created, with two bindings to the client queue and Config Server queue (I have already run it with the changes described in the next section). At this stage, I wouldn't like to go into the detail about RabbitMQ and its architecture. A good place for such a discussion would be in the `Chapter 11`, *Message-Driven Microservices* on the Spring Cloud Stream project:

Monitoring repository changes on a Config Server

Spring Cloud Config Server has to perform two tasks in the previously described process. First of all, it has to detect changes in a `property` file stored in a Git repository. This may be achieved by exposing a special endpoint, which would be called through a WebHook by the repository provider. The second step is to prepare and send a `RefreshRemoteApplicationEvent` targeted at the applications that might have been changed. This in turn requires us to establish connection with a message broker. The `spring-cloud-config-monitor` library is responsible for enabling the `/monitor` endpoint. To enable support for the RabbitMQ broker, we should include the same starter artifact as for the client application:

```
<dependency>
 <groupId>org.springframework.cloud</groupId>
 <artifactId>spring-cloud-config-monitor</artifactId>
</dependency>
<dependency>
 <groupId>org.springframework.cloud</groupId>
 <artifactId>spring-cloud-starter-bus-amqp</artifactId>
</dependency>
```

That's not all. The configuration monitor should also be activated in `application.yml`. Because each repository provider has a dedicated implementation in Spring Cloud, it is necessary to select which of them should be enabled:

```
spring:
 application:
   name: config-server
 cloud:
   config:
     server:
       monitor:
         github:
           enabled: true
```

The change detection mechanism may be customized. By default, it detects changes in files that match the application name. To override that behavior, you need to provide a custom implementation of `PropertyPathNotificationExtractor`. It accepts the request headers and body parameters, and returns a list of file paths that have been changed. To support notifications from GitHub, we may use `GithubPropertyPathNotificationExtractor` provided by `spring-cloud-config-monitor`:

```
@Bean
public GithubPropertyPathNotificationExtractor
githubPropertyPathNotificationExtractor() {
    return new GithubPropertyPathNotificationExtractor();
}
```

Simulating change events manually

A monitor endpoint can be invoked by a WebHook configured on a Git repository provider such as GitHub, Bitbucket, or GitLab. Testing such a feature with the application running on localhost is troublesome. It turns out that we may easily simulate such a WebHook activation by calling `POST /monitor` manually. For example, the `Github` command should have the header `X-Github-Event` included in the request. The JSON body with changes in the `property` files should look as shown in this cURL request:

```
$ curl -H "X-Github-Event: push" -H "Content-Type: application/json" -X
POST -d '{"commits": [{"modified": ["client-service-zone1.yml"]}]}'
http://localhost:8889/monitor
```

Now, let's change and commit a value of one property in the `client-service-zone1.yml` file, for example, `sample.int.property`. Then, we may call the `POST /monitor` method with the parameters shown in the previous example command. If you configured everything according to my descriptions, you should see the following log line on your client application side, `Received remote refresh request. Keys refreshed [sample.int.property]`. If you call the `/ping` endpoint exposed by the client microservice, it should return the newest value of the changed property.

Testing locally with a GitLab instance

For those who do not prefer simulating events, I'm proposing a more practical exercise. However, I would point out that it requires not only development skills from you, but also a basic knowledge of Continuous Integration tools. We will start by running a GitLab instance locally using its Docker image. GitLab is an open sourced web-based Git repository manager with wiki and issue tracking features. It is very similar to such tools as GitHub or Bitbucket, but may be easily deployed on your local machine:

```
docker run -d --name gitlab -p 10443:443 -p 10080:80 -p 10022:22
gitlab/gitlab-ce:latest
```

A web dashboard is available at `http://192.168.99.100:10080`. The first step is to create an admin user and then log in using the credentials provided. I won't go into the details of GitLab. It has a user-friendly and intuitive GUI interface, so I'm pretty sure you will able to handle it without too much effort. Anyway, going forward, I created a project in GitLab with the name `sample-spring-cloud-config-repo`. It may be cloned from `http://192.168.99.100:10080/root/sample-spring-cloud-config-repo.git`. I committed there the same set of configuration files, which is available in our example repository on GitHub. The next step is to define a WebHook that invokes the Config Server's `/monitor` endpoint with a push notification. To add a new WebHook for the project, you need to go to the **Settings** | **Integration** section and then fill in the **URL** field with the server address (use your hostname instead of localhost). Leave the **Push events** checkbox selected:

In comparison with the Config Server implementation with GitHub as a backend repository provider, we need to change the enabled monitor type in `application.yml` and of course provide a different address:

```
spring:
 application:
   name: config-server
 cloud:
   config:
     server:
       monitor:
         gitlab:
           enabled: true
       git:
         uri:
http://192.168.99.100:10080/root/sample-spring-cloud-config-repo.git
         username: root
         password: root123
         cloneOnStart: true
```

We should also register another bean implementing `PropertyPathNotificationExtractor`:

```
@Bean
public GitlabPropertyPathNotificationExtractor
gitlabPropertyPathNotificationExtractor() {
    return new GitlabPropertyPathNotificationExtractor();
}
```

Finally, you may make and push some changes in the configuration files. The WebHook should be activated and the client application's configuration should be refreshed. That is the last example in this chapter; we may proceed to the conclusion.

Summary

In this chapter, I have described the most important features of a Spring Cloud Config project. The same as for service discovery, we started from the basics, a simple use case on the client and server sides. We discussed the different backend repository types for a Config Server. I implemented the examples illustrating how to use filesystem, Git, and even third-party tools such as Vault as a repository for your `property` files. I put particular focus on interoperability with other components, such as service discovery or multiple instances of microservices within a larger system. Finally, I showed you how to reload an application's configuration without restart, based on WebHooks and a message broker. To conclude, after reading this chapter you should be able to use Spring Cloud Config as one element of your microservice-based architecture and take an advantage of its main features.

After we have discussed an implemetation of service discovery and configuration server with Spring Cloud, we may proceed to an inter-service communication. In the next two chapters we will analyze basic and some more advanced samples that illustrate synchronous communication between a few microservices.

6
Communication Between
Microservices

In the last two chapters, we discussed details related to very important elements in microservice architecture—service discovery and the configuration server. However, it is worth remembering that the main reason for their existence in the system is just to help in the management of the whole set of independent, standalone applications. One aspect of this management is communication between microservices. Here, a particularly important role is played by service discovery, which is responsible for storing and serving the network locations of all available applications. Of course, we may imagine our system architecture without a service discovery server. Such an example will also be presented in this chapter.

However, the most important components taking part in an inter-service communication are HTTP clients and client-side load balancers. In this chapter, we are going to focus just on them.

The topics we will cover in this chapter include:

- Using Spring `RestTemplate` for inter-service communication with and without service discovery
- Customizing the Ribbon client
- Description of the main features provided by the Feign client, such as integration with the Ribbon client, service discovery, inheritance, and zoning support

Different styles of communication

We can identify different styles of communication between microservices. It is possible to classify them into two dimensions. The first of them is a division into synchronous and asynchronous communication protocols. The key point of asynchronous communication is that the client should not have blocked a thread while waiting for a response. The most popular protocol for that type of communication is AMQP, and we already had the opportunity to run an example of that protocol usage at the end of the previous chapter. However, the main way of communication between services is still synchronous HTTP protocol. We will be only talking about it in this chapter.

The second division is into different communication types based on whether there is a single message receiver or multiple receivers. In one-to-one communication, each request is processed by exactly one service instance. In one-to-many communication, each request may be processed by many different services. This will be discussed in `Chapter 11`, *Message Driven Microservices*.

Synchronous communication with Spring Cloud

Spring Cloud provides a set of components to help you in implementing communication between microservices. The first of them is `RestTemplate`, which is always used for consuming RESTful web services by a client. It is included in a Spring Web project. To use it effectively in a microservices environment, it should be annotated with the `@LoadBalanced` qualifier. Thanks to that, it will be automatically configured to use Netflix Ribbon and it will be able to take an advantage of service discovery by using service names instead of IP addresses. Ribbon is a client-side load balancer, which provides a simple interface allowing control over the behavior of HTTP and TCP clients. It can be easily integrated with other Spring Cloud components, such as service discovery or circuit breaker, and, furthermore, it is fully transparent to a developer. The next available component is Feign, a declarative REST client also from the Netflix OSS stack. Feign already uses Ribbon for load balancing and fetching data from service discovery. It may be easily declared on the interface by annotating a method with `@FeignClient`. In this chapter, we will take a closer look at all the components listed here.

Load balancing with Ribbon

The main concept around Ribbon is a named **client**. That's why we may call other services using their names instead of the full address with hostname and port, without connecting to a service discovery. In that case, the list of addresses should be provided in the Ribbon configuration settings inside the `application.yml` file.

Enabling communication between microservices using the Ribbon client

Let's proceed with the example. It consists of four independent microservices. Some of them may call endpoints exposed by the others. The application source code is available here:

`https://github.com/piomin/sample-spring-cloud-comm.git`

In this example, we will try to develop a simple order system where customers may buy products. If a customer decides to confirm a selected list of products to buy, the POST request is sent to the `order-service`. It is processed by the `Order prepare(@RequestBody Order order) {...}` method inside REST controller. This method is responsible for order preparation. First, it calculates the final price, considering the price of each product from the list, customer order history, and their category in the system by calling the proper API method from the `customer-service`. Then, it verifies the customer's account balance is high enough to execute the order by calling the account service, and, finally, it returns the calculated price. If the customer confirms the action, the PUT /{id} method is called. The request is processed by the method `Order accept(@PathVariable Long id) {...}` inside REST controller. It changes the order status and withdraws money from the customer's account. The system architecture is broken down into the individual microservices as shown here:

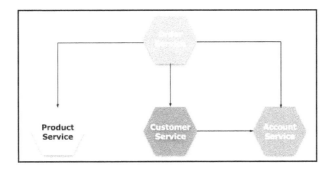

Static load balancing configuration

Our `order-service` has to communicate with all other microservices from the example to perform the required operations. So, we need to define three different Ribbon clients with network addresses set using the `ribbon.listOfServers` property. The second important thing in the example is to disable discovery services in Eureka, which are enabled by default. Here are all the defined properties for `order-service` inside its `application.yml` file:

```yaml
server:
 port: 8090

account-service:
 ribbon:
   eureka:
     enabled: false
   listOfServers: localhost:8091
customer-service:
 ribbon:
   eureka:
     enabled: false
   listOfServers: localhost:8092
product-service:
 ribbon:
   eureka:
     enabled: false
   listOfServers: localhost:8093
```

We should include the following dependencies in the project to use `RestTemplate` in conjunction with the Ribbon client:

```xml
<dependency>
 <groupId>org.springframework.cloud</groupId>
 <artifactId>spring-cloud-starter-ribbon</artifactId>
</dependency>
<dependency>
 <groupId>org.springframework.boot</groupId>
 <artifactId>spring-boot-starter-web</artifactId>
</dependency>
```

Then, we should enable the Ribbon client by declaring a list of the names configured in `application.yml`. To achieve this, you may annotate the main class or any other Spring configuration class with `@RibbonClients`. You should also register the `RestTemplate` bean and annotate it with `@LoadBalanced` to enable interaction with Spring Cloud components:

```
@SpringBootApplication
@RibbonClients({
 @RibbonClient(name = "account-service"),
 @RibbonClient(name = "customer-service"),
 @RibbonClient(name = "product-service")
})
public class OrderApplication {

 @LoadBalanced
 @Bean
 RestTemplate restTemplate() {
     return new RestTemplate();
 }

 public static void main(String[] args) {
     new
 SpringApplicationBuilder(OrderApplication.class).web(true).run(args);
 }
 // ...
}
```

Calling other services

Finally, we may begin to implement the `OrderController` responsible for serving HTTP methods exposed outside a microservice. It has the `RestTemplate` bean injected to be able to call other HTTP endpoints. You may see in the following source code fragment that uses the Ribbon client name configured in `application.yml` instead of IP address or hostname. Using the same `RestTemplate` bean, we can communicate with three different microservices. Let's just take a second here to discuss the methods available inside the controller. In the first of the implemented methods, we call the GET endpoint from `product-service`, which returns a list with details of selected products. Then, we invoke the GET `/withAccounts/{id}` method exposed by `customer-service`. It returns the customer details with the list of their accounts.

Now, we have all the information needed to calculate the final order price and validate the customer has sufficient funds in their main account. The PUT method calls the endpoint from `account-service` to withdraw money from the customer account. I have spent quite a bit of time discussing methods available in `OrderController`. However, I think that it was needed because the same example will be used to show the main features of Spring Cloud components that provide mechanisms for synchronous communication between microservices:

```
@RestController
public class OrderController {

 @Autowired
 OrderRepository repository;
 @Autowired
 RestTemplate template;

 @PostMapping
 public Order prepare(@RequestBody Order order) {
     int price = 0;
     Product[] products =
template.postForObject("http://product-service/ids", order.getProductIds(),
Product[].class);
     Customer customer =
template.getForObject("http://customer-service/withAccounts/{id}",
Customer.class, order.getCustomerId());
     for (Product product : products)
         price += product.getPrice();
     final int priceDiscounted = priceDiscount(price, customer);
     Optional<Account> account = customer.getAccounts().stream().filter(a
-> (a.getBalance() > priceDiscounted)).findFirst();
     if (account.isPresent()) {
         order.setAccountId(account.get().getId());
         order.setStatus(OrderStatus.ACCEPTED);
         order.setPrice(priceDiscounted);
     } else {
         order.setStatus(OrderStatus.REJECTED);
     }
     return repository.add(order);
 }

 @PutMapping("/{id}")
 public Order accept(@PathVariable Long id) {
     final Order order = repository.findById(id);
     template.put("http://account-service/withdraw/{id}/{amount}", null,
order.getAccountId(), order.getPrice());
     order.setStatus(OrderStatus.DONE);
```

```
        repository.update(order);
        return order;
    }
    // ...
}
```

It is interesting to note that the `GET /withAccounts/{id}` method from `customer-service`, which is called by `order-service`, also uses the Ribbon client to communicate with another microservice, `account-service`. Here's the fragment from `CustomerController` with the implementation of the preceding method:

```
@GetMapping("/withAccounts/{id}")
public Customer findByIdWithAccounts(@PathVariable("id") Long id) {
  Account[] accounts =
template.getForObject("http://account-service/customer/{customerId}",
Account[].class, id);
  Customer c = repository.findById(id);
  c.setAccounts(Arrays.stream(accounts).collect(Collectors.toList()));
  return c;
}
```

First, build the whole project with the Maven command `mvn clean install`. Then, you may launch all the microservices in any order using the `java -jar` command without any additional parameters. Optionally, you can run the application from your IDE. The test data is prepared for every microservice on startup. There is no persistence storage, so all objects will be removed after a restart. We can test the whole system by calling the `POST` method exposed by `order-service`. The example request is shown here:

```
$ curl -d '{"productIds": [1,5],"customerId": 1,"status": "NEW"}' -H
"Content-Type: application/json" -X POST http://localhost:8090
```

If you try to send this request, you will able to see the following logs printed by the Ribbon client:

```
DynamicServerListLoadBalancer for client customer-service initialized:
DynamicServerListLoadBalancer:{NFLoadBalancer:name=customer-service,current
list of Servers=[localhost:8092],Load balancer stats=Zone stats:
{unknown=[Zone:unknown; Instance count:1; Active connections count: 0;
Circuit breaker tripped count: 0; Active connections per server: 0.0;]
},Server stats: [[Server:localhost:8092; Zone:UNKNOWN; Total Requests:0;
Successive connection failure:0; Total blackout seconds:0; Last connection
made:Thu Jan 01 01:00:00 CET 1970; First connection made: Thu Jan 01
01:00:00 CET 1970; Active Connections:0; total failure count in last (1000)
msecs:0; average resp time:0.0; 90 percentile resp time:0.0; 95 percentile
resp time:0.0; min resp time:0.0; max resp time:0.0; stddev resp time:0.0]
]}ServerList:com.netflix.loadbalancer.ConfigurationBasedServerList@7f1e23f6
```

The approach described in this section has one big disadvantage, which makes it not very usable in a system composed of several microservices. The problem is more severe if you have auto-scaling. It is easy to see that all the network addresses of services have be managed manually. Of course, we may move the configuration settings from the `application.yml` file inside every fat JAR to the configuration server. However, it does not change the fact that management of a large number of interactions will still be troublesome. Such a problem would be easily solved by the ability for the client-side load balancer and service discovery to interact.

Using RestTemplate together with service discovery

In fact, an integration with service discovery is the default behavior of the Ribbon client. As you probably remember, we disabled Eureka for the client-side balancer by setting the `ribbon.eureka.enabled` property to `false`. The existence of service discovery simplifies a configuration of Spring Cloud components during inter-service communication, examples in this section.

Building example application

The system architecture is the same as for the previous example. To view the source code for the current exercise, you have to switch to the `ribbon_with_discovery` branch (`https://github.com/piomin/shown here-spring-cloud-comm/tree/ribbon_with_discovery`). The first thing you will see there is a new module, `discovery-service`. We have discussed in detail almost all aspects related to Eureka in Chapter 4, *Service Discovery*, so you should not have any problems with launching it. We run a single standalone Eureka server with really basic settings. It is available on the default port, `8761`.

In comparison with the previous example, we should remove all the configuration and annotations strictly related to the Ribbon client. In their place, the Eureka discovery client has to be enabled with `@EnableDiscoveryClient` and the Eureka server address is provided in the `application.yml` file. Now, the main class of `order-service` looks like this:

```
@SpringBootApplication
@EnableDiscoveryClient
public class OrderApplication {
```

```
@LoadBalanced
@Bean
RestTemplate restTemplate() {
return new RestTemplate();
}

public static void main(String[] args) {
    new
SpringApplicationBuilder(OrderApplication.class).web(true).run(args);
}
// ...
}
```

Here's the current configuration file. I set the name of the service with the `spring.application.name` property:

```
spring:
 application:
   name: order-service

server:
 port: ${PORT:8090}

eureka:
 client:
   serviceUrl:
     defaultZone: ${EUREKA_URL:http://localhost:8761/eureka/}
```

This is the same as earlier; we also launch all microservices. But, this time `account-service` and `product-service` will be multiplied by two instances. When starting a second instance of each service, the default server port may be overridden with the `-DPORT` or `-Dserver.port` parameter, for example, `java -jar -DPORT=9093 product-service-1.0-SNAPSHOT.jar`. All the instances have been registered in the Eureka server. This can be easily checked out using its UI dashboard:

Instances currently registered with Eureka			
Application	**AMIs**	**Availability Zones**	**Status**
ACCOUNT-SERVICE	n/a (2)	(2)	UP (2) - minkowpi.p4.org.account-service:8091 , minkowpi.p4.org.account-service:8061
CUSTOMER-SERVICE	n/a (1)	(1)	UP (1) - minkowpi.p4.org.customer-service:8092
ORDER-SERVICE	n/a (1)	(1)	UP (1) - minkowpi.p4.org.order-service:8090
PRODUCT-SERVICE	n/a (2)	(2)	UP (2) - minkowpi.p4.org.product-service:8093 , minkowpi.p4.org.product-service:9093

This is the first time in this book we have seen a practical example of load balancing. By default, the Ribbon client distributes traffic equally among all the registered instances of the microservice. That algorithm is called **round robin**. In practice, it means that the client remembers where it forwarded the last request and then sends the current request to the service next in the row. This approach may be overridden by the other rule I'm going to show you in detail in the next chapter. Load balancing may also be configured for the previous example without service discovery, by setting a comma-separated list of service addresses in `ribbon.listOfServers`, for example, `ribbon.listOfServers=localhost:8093,localhost:9093`. Getting back to the example application, the requests sent by `order-service` will be load balanced between two instances of `account-service` and `product-service`. This looks similar to `customer-service`, which distributes traffic between two instances of `account-service`. If you launch all the instances of the service visible on the Eureka dashboard in the previous screenshot and send some test requests to `order-service`, you will certainly see the following log which I have posted. I have highlighted the fragment where the Ribbon client displays a list of addresses found for the target service:

```
DynamicServerListLoadBalancer for client account-service initialized:
DynamicServerListLoadBalancer:{NFLoadBalancer:name=account-service,current
list of Servers=[minkowp-1.p4.org:8091, minkowp-1.p4.org:9091],Load
balancer stats=Zone stats: {defaultzone=[Zone:defaultzone; Instance
count:2; Active connections count: 0; Circuit breaker tripped count: 0;
Active connections per server: 0.0;]
  },Server stats: [[Server:minkowp-1.p4.org:8091; Zone:defaultZone; Total
Requests:0; Successive connection failure:0; Total blackout seconds:0; Last
connection made:Thu Jan 01 01:00:00 CET 1970; First connection made: Thu
Jan 01 01:00:00 CET 1970; Active Connections:0; total failure count in last
(1000) msecs:0; average resp time:0.0; 90 percentile resp time:0.0; 95
percentile resp time:0.0; min resp time:0.0; max resp time:0.0; stddev resp
time:0.0]
  , [Server:minkowp-1.p4.org:9091; Zone:defaultZone; Total Requests:0;
Successive connection failure:0; Total blackout seconds:0; Last connection
made:Thu Jan 01 01:00:00 CET 1970; First connection made: Thu Jan 01
01:00:00 CET 1970; Active Connections:0; total failure count in last (1000)
msecs:0; average resp time:0.0; 90 percentile resp time:0.0; 95 percentile
resp time:0.0; min resp time:0.0; max resp time:0.0; stddev resp time:0.0]
]}ServerList:org.springframework.cloud.netflix.ribbon.eureka.DomainExtracti
ngServerList@3e878e67
```

Using Feign client

`RestTemplate` is a Spring component specially adapted to interact with Spring Cloud and microservices. However, Netflix has developed their own tool that acts as a web service client for providing out-of-the-box communication between independent REST services. Feign client, which is in it, generally does the same as `RestTemplate` with the `@LoadBalanced` annotation, but in a more elegant way. It is a Java to HTTP client binder that works by processing annotations into a templatized request. When using Open Feign client, you only have to create an interface and annotate it. It integrates with Ribbon and Eureka to provide a load balanced HTTP client, fetching all the necessary network addresses from service discovery. Spring Cloud adds support for Spring MVC annotations and for using the same HTTP message converters as in Spring Web.

Support for different zones

Let me back up for a moment to the last example. I'm going to propose some changes to complicate our system architecture a little. The current architecture is visualized in the following diagram. The communication model between microservices is still the same, but now we launch two instances of every microservice and divide them into two different zones. A zoning mechanism has been already discussed in Chapter 4, *Service Discovery*, when talking about service discovery with Eureka, so I assume it is well known to you. The main purpose of this exercise is not only to show how to use Feign client, but also how a zoning mechanism works in communication between instances of microservices. Let's start with the basics then:

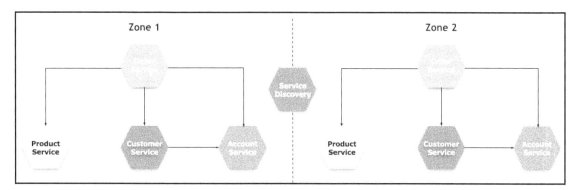

Enabling Feign for an application

To include Feign in the project, we have to add to the dependencies the `spring-cloud-starter-feign` artifact or `spring-cloud-starter-openfeign` for Spring Cloud Netflix in minimal version 1.4.0:

```
<dependency>
 <groupId>org.springframework.cloud</groupId>
 <artifactId>spring-cloud-starter-feign</artifactId>
</dependency>
```

The next step is to enable Feign for the application by annotating a main or a configuration class with `@EnableFeignClients`. This annotation will result in a search for all clients implemented in the application. We may also reduce the number of client used by setting the `clients` or `basePackages` annotation properties, for example, `@EnableFeignClients(clients = {AccountClient.class, Product.class})`. Here's the main class of the `order-service` application:

```
@SpringBootApplication
@EnableDiscoveryClient
@EnableFeignClients
public class OrderApplication {

    public static void main(String[] args) {
        new
SpringApplicationBuilder(OrderApplication.class).web(true).run(args);
    }

    @Bean
    OrderRepository repository() {
        return new OrderRepository();
    }

}
```

Building Feign interfaces

An approach where only an interface with some annotations has to be created to provide a component is standard for Spring Framework. For Feign, an interface must be annotated with `@FeignClient(name = "...")`. It has one required property name, which corresponds to the invoked microservice name if service discovery is enabled. Otherwise, it is used together with the `url` property, where we can set a concrete network address. `@FeignClient` is not the only annotation that needs to be used here. Every method in our client interface is associated with a specific HTTP API endpoint by marking it with `@RequestMapping` or more concrete annotations, such as `@GetMapping`, `@PostMapping`, or `@PutMapping`, as in this example source code fragment:

```
@FeignClient(name = "account-service")
public interface AccountClient {
    @PutMapping("/withdraw/{accountId}/{amount}")
    Account withdraw(@PathVariable("accountId") Long id,
@PathVariable("amount") int amount);
}

@FeignClient(name = "customer-service")
public interface CustomerClient {
    @GetMapping("/withAccounts/{customerId}")
    Customer findByIdWithAccounts(@PathVariable("customerId") Long
customerId);
}

@FeignClient(name = "product-service")
public interface ProductClient {
    @PostMapping("/ids")
    List<Product> findByIds(List<Long> ids);
}
```

Such components may be injected into the controller bean as they are also Spring Beans. Then, we just have to invoke their methods. Here's the current implementation of the REST controller in `order-service`:

```
@Autowired
OrderRepository repository;
@Autowired
AccountClient accountClient;
@Autowired
CustomerClient customerClient;
@Autowired
ProductClient productClient;

@PostMapping
```

```
public Order prepare(@RequestBody Order order) {
    int price = 0;
    List<Product> products =
productClient.findByIds(order.getProductIds());
    Customer customer =
customerClient.findByIdWithAccounts(order.getCustomerId());
    for (Product product : products)
        price += product.getPrice();
    final int priceDiscounted = priceDiscount(price, customer);
    Optional<Account> account = customer.getAccounts().stream().filter(a ->
(a.getBalance() > priceDiscounted)).findFirst();
    if (account.isPresent()) {
        order.setAccountId(account.get().getId());
        order.setStatus(OrderStatus.ACCEPTED);
        order.setPrice(priceDiscounted);
    } else {
        order.setStatus(OrderStatus.REJECTED);
    }
    return repository.add(order);
}
```

Launching microservices

I have changed a configuration for all the microservices in `application.yml`. Now, there are two different profiles, the first used for assigning an application to `zone1` and the second for `zone2`. You may check out the version from the `feign_with_discovery` branch (`https://github.com/piomin/shown here-spring-cloud-comm/tree/feign_with_ discovery`). Then, build the whole project using the `mvn clean install` command. The application should be launched with the `java -jar --spring.profiles.active=zone[n]` command, where `[n]` is the number of the zone. Because you have to start many instances to perform that test, it is worth considering a limit on heap size by setting the `-Xmx` parameter, for example, `-Xmx128m`. Here are the current configuration settings for one of the microservices:

```
spring:
 application:
    name: account-service

---
spring:
 profiles: zone1
eureka:
 instance:
    metadataMap:
```

```
          zone: zone1
  client:
      serviceUrl:
          defaultZone: http://localhost:8761/eureka/
          preferSameZoneEureka: true
server:
 port: ${PORT:8091}

---

spring:
 profiles: zone2
eureka:
 instance:
     metadataMap:
         zone: zone2
  client:
      serviceUrl:
          defaultZone: http://localhost:8761/eureka/
          preferSameZoneEureka: true
server:
 port: ${PORT:9091}
```

We will launch one instance of every microservice per single zone. So, there are nine running Spring Boot applications, including the service discovery server, as shown in this screenshot:

Instances currently registered with Eureka			
Application	**AMIs**	**Availability Zones**	**Status**
ACCOUNT-SERVICE	n/a (2)	(2)	UP (2) - minkowp-l.p4.org:account-service:8091 , minkowp-l.p4.org:account-service:9091
CUSTOMER-SERVICE	n/a (2)	(2)	UP (2) - minkowp-l.p4.org:customer-service:9092 , minkowp-l.p4.org:customer-service:8092
ORDER-SERVICE	n/a (2)	(2)	UP (2) - minkowp-l.p4.org:order-service:9090 , minkowp-l.p4.org:order-service:8090
PRODUCT-SERVICE	n/a (2)	(2)	UP (2) - minkowp-l.p4.org:product-service:8093 , minkowp-l.p4.org:product-service:9093

If you send the test request to the instance of order-service running in zone1 (http://localhost:8090), all the traffic will be forwarded to the other services in that zone, and the same for zone2 (http://localhost:9090). I have highlighted the fragment where the Ribbon client prints a list of found addresses of the target service registered in the current zone:

```
DynamicServerListLoadBalancer for client product-service initialized:
DynamicServerListLoadBalancer:{NFLoadBalancer:name=product-service,current
list of Servers=[minkowp-1.p4.org:8093],Load balancer stats=Zone stats:
{zone1=[Zone:zone1; Instance count:1; Active connections count: 0; Circuit
breaker tripped count: 0; Active connections per server: 0.0;]...
```

Inheritance support

You have probably noticed that the annotations inside a controller implementation and the Feign client implementation for a REST service served by that controller are identical. We may create an interface that contains abstract REST method definitions. That interface can be implemented by a controller class or extended by a Feign client interface:

```
public interface AccountService {

    @PostMapping
    Account add(@RequestBody Account account);

    @PutMapping
    Account update(@RequestBody Account account);

    @PutMapping("/withdraw/{id}/{amount}")
    Account withdraw(@PathVariable("id") Long id, @PathVariable("amount")
int amount);

    @GetMapping("/{id}")
    Account findById(@PathVariable("id") Long id);

    @GetMapping("/customer/{customerId}")
    List<Account> findByCustomerId(@PathVariable("customerId") Long
customerId);

    @PostMapping("/ids")
    List<Account> find(@RequestBody List<Long> ids);

    @DeleteMapping("/{id}")
    void delete(@PathVariable("id") Long id);

}
```

Now, the controller class provides an implementation for all methods from the base interface, but does not contain any annotations for REST mappings instead of `@RestController`. Here's a fragment of the `account-service` controller:

```
@RestController
public class AccountController implements AccountService {

    @Autowired
    AccountRepository repository;

    public Account add(@RequestBody Account account) {
        return repository.add(account);
    }
```

```
        // ...
    }
```

The Feign client interface for calling `account-service` does not provide any methods. It just extends the base interface, `AccountService`. To see the full implementation based on interfaces and Feign inheritance, switch to the `feign_with_inheritance` branch:

```
https://github.com/piomin/shown here-spring-cloud-comm/tree/feign_with_
inheritance
```

Here's an example Feign client declaration with inheritance support. It extends the `AccountService` interface, and hence handles all the methods exposed by `@RestController`:

```
@FeignClient(name = "account-service")
public interface AccountClient extends AccountService {
}
```

Creating a client manually

If you are not convinced by the annotation-like style, you may always create a Feign client manually using the Feign Builder API. Feign has several features that can be customized, such as encoders and decoders for messages or HTTP client implementation:

```
AccountClient accountClient = Feign.builder().client(new OkHttpClient())
    .encoder(new JAXBEncoder())
    .decoder(new JAXBDecoder())
    .contract(new JAXRSContract())
    .requestInterceptor(new BasicAuthRequestInterceptor("user",
"password"))
    .target(AccountClient.class, "http://account-service");
```

Client customization

Client customization can be performed not only with the Feign Builder API, but also by using the annotation-like style. We may provide a configuration class by setting it with the `configuration` property of `@FeignClient`:

```
@FeignClient(name = "account-service", configuration =
AccountConfiguration.class)
```

An example configuration bean is shown here:

```
@Configuration
public class AccountConfiguration {
 @Bean
 public Contract feignContract() {
     return new JAXRSContract();
 }

 @Bean
 public Encoder feignEncoder() {
     return new JAXBEncoder();
 }

 @Bean
 public Decoder feignDecoder() {
     return new JAXBDecoder();
 }

 @Bean
 public BasicAuthRequestInterceptor basicAuthRequestInterceptor() {
     return new BasicAuthRequestInterceptor("user", "password");
 }
}
```

Spring Cloud supports the following properties to override by declaring Spring Beans:

- `Decoder`: By default, `ResponseEntityDecoder`.
- `Encoder`: By default, `SpringEncoder`.
- `Logger`: By default, `Slf4jLogger`.
- `Contract`: By default, `SpringMvcContract`.
- `Feign.Builder`: By default, `HystrixFeign.Builder`.
- `Client`: If Ribbon is enabled, it is `LoadBalancerFeignClient`; otherwise, the default Feign client is used.
- `Logger.Level`: It sets a default log level for Feign. You can choose between `NONE`, `BASIC`, `HEADERS` and `FULL`.
- `Retryer`: It allows the implementing of the retry algorithm in case of communication failure.
- `ErrorDecoder`: It allows the mapping of the HTTP status code into application-specific exception.

- `Request.Options`: It allows setting read and connects timeout for the request.
- `Collection<RequestInterceptor>`: Collection of registered `RequestInterceptor` implementations that perform some actions basing on data taken from request.

Feign client can also be customized using configuration properties. It is possible to override settings for all available clients or only for a single selected client by providing its name after the `feign.client.config` property prefix. If we set the name `default` instead of a specific client name, it will apply it to all Feign clients. Default configurations can also be specified when using the `@EnableFeignClients` annotation and its `defaultConfiguration` attribute in a similar way to what was described previously. The settings provided in the `appplication.yml` file always have a higher priority than the `@Configuration` bean. To change that approach and prefer `@Configuration` instead of the YAML file, you should set the `feign.client.default-to-properties` property to `false`. Here's an example Feign client configuration for `account-service` that sets connect timeout, read timeout of HTTP connection, and log level:

```
feign:
  client:
    config:
      account-service:
        connectTimeout: 5000
        readTimeout: 5000
        loggerLevel: basic
```

Summary

In this chapter, we have launched a couple of microservices that communicate with one another. We discussed such topics as different implementations of REST clients, load balancing between multiple instances, and integration with service discovery. In my opinion, these aspects are so important that I decided to describe them in two chapters. This chapter should be treated as an introduction to the subject of inter-service communication and a discussion of integration with other important components of microservice architecture. The next chapter will show more advanced use of load balancers and REST clients, with particular attention on network and communication problems. After reading this chapter, you should be able to use Ribbon, Feign, and even `RestTemplate` properly in your applications and connect them to other Spring Cloud components.

In most cases, this knowledge is enough. However, sometimes you will need to customize client-side load balancer configuration or enable more advanced communication mechanisms like a circuit breaker or fallback. It is important to understand these solutions and their impact on the inter-service communication in your system. We will discuss them in the next chapter.

7
Advanced Load Balancing and Circuit Breakers

In this chapter, we will continue the subject discussed in the previous chapter, inter-service communication. We will extend it to more advanced samples of load balancing, timeouts, and circuit breaking.

Spring Cloud provides features that make implementation of communication between microservices nice and simple. However, we must not forget that the major difficulties we would face with such communication concern the processing time of the systems involved. If you have many microservices in your system, one of the first issues you need to deal with is the problem of latency. In this chapter, I would like to discuss a few Spring Cloud features that help us to avoid latency problems that are caused by many hops between services when processing a single input request, slow responses from several services, or a temporary unavailability of services. There are several strategies for dealing with partial failures. These include setting network timeouts, limiting the number of waiting requests, implementing different load balancing methods, or setting up a circuit breaker pattern and fallback implementation.

We will also talk about Ribbon and Feign clients once again, this time focusing on their more advanced configuration features. An entirely new library that will be introduced here is Netflix Hystrix. This library implements the circuit breaker pattern.

The topics we will cover in this chapter include the following:

- Different load balancing algorithms with Ribbon clients
- Enabling a circuit breaker for the application
- Customizing Hystrix with configuration properties
- Monitoring interservice communication with the Hystrix dashboard
- Using Hystrix together with Feign clients

Load balancing rules

Spring Cloud Netflix provides different load balancing algorithms in order to provide different benefits to the user. Your choice of supported method depends on your needs. In the Netflix OSS nomenclature, this algorithm is called a **rule**. The custom rule class should have implemented an `IRule` base interface. The following implementations are available by default inside Spring Cloud:

- `RoundRobinRule`: This rule simply chooses servers using the well-known round robin algorithm, where incoming requests are distributed across all instances sequentially. It is often used as the default rule or fallbacks for more advanced rules, such as `ClientConfigEnabledRoundRobinRule` and `ZoneAvoidanceRule`. `ZoneAvoidanceRule` is the default rule for Ribbon clients.

- `AvailabilityFilteringRule`: This rule will skip servers that are marked as circuit tripped or with a high number of concurrent connections. It also uses `RoundRobinRule` as a base class. By default, an instance is circuit tripped if an HTTP client fails to establish a connection with it three times in a row. This approach may be customized with the `niws.loadbalancer.<clientName>.connectionFailureCountThreshold` property. Once an instance is circuit tripped, it will remain in this state for the next 30 seconds before the next retry. This property may also be overridden in the configuration settings.

- `WeightedResponseTimeRule`: With this implementation, a traffic volume forwarder to the instance is inversely proportional to the instance's average response time. In other words, the longer the response time, the less weight it will get. In these circumstances, a load balancing client will record the traffic and response time of every instance of the service.

- `BestAvailableRule`: According to the description from the class documentation, this rule skips servers with *tripped* circuit breakers and picks the server with the lowest concurrent requests.

Tripped circuit breaker is a term taken from electrical engineering, and means that there's no current flowing through a circuit. In IT terminology, it refers to the situation where too many consecutive requests that are sent to a service fail, and therefore any further attempts to invoke the remote service will be interrupted immediately by the software on the client side in order to relieve the server-side application.

The WeightedResponseTime rule

Until now, we have usually tested our services manually by calling them from a web browser or a REST client. The current changes do not allow such an approach because we need to set fake delays for the services, as well as generate many HTTP requests.

Introducing Hoverfly for testing

At this point, I would like to introduce an interesting framework that may be a perfect solution for these kinds of tests. I am talking about Hoverfly, a lightweight service virtualization tool that is used to stub or simulate HTTP services. It is originally written in Go, but also gives you an expressive API for managing Hoverfly in Java. Hoverfly Java, maintained by SpectoLabs, provides classes that abstract away the binary and API calls, a DSL for creating simulations, and an integration with the JUnit test framework. This framework has a feature that I really like. You may easily add a delay to every simulated service by calling one method in your DSL definition. To enable Hoverfly for your project, you have to include the following dependency in your Maven `pom.xml`:

```
<dependency>
    <groupId>io.specto</groupId>
    <artifactId>hoverfly-java</artifactId>
    <version>0.9.0</version>
    <scope>test</scope>
</dependency>
```

Testing the rule

The sample we are discussing here is available on GitHub. To access it, you have to switch to `weighted_lb` branch (`https://github.com/piomin/sample-spring-cloud-comm/tree/weighted_lb`). Our JUnit test class, called `CustomerControllerTest`, is available under the `src/test/java` directory. To enable Hoverfly for the test, we should define the JUnit `@ClassRule`. The `HoverflyRule` class provides an API that allows us to simulate many services with different addresses, characteristics, and responses. In the following source code fragment, you may see that two instances of our sample microservice `account-service` have been declared inside `@ClassRule`. As you probably remember, that service has been invoked by `customer-service` and `order-service`.

Let's take a look at a test class from the `customer-service` module. It simulates the `GET` `/customer/*` method with a predefined response for two instances of `account-service` available on ports `8091` and `9091`. The first of them has been delayed by `200` milliseconds, while the second is delayed by `50` milliseconds:

```
@ClassRule
public static HoverflyRule hoverflyRule = HoverflyRule
  .inSimulationMode(dsl(
  service("account-service:8091")
      .andDelay(200, TimeUnit.MILLISECONDS).forAll()
      .get(startsWith("/customer/"))
.willReturn(success("[{\"id\":\"1\",\"number\":\"1234567890\",\"balance\":5
000}]", "application/json")),
  service("account-service:9091")
      .andDelay(50, TimeUnit.MILLISECONDS).forAll()
      .get(startsWith("/customer/"))
.willReturn(success("[{\"id\":\"2\",\"number\":\"1234567891\",\"balance\":8
000}]", "application/json")))))
  .printSimulationData();
```

Before running the test, we should also modify the `ribbon.listOfServers` configuration file by changing it to `listOfServers: account-service:8091, account-service:9091`. We should only make such a modification when working with Hoverfly.

Here's a `test` method that invokes the `GET /withAccounts/ {id}` endpoint exposed by `customer-service` a thousand times. This, in turn, invokes the `GET` `customer/{customerId}` endpoint from `account-service`, with a list of accounts owned by the customer. Every request is load balanced between two instances of `account-service` using `WeightedResponseTimeRule`:

```
@RunWith(SpringRunner.class)
@SpringBootTest(webEnvironment = WebEnvironment.DEFINED_PORT)
public class CustomerControllerTest {

    private static Logger LOGGER =
LoggerFactory.getLogger(CustomerControllerTest.class);

    @Autowired
    TestRestTemplate template;
    // ...

    @Test
    public void testCustomerWithAccounts() {
        for (int i = 0; i < 1000; i++) {
            Customer c = template.getForObject("/withAccounts/{id}",
```

```
Customer.class, 1);
            LOGGER.info("Customer: {}", c);
        }
    }

}
```

The method of working with a weighted response rule implementation is really interesting. Just after starting the test, the incoming requests are load balanced at a ratio of 50:50 between two instances of `account-service`. But, after some time, most of them are forwarded to the instance with the lesser delay.

Finally, 731 requests were processed by the instance available on port `9091` and 269 by the instance at port `8091` for a JUnit test launched on my local machine. However, at the end of the test, the proportion looked a bit different and was weighted in favor of the instance with the lesser delay, where incoming traffic is divided 4:1 between the two instances.

Now, we will change our test case a little by adding a third instance of `account-service` with a big delay of around 10 seconds. This modification aims to simulate a timeout in HTTP communication. Here's the fragment from the JUnit `@ClassRule` definition with the newest service instance listening on port `10091`:

```
service("account-service:10091")
    .andDelay(10000, TimeUnit.MILLISECONDS).forAll()
    .get(startsWith("/customer/"))
.willReturn(success("[{\"id\":\"3\",\"number\":\"1234567892\",\"balance\":1
0000}]", "application/json"))
```

We should accordingly perform a change in the Ribbon configuration to enable load balancing to the newest instance of `account-service`:

```
listOfServers: account-service:8091, account-service:9091, account-
service:10091
```

The last thing that has to be changed, but which is left as it is in the previous test case, is the `RestTemplate` bean declaration. In this instance, I have set both the read and the connect timeout to one second because the third instance of `account-service` launched during the test is delayed by 10 seconds. Every request sent there would be terminated by the timeout after one second:

```
@LoadBalanced
@Bean
RestTemplate restTemplate(RestTemplateBuilder restTemplateBuilder) {
    return restTemplateBuilder
        .setConnectTimeout(1000)
```

```
        .setReadTimeout(1000)
        .build();
}
```

If you run the same test as before, the result would not be satisfactory. The distribution between all declared instances will be 420, processed by the instance listening on port `8091` (with a delay of `200` milliseconds), 468, processed by the instance listening on port `9091` (with a delay of `50` milliseconds), and 112 sent to the third instance, terminated by the timeout. Why am I quoting all these statistics? We may change a default load balancing rule from `WeightedResponseTimeRule` to `AvailabilityFilteringRule` and rerun the test. If we do this, 496 requests will be sent to both the first and second instance, while only 8 will be sent to the third instance, with a one second timeout. Interestingly, if you set `BestAvailableRule` as the default rule, all requests would be sent to the first instance.

Now that you have read through this example, you can easily see the differences between all available load balancing rules for the Ribbon client.

Customizing the Ribbon client

Several configuration settings of the Ribbon client may be overridden with Spring bean declarations. As with Feign, it should be declared in the client annotation field named configuration, for example,`@RibbonClient(name = "account-service", configuration = RibbonConfiguration.class)`. The following features may be customized with this approach:

- `IClientConfig`: The default implementation of this is `DefaultClientConfigImpl`.
- `IRule`: This component is used to determine which service instance should be selected from a list. The `ZoneAvoidanceRule` implementation class is auto-configured.
- `IPing`: This is a component that runs in the background. It is responsible for ensuring that the instances of service are running.

- `ServerList<Server>`: This can be static or dynamic. If it is dynamic (as used by `DynamicServerListLoadBalancer`), a background thread will refresh and filter the list at a predefined interval. By default, Ribbon uses a static list of servers taken from configuration file. It is implemented by `ConfigurationBasedServerList`.

- `ServerListFilter<Server>`: `ServerListFilter` is a component used by `DynamicServerListLoadBalancer` to filter the servers returned from a `ServerList` implementation. There are two implementations of that interface—auto-configured `ZonePreferenceServerListFilter` and `ServerListSubsetFilter`.

- `ILoadBalancer`: This is responsible for performing load balancing between available instances of a service on the client side. By default, Ribbon uses `ZoneAwareLoadBalancer`.

- `ServerListUpdater`: This is responsible for updating the list of available instances of a given application. By default, Ribbon uses `PollingServerListUpdater`.

Let's look at an example configuration class that defines the default implementation of the `IRule` and `IPing` components. Such a configuration may be defined for a single Ribbon client, as well as for all Ribbon clients available in the application classpath, by providing the `@RibbonClients(defaultConfiguration = RibbonConfiguration.class)` annotation:

```
@Configuration
public class RibbonConfiguration {

    @Bean
    public IRule ribbonRule() {
        return new WeightedResponseTimeRule();
    }

    @Bean
    public IPing ribbonPing() {
        return new PingUrl();
    }

}
```

Even if you don't have any experience with Spring, you may probably have guessed (based on the previous samples) that the configuration can also be customized using the `properties` file. In that case, Spring Cloud Netflix is compatible with the properties described in the Ribbon documentation provided by Netflix. The following classes are the supported properties, and they should be prefixed by `<clientName>.ribbon`, or, if they apply to all clients, by `ribbon`:

- `NFLoadBalancerClassName`: `ILoadBalancer` default implementation class
- `NFLoadBalancerRuleClassName`: `IRule` default implementation class
- `NFLoadBalancerPingClassName`: `IPing` default implementation class
- `NIWSServerListClassName`: `ServerList` default implementation class
- `NIWSServerListFilterClassName`: `ServerListFilter` default implementation class

Here's a similar sample to the preceding `@Configuration` class that overrides the `IRule` and `IPing` default implementations used by the Spring Cloud application:

```
account-service:
  ribbon:
    NFLoadBalancerPingClassName: com.netflix.loadbalancer.PingUrl
    NFLoadBalancerRuleClassName:
com.netflix.loadbalancer.WeightedResponseTimeRule
```

The circuit breaker pattern with Hystrix

We have already discussed the different implementations of load balancer algorithms in Spring Cloud Netflix. Some of them are based on monitoring the instance response time or the number of failures. In these cases, a load balancer makes decisions about which instance should be invoked based on these statistics. The circuit breaker pattern should be treated as an extension of that solution. The main idea behind a circuit breaker is very simple. A protected function call is wrapped in a circuit breaker object, which is responsible for monitoring a number of failure calls. If the failures reach a threshold, the circuit is opened, and all further calls will be failed automatically. Usually, it is also desirable to have some kind of monitor alert if a circuit breaker trips. Some crucial benefits derived from the usage of the circuit breaker pattern in your applications are the ability to continue operating when a related service fails, the prevention of a cascaded failure, and giving a failing service time to recover.

Building an application with Hystrix

Netflix provides an implementation of the circuit breaker pattern in their library called **Hystrix**. That library has also been included as a default implementation of the circuit breaker for Spring Cloud. Hystrix has some other interesting features, and should also be treated as a comprehensive tool for dealing with latency and fault tolerance for distributed systems. What is important is that if the circuit breaker is opened, Hystrix redirects all calls to the specified fallback method. The fallback method is designed to provide a generic response without any dependency on a network, usually read from an in-memory cache or just implemented as static logic. If it becomes necessary to perform a network call, it is recommended that you implement it using another `HystrixCommand` or `HystrixObservableCommand`. To include Hystrix in your project, you should use the `spring-cloud-starter-netflix-hystrix` or `spring-cloud-starter-hystrix` starter for Spring Cloud Netflix versions older than 1.4.0:

```
<dependency>
    <groupId>org.springframework.cloud</groupId>
    <artifactId>spring-cloud-starter-hystrix</artifactId>
</dependency>
```

Implementing Hystrix's commands

Spring Cloud Netflix Hystrix looks for a method that is annotated with the `@HystrixCommand` annotation, and then wraps it in a proxy object connected to a circuit breaker. Thanks to this, Hystrix is able to monitor all calls of such a method. This annotation currently works only for a class marked with `@Component` or `@Service`. That's important information for us, because we have implemented the logic related to other services calling in all the previous samples inside the REST controller class, which is marked with the `@RestController` annotation. So, in the `customer-service` application, all that logic has been moved to the newly created `CustomerService` class, which is then injected into the controller bean. The method responsible for communication with `account-service` has been annotated with `@HystrixCommand`. I have also implemented a fallback method, the name of which passes into the `fallbackMethod` annotation's field. This method only returns an empty list:

```
@Service
public class CustomerService {

    @Autowired
    RestTemplate template;
    @Autowired
    CustomerRepository repository;
```

```
// ...

@HystrixCommand(fallbackMethod = "findCustomerAccountsFallback")
public List<Account> findCustomerAccounts(Long id) {
    Account[] accounts =
template.getForObject("http://account-service/customer/{customerId}",
Account[].class, id);
    return Arrays.stream(accounts).collect(Collectors.toList());
}

public List<Account> findCustomerAccountsFallback(Long id) {
    return new ArrayList<>();
}

}
```

Don't forget to mark your main class with @EnableHystrix, which is needed to tell Spring Cloud that it should use circuit breakers for the application. We may also optionally annotate a class with @EnableCircuitBreaker, which does the same. For test purposes, the account-service.ribbon.listOfServers property should have included the network addresses of two instances of the localhost:8091, localhost:9091 service. Although we have declared two instances of account-service for the Ribbon client, we will start the only one that is available on the 8091 port. If you call the customer-service method GET http://localhost:8092/withAccounts/{id}, Ribbon will try to load balance every incoming request between those two declared instances, that is, once you receive the response containing a list of accounts and the second time you receive an empty account list, or vice versa. This is illustrated by the following fragment of the application logs. This is illustrated by the following fragment of application's logs. To access the sample application's source code, you should switch to the hystrix_basic branch (https://github.com/piomin/sample-spring-cloud-comm/tree/hystrix_basic) in the same GitHub repository as the samples from the previous chapter:

```
{"id":1,"name":"John Scott","type":"NEW","accounts":[]}

{"id":1,"name":"John
Scott","type":"NEW","accounts":[{"id":1,"number":"1234567890","balance":500
0},{"id":2,"number":"1234567891","balance":5000},{"id":3,"number":"12345678
92","balance":0}]}
```

Implementing fallback with cached data

The fallback implementation presented in the previous example is very simple. Returning an empty list does not make much sense for an application running in production. It makes more sense to use the fallback method in your application when you read data from a cache in case of a request failure, for example. Such a cache may be implemented inside the client application or with the use of third-party tools, such as Redis, Hazelcast, or EhCache. The simplest implementation is available within the Spring Framework, and can be used after including the `spring-boot-starter-cache` artifact with your dependencies. To enable caching for the Spring Boot application, you should annotate the main or configuration class with `@EnableCaching` and provide the `CacheManager` bean in the following context:

```
@SpringBootApplication
@RibbonClient(name = "account-service")
@EnableHystrix
@EnableCaching
public class CustomerApplication {

    @LoadBalanced
    @Bean
    RestTemplate restTemplate() {
        return new RestTemplate();
    }

    public static void main(String[] args) {
        new
SpringApplicationBuilder(CustomerApplication.class).web(true).run(args);
    }

    @Bean
    public CacheManager cacheManager() {
        return new ConcurrentMapCacheManager("accounts");
    }
    // ...

}
```

Then you can mark the method wrapped with the circuit breaker using the `@CachePut` annotation. This will add the result returning from the calling method to the cache map. In that case, our map is named `accounts`. Finally, you may read the data inside your fallback method implementation by invoking the `CacheManager` bean directly. If you retry the same request a couple of times, you will see that the empty list of accounts is no longer returned as a response. Instead, the service always returns data that is cached during the first successful call:

```
@Autowired
CacheManager cacheManager;
@CachePut("accounts")
@HystrixCommand(fallbackMethod = "findCustomerAccountsFallback")
public List<Account> findCustomerAccounts(Long id) {
    Account[] accounts =
template.getForObject("http://account-service/customer/{customerId}",
Account[].class, id);
    return Arrays.stream(accounts).collect(Collectors.toList());
}

public List<Account> findCustomerAccountsFallback(Long id) {
    ValueWrapper w = cacheManager.getCache("accounts").get(id);
    if (w != null) {
        return (List<Account>) w.get();
    } else {
    return new ArrayList<>();
    }
}
```

The tripping circuit breaker

Let me suggest an exercise for you to do. Until now, you have learned how to enable and implement circuit breakers in your application using Hystrix, in conjunction with Spring Cloud, and how to use a fallback method to take data from the cache. But you still have not used a tripped circuit breaker to prevent the failure instance from being invoked by a load balancer. Now, I would like to configure Hystrix to open the circuit after three failed call attempts if the failure percentage is greater than 30 percent and prevent the API method from being called for the next 5 seconds. The measurement time window is around 10 seconds. To meet these requirements, we have to override several default Hystrix configuration settings. It may be performed using the `@HystrixProperty` annotation inside `@HystrixCommand`.

Here's the current implementation of the method responsible for getting the account list from `customer-service`:

```
@CachePut("accounts")
@HystrixCommand(fallbackMethod = "findCustomerAccountsFallback",
  commandProperties = {
    @HystrixProperty(name =
"execution.isolation.thread.timeoutInMilliseconds", value = "500"),
    @HystrixProperty(name = "circuitBreaker.requestVolumeThreshold", value
= "10"),
    @HystrixProperty(name = "circuitBreaker.errorThresholdPercentage",
value = "30"),
    @HystrixProperty(name = "circuitBreaker.sleepWindowInMilliseconds",
value = "5000"),
    @HystrixProperty(name = "metrics.rollingStats.timeInMilliseconds",
value = "10000")
  }
)
public List<Account> findCustomerAccounts(Long id) {
    Account[] accounts =
template.getForObject("http://account-service/customer/{customerId}",
Account[].class, id);
    return Arrays.stream(accounts).collect(Collectors.toList());
}
```

The full list of Hystrix's configuration properties is available on Netflix's GitHub site at `https://github.com/Netflix/Hystrix/wiki/Configuration`. I won't discuss all of them, only the most important properties for communication between microservices. Here's the list of the properties used in our sample, along with their descriptions:

- `execution.isolation.thread.timeoutInMilliseconds`: This property sets the time in milliseconds, after which a read or connect timeout will occur and the client will walk away from the command execution. Hystrix marks such a method call as a failure, and performs fallback logic. That timeout may be completely turned off by setting the `command.timeout.enabled` property to `false`. The default is 1,000 milliseconds.

- `circuitBreaker.requestVolumeThreshold`: This property sets the minimum number of requests in a rolling window that will trip the circuit. The default value is 20. In our sample, this property is set to `10`, which means that the first nine will not trip the circuit, even if all of them fail. I set that value because we have assumed that the circuit should be opened if `30` percent of incoming requests fail, but the minimum number of incoming requests is three.

- `circuitBreaker.errorThresholdPercentage`: This property sets the minimum error percentage. Exceeding this percentage results in opening the circuit, and the system starts short-circuiting requests to fallback logic. The default value is 50. I set it to 30 because, in our sample, I want 30 percent of failed requests should open the circuit.
- `circuitBreaker.sleepWindowInMilliseconds`: This property sets a period of time between tripping the circuit and allowing attempts taken in order to determine whether the circuit should be closed again. During this time, all incoming requests are rejected. The default value is 5,000. Because we would like to wait 10 seconds before the first call is retired after the circuit has been opened, I set it to 10,000.
- `metrics.rollingStats.timeInMilliseconds`: This property sets the duration of the statistical rolling window in milliseconds. This is how long Hystrix keeps metrics for the circuit breaker to use, and for publishing.

With these settings, we may run the same JUnit test as for the previous example. We launch two stubs of `account-service` using `HoverflyRule`. The first of them would be delayed by 200 milliseconds, while a second one that is delayed by 2,000 milliseconds is greater than the timeout set for `@HystrixCommand` with the `execution.isolation.thread.timeoutInMilliseconds` property. After running JUnit `CustomerControllerTest`, take a look at the printed logs. I have inserted the logs taken from the test launched on my machine. The first request from `customer-service` is load balanced to the first instance, delayed by 200 ms `(1)`. Every request sent to the instance available on `9091` finishes with a timeout after one second. After sending 10 requests, the first failure causes a trip of the circuit `(2)`. Then, for the next 10 seconds, every single request is handled by a fallback method, which returns cached data `(3)`, `(4)`. After 10 seconds, the client tries to call an instance of `account-service` again and succeeds `(5)` because it hits on the instance delayed by 200 ms. That success results in the closure of the circuit. Unfortunately, the second instance of `account-service` still responds slowly, so the scenario happens all over again until the JUnit test finishes `(6)` and `(7)`. This detailed description shows you exactly how a circuit breaker with Hystrix works for Spring Cloud:

```
16:54:04+01:00 Found response delay setting for this request host:
{account-service:8091 200} // (1)
16:54:05+01:00 Found response delay setting for this request host:
{account-service:9091 2000}
16:54:05+01:00 Found response delay setting for this request host:
{account-service:8091 200}
16:54:06+01:00 Found response delay setting for this request host:
{account-service:9091 2000}
16:54:06+01:00 Found response delay setting for this request host:
```

```
{account-service:8091 200}
...
16:54:09+01:00 Found response delay setting for this request host:
{account-service:9091 2000} // (2)
16:54:10.137 Customer [id=1, name=John Scott, type=NEW, accounts=[Account
[id=1, number=1234567890, balance=5000]]] // (3)
...
16:54:20.169 Customer [id=1, name=John Scott, type=NEW, accounts=[Account
[id=1, number=1234567890, balance=5000]]] // (4)
16:54:20+01:00 Found response delay setting for this request host:
{account-service:8091 200} // (5)
16:54:20+01:00 Found response delay setting for this request host:
{account-service:9091 2000}
16:54:21+01:00 Found response delay setting for this request host:
{account-service:8091 200}
...
16:54:25+01:00 Found response delay setting for this request host:
{account-service:8091 200} // (6)
16:54:26.157 Customer [id=1, name=John Scott, type=NEW, accounts=[Account
[id=1, number=1234567890, balance=5000]]] // (7)
```

Monitoring latency and fault tolerance

As I have already mentioned, Hystrix is not only a simple tool implementing a circuit breaker pattern. It is a solution that deals with latency and fault tolerance in distributed systems. One interesting feature provided by Hystrix is the ability to expose the most important metrics related to interservice communication and display them using a UI dashboard. This function is available for clients wrapped with the Hystrix command. In some previous samples, we have analyzed only a part of our system to simulate a delay in communication between `customer-service` and `account-service`. That's a really good approach when testing advanced load balancing algorithms or different circuit breaker configuration settings, but now we will go back to analyzing the whole of our sample system setup as a set of standalone Spring Boot applications. This allows us to observe how Spring Cloud, in conjunction with Netflix OSS tools, helps us to monitor and react to latency issues and failures in communication between our microservices. The sample system simulates a failure in a simple way. It has a static configuration with the network addresses of two instances, `account-service`, and `product-service`, but only one of them for each service is running.

In order to refresh your memory, the architecture of our sample system, taking into consideration assumptions about failure, is shown in the following diagram:

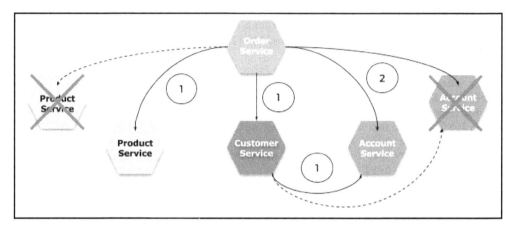

This time, we'll begin a bit differently, with a test. Here's the fragment of the test method, which is being invoked in a loop. First, it calls the POST http://localhost:8090/ endpoint from order-service, sending an Order object, and it receives a response with the id, status, and price set. Within that request, which has been labeled in the preceding diagram as (1), order-service communicates with product-service and customer-service and, in addition, customer-service calls the endpoint from account-service. If the order has been accepted, the test client calls the PUT http://localhost:8090/{id} method with the order's id to accept it and withdraw funds from the account. On the server side, there is only one interservice communication in that case, which is labeled (2) in the preceding diagram. Before running this test, you have to launch all microservices that are a part of our system:

```
Random r = new Random();
Order order = new Order();
order.setCustomerId((long) r.nextInt(3)+1);
order.setProductIds(Arrays.asList(new Long[] {(long) r.nextInt(10)+1, (long)
r.nextInt(10)+1}));
order = template.postForObject("http://localhost:8090", order,
Order.class); // (1)
if (order.getStatus() != OrderStatus.REJECTED) {
    template.put("http://localhost:8090/{id}", null, order.getId()); // (2)
}
```

Exposing Hystrix's metrics stream

Each microservice that uses Hystrix in communication with other microservices may expose metrics of every integration wrapped with the Hystrix command. To enable such a metrics stream, you should include a dependency on `spring-boot-starter-actuator`. This will expose the `/hystrix.stream` object as a management endpoint. It is also necessary to include `spring-cloud-starter-hystrix`, which has already been added to our sample application:

```
<dependency>
    <groupId>org.springframework.boot</groupId>
    <artifactId>spring-boot-starter-actuator</artifactId>
</dependency>
```

A generated stream is exposed as further JSON entries containing metrics characterizing a single call within a method. Here's a single entry for a call within the `GET` `/withAccounts/{id}` method from `customer-service`:

`{"type":"HystrixCommand","name":"`**`customer-`** **`service.findWithAccounts`**`","group":"CustomerService","currentTime":151308920 4882,"isCircuitBreakerOpen":false,"errorPercentage":0,"errorCount":0,"reque stCount":`**`74`**`,"rollingCountBadRequests":0,"rollingCountCollapsedRequests":0," rollingCountEmit":0,"rollingCountExceptionsThrown":0,"rollingCountFailure": 0,"rollingCountFallbackEmit":0,"rollingCountFallbackFailure":0,"rollingCoun tFallbackMissing":0,"rollingCountFallbackRejection":0,"rollingCountFallback Success":0,"rollingCountResponsesFromCache":0,"rollingCountSemaphoreRejecte d":0,"rollingCountShortCircuited":0,"rollingCountSuccess":`**`75`**`,"rollingCountT hreadPoolRejected":0,"rollingCountTimeout":0,"currentConcurrentExecutionCou nt":0,"rollingMaxConcurrentExecutionCount":1,"latencyExecute_mean":`**`5`**`,"laten cyExecute":{"0":0,"25":0,"50":0,"75":15,"90":16,"95":31,"99":47,"99.5":47," 100":62},"latencyTotal_mean":5,"latencyTotal":{"0":0,"25":0,"50":0,"75":15, "90":16,"95":31,"99":47,"99.5":47,"100":62},"propertyValue_circuitBreakerRe questVolumeThreshold":10,"propertyValue_circuitBreakerSleepWindowInMillisec onds":10000,"propertyValue_circuitBreakerErrorThresholdPercentage":30,"prop ertyValue_circuitBreakerForceOpen":false,"propertyValue_circuitBreakerForce Closed":false,"propertyValue_circuitBreakerEnabled":true,"propertyValue_exe cutionIsolationStrategy":"THREAD","propertyValue_executionIsolationThreadTi meoutInMilliseconds":2000,"propertyValue_executionTimeoutInMilliseconds":20 00,"propertyValue_executionIsolationThreadInterruptOnTimeout":true,"propert yValue_executionIsolationThreadPoolKeyOverride":null,"propertyValue_executi onIsolationSemaphoreMaxConcurrentRequests":10,"propertyValue_fallbackIsolat ionSemaphoreMaxConcurrentRequests":10,"propertyValue_metricsRollingStatisti calWindowInMilliseconds":10000,"propertyValue_requestCacheEnabled":true,"pr opertyValue_requestLogEnabled":true,"reportingHosts":1,"threadPool":"Custom erService"}`

Hystrix dashboard

Hystrix dashboard visualizes the following information:

- Health and traffic volume is displayed as a circle that is changing its color and size together with the changes in incoming statistics
- The error percentage over the last 10 seconds
- The request rate over the last two minutes by number, displaying the results on a graph
- The circuit breaker status (open/closed)
- The number of service hosts
- The latency percentiles over the last minute
- The service's thread pools

Building an application with the dashboard

The Hystrix dashboard is integrated with Spring Cloud. The best approach when implementing the dashboard inside a system is to separate out an independent Spring Boot application with the dashboard. To include the Hystrix dashboard in your project, use the `spring-cloud-starter-hystrix-netflix-dashboard` **starter** or `spring-cloud-starter-hystrix-dashboard` for Spring Cloud Netflix versions older than 1.4.0:

```
<dependency>
    <groupId>org.springframework.cloud</groupId>
    <artifactId>spring-cloud-starter-hystrix-dashboard</artifactId>
</dependency>
```

The application's main class should be annotated with `@EnableHystrixDashboard`. After launching it, the Hystrix dashboard is available under the `/hystrix` context path:

```
@SpringBootApplication
@EnableHystrixDashboard
public class HystrixApplication {

    public static void main(String[] args) {
        new
SpringApplicationBuilder(HystrixApplication.class).web(true).run(args);
    }

}
```

I configured port `9000` as the default for the Hystrix application in our sample system, which is implemented in the `hystrix-dashboard` module. So, if you call the `http://localhost:9000/hystrix` address in a web browser after launching `hystrix-dashboard`, it will display the page as shown in the following screenshot. There, you should provide the Hystrix stream endpoint's address, and, optionally, a title. If you would like to display metrics for all the endpoints that are called from `order-service`, type the address `http://localhost:8090/hystrix.stream` and then click the **Monitor Stream** button :

Hystrix Dashboard

http://localhost:8090/hystrix.stream

Cluster via Turbine (default cluster): http://turbine-hostname:port/turbine.stream
Cluster via Turbine (custom cluster): http://turbine-hostname:port/turbine.stream?cluster=[clusterName]
Single Hystrix App: http://hystrix-app:port/hystrix.stream

Delay: 2000   ms   Title: order-service

Monitor Stream

Monitoring metrics on the dashboard

In this section, we will look at calling the GET /withAccounts/{id} method from customer-service. It is wrapped with @HystrixCommand. It is displayed on the Hystrix dashboard under the title customer-service.findWithAccounts, taken from a commandKey attribute. In addition, the UI dashboard also shows information about the thread pools that are assigned to every Spring Bean that provides an implementation of methods wrapped with Hystrix's command. In this case, it is CustomerService:

```
@Service
public class CustomerService {

    // ...
    @CachePut("customers")
    @HystrixCommand(commandKey = "customer-service.findWithAccounts",
fallbackMethod = "findCustomerWithAccountsFallback",
        commandProperties = {
            @HystrixProperty(name =
"execution.isolation.thread.timeoutInMilliseconds", value = "2000"),
            @HystrixProperty(name =
"circuitBreaker.requestVolumeThreshold", value = "10"),
            @HystrixProperty(name =
"circuitBreaker.errorThresholdPercentage", value = "30"),
            @HystrixProperty(name =
"circuitBreaker.sleepWindowInMilliseconds", value = "10000"),
            @HystrixProperty(name =
"metrics.rollingStats.timeInMilliseconds", value = "10000")
        })
    public Customer findCustomerWithAccounts(Long customerId) {
        Customer customer =
template.getForObject("http://customer-service/withAccounts/{id}",
Customer.class, customerId);
        return customer;
    }

    public Customer findCustomerWithAccountsFallback(Long customerId) {
        ValueWrapper w =
cacheManager.getCache("customers").get(customerId);
        if (w != null) {
            return (Customer) w.get();
        } else {
            return new Customer();
        }
    }

}
```

Here's the screen from the Hystrix dashboard just after the start of a JUnit test. We monitor the state of all three methods wrapped with @HystrixCommand. The circuit has been opened for the findByIds method from product-service, as expected. After a few seconds, the circuit has also been opened for the withdraw method from account-service:

Hystrix Stream: order-service

Circuit   Sort: Error then Volume | Alphabetical | Volume | Error | Mean | Median | 90 | 99 | 99.5   Succe

product-service.findByIds	cust...ice.findWithAccounts	account-service.withdraw
5 0 28.0 % 18 0 0	5 0 16.0 % 0 0 0	1 0 33.0 % 0 0 0
Host 0.7/s	Host 0.6/s	Host 0.3/s
Cluster 0.7/s	Cluster 0.6/s	Cluster 0.3/s
Circuit Open	Circuit Closed	Circuit Closed
Hosts 1 90th 1044ms Median 95ms 99th 1202ms Mean 491ms 99.5th 1202ms	Hosts 1 90th 634ms Median 524ms 99th 2002ms Mean 624ms 99.5th 2002ms	Hosts 1 90th 0ms Median 0ms 99th 0ms Mean 0ms 99.5th 0ms

Thread Pools   Sort: Alphabetical | Volume |

ProductService	CustomerService	AccountService
Host 0.7/s	Host 0.5/s	Host 0.2/s
Cluster 0.7/s	Cluster 0.5/s	Cluster 0.2/s
Active 0 Max Active 1 Queued 0 Executions 7 Pool Size 10 Queue Size 5	Active 0 Max Active 1 Queued 0 Executions 5 Pool Size 6 Queue Size 5	Active 0 Max Active 1 Queued 0 Executions 2 Pool Size 3 Queue Size 5

After a few moments, the situation will be stabilized. All the circuits remain closed because only a small percentage of traffic is sent to the inactive instances of applications. This shows the power of Spring Cloud with Hystrix and Ribbon. The system was able to automatically reconfigure itself in order to redirect most of the incoming requests to the working instances based on the metrics generated by the load balancers and circuit breakers:

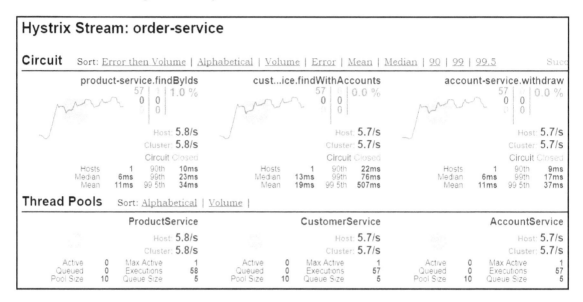

Aggregating Hystrix's streams with Turbine

You have probably noticed that we were only able to look at an individual instance of the service in the Hystrix dashboard. There were no metrics from communication between `customer-service` and `account-service` when we were displaying the state of commands for `order-service`, and vice versa. We might also imagine that there is more than one instance of `order-service` running, which makes it necessary to switch regularly between different instances or services in the Hystrix dashboard. Fortunately, there is an application called **Turbine** that aggregates all of the relevant `/hystrix.stream` endpoints into a combined `/turbine.stream` and makes it possible for us to monitor the overall health of the whole system.

Enabling Turbine

Before making any changes to enable Turbine for our application, we should start by enabling service discovery, which is required here. Switch to the `hystrix_with_turbine` branch to access the version of our sample system that supports service discovery with Eureka and aggregates Hystrix's streams using Turbine. To enable Turbine for the project exposing the UI dashboard, just include `spring-cloud-starter-turbine` in the dependencies and annotate the main application class with `@EnableTurbine`:

```
<dependency>
    <groupId>org.springframework.cloud</groupId>
    <artifactId>spring-cloud-starter-turbine</artifactId>
</dependency>
```

The `turbine.appConfig` configuration property is a list of Eureka service names that Turbine will use to look up instances. The Turbine stream is then available in the Hystrix dashboard under the URL `http://localhost:9000/turbine.stream`. The address is also determined by a value of the `turbine.aggregator.clusterConfig` property, `http://localhost:9000/turbine.stream?cluster=<clusterName>`. The cluster parameter can be omitted if the name is `default`. Here's the Turbine configuration that combines all of Hystrix's visualization metrics in a single UI dashboard:

```
turbine:
  appConfig: order-service,customer-service
    clusterNameExpression: "'default'"
```

Now, all of Hystrix's metrics for the whole sample system are displayed in a single dashboard site. All we need to display them is to monitor the statistics stream, available under `http://localhost:9000/turbine.stream`:

Alternatively, we can configure a cluster per service by providing a list of services with the `turbine.aggregator.clusterConfig` property. In that case, you may switch between clusters by providing the service name `cluster` with the `http://localhost:9000/turbine.stream?cluster=ORDER-SERVICE` parameter. The cluster name must be provided in uppercase because values returned by the Eureka server are in uppercase:

```
turbine:
  aggregator:
    clusterConfig: ORDER-SERVICE,CUSTOMER-SERVICE
    appConfig: order-service,customer-service
```

By default, Turbine is looking for the `/hystrix.stream` endpoint on a registered instance under its `homePageUrl` address in Eureka. Then it appends `/hystrix.stream` to that URL. Our sample application `order-service` is launched under port `8090`, so we should also override the default management port to `8090`. The current configuration of `order-service` is shown in the following code fragment. Alternatively, you may also change that port with the `eureka.instance.metadata-map.management.port` property:

```
spring:
 application:
   name: order-service

server:
 port: ${PORT:8090}

eureka:
 client:
   serviceUrl:
     defaultZone: ${EUREKA_URL:http://localhost:8761/eureka/}

management:
 security:
   enabled: false
     port: 8090
```

Enabling Turbine with streaming

The classic Turbine model of pulling metrics from all the distributed Hystrix commands is not always a good choice. An operation such as collecting metrics from HTTP endpoints may also be realized asynchronously with a message broker. To enable Turbine with streaming, we should include the following dependencies with the project and then annotate the main application with `@EnableTurbineStream`. The following sample uses RabbitMQ as a default message broker, but you may use Apache Kafka by including `spring-cloud-starter-stream-kafka`:

```
<dependency>
  <groupId>org.springframework.cloud</groupId>
  <artifactId>spring-cloud-starter-turbine-stream</artifactId>
</dependency>
<dependency>
  <groupId>org.springframework.cloud</groupId>
  <artifactId>spring-cloud-starter-stream-rabbit</artifactId>
</dependency>
```

The dependencies visible in the preceding code should be included on the server side. For client applications, these are `order-service` and `customer-service`, and we need to add the `spring-cloud-netflix-hystrix-stream` library. If you have run your message broker locally, it should have worked successfully on auto-configured settings. You may also run RabbitMQ using a Docker container, as we did in the example of the Spring Cloud Config with AMQP bus described in `Chapter 5`, *Distributed Configuration with Spring Cloud Config*. Then you should override the following properties in `application.yml` for both the client-side and server-side applications:

```
spring:
  rabbitmq:
    host: 192.168.99.100
    port: 5672
    username: guest
    password: guest
```

If you log in to the RabbitMQ management console, available under `http://192.168.99.100:15672`, you will see that the new exchange with the name `springCloudHystrixStream` has been created after our sample application's startup. Now, the only thing left to do is to run the same JUnit test as we did for the sample that illustrated the classic Turbine approach, described in the previous section. All metrics are sent through the message broker and may be observed under the `http://localhost:9000` endpoint. If you would like to try it by yourself, switch to the `hystrix_with_turbine_stream` branch (see `https://github.com/piomin/sample-spring-cloud-comm/tree/hystrix_with_turbine_stream` for more information).

Failures and the circuit breaker pattern with Feign

The Feign client is, by default, integrated with Ribbon and Hystrix. This means that, if you wish, you can apply different approaches to deal with latency and timeouts in your system when using that library. The first of these approaches is a connection retry mechanism provided by the Ribbon client. The second is a circuit breaker pattern and a fallback implementation available under the Hystrix project, which has already been discussed in the previous sections of this chapter.

Retrying the connection with Ribbon

Hystrix is enabled by default for the application when using a Feign library. This means that you should disable it in the configuration settings if you do not want to use it. For the purpose of testing a retry mechanism with Ribbon, I suggest that you disable Hystrix. In order to enable connection retrying for Feign, you only have to set two configuration properties—`MaxAutoRetries` and `MaxAutoRetriesNextServer`. The important settings, in this case, are also `ReadTimeout` and `ConnectTimeout`. All of them may be overridden in the `application.yml` file. Here's the list of the most important Ribbon settings:

- `MaxAutoRetries`: This is the maximum number of retries on the same server or service instances. The first try is excluded from this count.
- `MaxAutoRetriesNextServer`: This is the maximum number of next servers or service instances to retry, excluding the first server.
- `OkToRetryOnAllOperations`: This states that all operations can be retried for this client.
- `ConnectTimeout`: This is the maximum time waiting to establish a connection to a server or service instance.
- `ReadTimeout`: This is the maximum time waiting for a response from the server after establishing a connection.

Let's assume that we have two instances of a target service. The connection to the first has been established, but it responds too slowly and a timeout occurs. The client performs one retry to that instance in accordance with the `MaxAutoRetries=1` property. If it has still not been successful, it tries to connect with a second available instance of that service. This action is repeated twice in the case of a failure, according to what has been set in the `MaxAutoRetriesNextServer=2` property. If the described mechanism is ultimately *not successful*, the timeout is returned to the external client. In that case, it may happen even after more than four seconds. Take a look at the following configuration:

```
ribbon:
  eureka:
    enabled: true
  MaxAutoRetries: 1
  MaxAutoRetriesNextServer: 2
  ConnectTimeout: 500
  ReadTimeout: 1000

feign:
  hystrix:
    enabled: false
```

This solution is a standard retry mechanism implemented for a microservices-based environment. We may also look at some other scenarios related to the different configuration settings of Ribbon's timeouts and retries. There is no reason why we shouldn't use that mechanism together with Hystrix's circuit breaker. However, we have to remember that `ribbon.ReadTimeout` should be lower than the value of Hystrix's `execution.isolation.thread.timeoutInMilliseconds` property.

I suggest that you test the configuration settings that we just described as an exercise. You may use a previously introduced Hoverfly JUnit rule for simulating the delays and stubs of a service's instances.

Hystrix's support for Feign

To begin with, I would like to reiterate that Hystrix is enabled by default for the application when using a Feign library, but only for the older versions of Spring Cloud. According to the documentation for the newest version of Spring Cloud, we should set the `feign.hystrix.enabled` property to `true`, which forces Feign to wrap all methods with a circuit breaker.

Prior to the Spring Cloud Dalston release, if Hystrix was on the classpath, Feign would have wrapped all methods in a circuit breaker by default. This default behavior was changed in Spring Cloud Dalston in favor of an opt-in approach.

When using Hystrix together with a Feign client, the simplest way to provide configuration properties previously set with @HystrixProperty inside @HystrixCommand is through the application.yml file. Here's the equivalent configuration of the samples presented before:

```
hystrix:
  command:
    default:
      circuitBreaker:
        requestVolumeThreshold: 10
        errorThresholdPercentage: 30
        sleepWindowInMilliseconds: 10000
      execution:
        isolation:
          thread:
            timeoutInMilliseconds: 1000
      metrics:
        rollingStats:
          timeInMilliseconds: 10000
```

Feign supports the notation of a fallback. To enable fallbacks for a given @FeignClient, we should set the fallback attribute with the class name that provides a fallback implementation. The implementation class should be defined as a Spring Bean:

```
@FeignClient(name = "customer-service", fallback =
CustomerClientFallback.class)
public interface CustomerClient {

    @CachePut("customers")
    @GetMapping("/withAccounts/{customerId}")
    Customer findByIdWithAccounts(@PathVariable("customerId") Long
customerId);

}
```

Fallback implementation is based on a cache, and implements the interface annotated with
`@FeignClient`:

```
@Component
public class CustomerClientFallback implements CustomerClient {

    @Autowired
    CacheManager cacheManager;

    @Override
    public Customer findByIdWithAccountsFallback(Long customerId) {
        ValueWrapper w =
cacheManager.getCache("customers").get(customerId);
        if (w != null) {
            return (Customer) w.get();
        } else {
            return new Customer();
        }
    }

}
```

Optionally, we may implement a `FallbackFactory` class. That approach has one big
advantage, it gives you access to the cause that made the fallback trigger. To declare a
`FallbackFactory` class for Feign, just use the `fallbackFactory` attribute inside
`@FeignClient`:

```
@FeignClient(name = "account-service", fallbackFactory =
AccountClientFallbackFactory.class)
public interface AccountClient {

    @CachePut
    @GetMapping("/customer/{customerId}")
    List<Account> findByCustomer(@PathVariable("customerId") Long
customerId);

}
```

The custom `FallbackFactory` class needs to implement a `FallbackFactory` interface, which declares the one `T create(Throwable cause)` method that has to be overridden:

```java
@Component
public class AccountClientFallbackFactory implements
FallbackFactory<AccountClient> {

    @Autowired
    CacheManager cacheManager;

    @Override
    public AccountClient create(Throwable cause) {
        return new AccountClient() {
            @Override
            List<Account> findByCustomer(Long customerId) {
                ValueWrapper w =
cacheManager.getCache("accounts").get(customerId);
                if (w != null) {
                    return (List<Account>) w.get();
                } else {
                    return new Customer();
                }
            }
        }
    }
}
```

Summary

You may not be aware of the configuration settings or tools described in this chapter if you have already been using auto-configured clients for inter-service communication. However, I think that it is worth having some knowledge about a few of the advanced mechanisms, even if they can run in the background and/or out of the box. In this chapter, I have tried to give you a closer view on topics, such as load balancers, retries, fallbacks, or circuit breakers by demonstrating how they work using simple examples. After reading this chapter, you should be able to customize Ribbon, Hystrix, or Feign clients to suit your needs related to communication between microservices, both on a small and large scale. You should also understand the when and why of using them in your system. With this chapter, we are closing the discussion about the core elements inside microservices-based architecture. Now, we have got one more important component to look at that is outside the system by quite a bit, the gateway. This hides the system complexity from an external client.

Routing and Filtering with API Gateway

8

In this chapter, we will discuss the next important element of microservice-based architecture, an API gateway. It is not our first encounter with that element in practice. We have already implemented a simple gateway pattern in `Chapter 4`, *Service Discovery*, for the purpose of presenting how a zoning mechanism works for service discovery with Eureka. We used Netflix's Zuul library, which is a JVM-based router and server-side load balancer. Netflix designed Zuul to provide features such as authentication, stress and canary testing, dynamic routing, and active/active multiregional traffic management. Although this is not explicitly stated, it also acts as a gateway in microservice architecture and its main task is to hide the complexity of your system from an external client.

Until now, Zuul, in fact, didn't have any competition when it came to API gateway pattern implementation inside the Spring Cloud framework. However, the situation is changing dynamically with the progressive development of a new project called Spring Cloud Gateway. It is built on the base of Spring Framework 5, Project Reactor, and Spring Boot 2.0. The last stable version of that library is 1.0.0, but there are many crucial changes in the version currently being developed, 2.0.0, which is still at the milestone stage. Spring Cloud Gateway aims to provide a simple, effective way to route to APIs and provide cross-cutting concerns related to them such as security, monitoring/metrics, and resiliency. Although the solution is relatively new, it is definitely worthy of attention.

The topics we will cover in this chapter include:

- Static routing and load balancing based on URLs
- Integrating Zuul and Spring Cloud Gateway with service discovery
- Creating custom filters with Zuul
- Customizing route configuration with Zuul
- Providing Hystrix fallback in case of route failure
- Description of the main components included in Spring Cloud Gateway—predicators and gateway filters

Using Spring Cloud Netflix Zuul

Spring Cloud has implemented an embedded Zuul proxy to allow frontend application's proxy calls to backend services. This feature is useful for external clients, because it hides system complexity and helps to avoid the need to manage CORS and authentication concerns independently for all microservices. To enable it, you should annotate a Spring Boot main class with `@EnableZuulProxy`, and this forwards incoming requests to the target service. Of course, Zuul is integrated with the Ribbon load balancer, Hystrix circuit breaker, and service discovery, for example with Eureka.

Building a gateway application

Let's go back to the example from the previous chapter to append the last element in the microservice-based architecture, API Gateway. What we haven't considered yet is how the external client would call our services. First, we would not want to expose the network addresses of all microservices running inside the system. We may also perform some operations such as request authentication or setting tracing headers in just one place. The solution is to share only a single edge network address, which proxies all the incoming requests to the appropriate service. The current example's system architecture is illustrated in the following diagram:

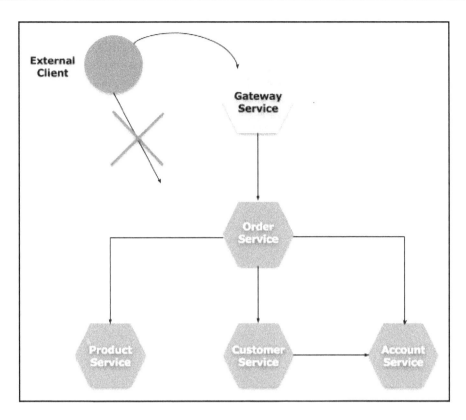

For the needs of our current sample, let me go back for a moment to the project already discussed in the previous chapter. It is available in GitHub (`https://github.com/piomin/sample-spring-cloud-comm.git`) in `master` branch. Now, we will add a new module called `gateway-service` to that project. The first step is to include Zuul with the Maven dependencies. We have to use the `spring-cloud-starter-zuul` starter:

```
<dependency>
    <groupId>org.springframework.cloud</groupId>
    <artifactId>spring-cloud-starter-zuul</artifactId>
</dependency>
```

After annotating a Spring Boot main class with `@EnableZuulProxy`, we may proceed to route configuration, which is provided in the `application.yml` file. By default, the Zuul starter artifact does not include the service discovery client. The routes are configured statically with the `url` property set to the network address of the service. Now, if you launch all the microservices and the gateway application, you may try to call them via the gateway. Each service is available under the path set in the configuration property `path` for every single route, for example, `http://localhost:8080/account/1` would be forwarded to `http://localhost:8091/1`:

```
server:
 port: ${PORT:8080}

zuul:
 routes:
  account:
   path: /account/**
   url: http://localhost:8091
  customer:
   path: /customer/**
   url: http://localhost:8092
  order:
   path: /order/**
   url: http://localhost:8090
  product:
   path: /product/**
   url: http://localhost:8093
```

Integration with service discovery

The static route configuration presented in the previous example is not enough for a microservice-based system. The main requirement for an API gateway is a built-in integration with service discovery. To enable service discovery with Eureka for Zuul, we have to include the `spring-cloud-starter-eureka` starter in the project dependencies and enable the client by annotating the application's main class with `@EnableDiscoveryClient`. In fact, it does not make sense to let the gateway register itself in discovery server, it must only fetch the current list of registered services. So we would disable that registration by setting the `eureka.client.registerWithEureka` property to `false`. The route's definition in the `application.yml` file is really simple. Each route's name is mapped to the application service name in Eureka:

```
zuul:
 routes:
  account-service:
```

```
    path: /account/**
  customer-service:
   path: /customer/**
  order-service:
   path: /order/**
  product-service:
   path: /product/**
```

Customizing route configuration

There are several configuration settings, which allow us to customize the behavior of the Zuul proxy. Some of them are strictly related to the service discovery integration.

Ignoring registered services

Spring Cloud Zuul by default exposes all the services registered in Eureka server. If you would like to skip the automatic addition of every service, you have to set the `zuul.ignored-services` property with a pattern matched to all the ignored service names from a discovery server. How does it work in practice? Even if you do not provide any configuration with `zuul.routes.*` properties, Zuul would fetch the list of services from Eureka and automatically bind them to the path with the service name. For example, `account-service` would be available under the gateway address `http://localhost:8080/account-service/**`. Now, if you set the following configuration in your `application.yml` file, it would ignore `account-service` and respond with an HTTP 404 status:

```
zuul:
  ignoredServices: 'account-service'
```

You may also ignore all registered services by setting `zuul.ignored-services` to `'*'`. If a service matches a pattern that is ignored, but also included in the routes map configuration, then it will be included by Zuul. In that case, only `customer-service` would be processed:

```
zuul:
  ignoredServices: '*'
    routes:
      customer-service: /customer/**
```

Explicity set service name

The service name from a discovery server may also be set in configuration using the `serviceId` property. It gives you fine-grained control over a route, because you can specify the path and the `serviceId` independently. Here's the equivalent configuration of the routes:

```
zuul:
  routes:
   accounts:
    path: /account/**
    serviceId: account-service
   customers:
    path: /customer/**
    serviceId: customer-service
   orders:
    path: /order/**
    serviceId: order-service
   products:
    path: /product/**
    serviceId: product-service
```

Route definition with the Ribbon client

There is another approach to configuring routes. We may disable Eureka discovery in order to rely solely on a list of network addresses provided with the `listOfServers` property of the Ribbon client. All incoming requests to the gateway are load balanced by default between all instances of the service through a Ribbon client. This rule is true even if you enable or disable service discovery, as in the following example code:

```
zuul:
 routes:
  accounts:
   path: /account/**
   serviceId: account-service

ribbon:
 eureka:
  enabled: false

account-service:
 ribbon:
  listOfServers: http://localhost:8091,http://localhost:9091
```

Adding a prefix to the path

Sometimes it is necessary to set a different path for services invoked via a gateway rather than allow them being available directly. In that case, Zuul provides the ability to add prefixes to all the defined mappings. This may be easily configured with the `zuul.prefix` property. By default, Zuul cuts that prefix before forwarding requests to the services. However, that behavior can also be disabled by setting the `zuul.stripPrefix` property to `false`. A `stripPrefix` property may be configured not only globally for all defined routes, but also per single route.

Here's an example that adds the `/api` prefix to all the forwarded requests. Now, for example, if you would like to call the `GET /{id}` endpoint from `account-service`, you should use the address `http://localhost:8080/api/account/1`:

```
zuul:
 prefix: /api
 routes:
   accounts:
    path: /account/**
    serviceId: account-service
   customers:
    path: /customer/**
    serviceId: customer-service
```

What would happen if we have provided the configuration with `stripPrefix` set to `false`? Zuul would try to look for endpoints in the target services under the context paths `/api/account` and `/api/customer`:

```
zuul:
 prefix: /api
 stripPrefix: false
```

Connection settings and timeouts

The main task of Spring Cloud Netflix Zuul is to route incoming requests to downstream services. Therefore, it has to use an HTTP client implementation to communicate with those services. The default HTTP client used by Zuul is now backed by the Apache HTTP Client instead of the deprecated Ribbon `RestClient`. If you would like to use Ribbon, you should set the `ribbon.restclient.enabled` property to `true`. You may also try `OkHttpClient` by setting the `ribbon.okhttp.enabled` property to `true`.

We may configure the basic settings for HTTP clients such as the connect or read timeout, and the maximum number of connections. There are two available options for such configurations depending on whether we are using service discovery or not. If you have defined Zuul routes with a specified network address through the `url` property, then you should set `zuul.host.connect-timeout-millis` and `zuul.host.socket-timeout-millis`. For the purpose of controlling the maximum number of connections, you should override the default value of the `zuul.host.maxTotalConnections` property, which is by default set to `200`. It is also possible to define the maximum number of connections per single route by setting the `zuul.host.maxPerRouteConnections` property, which is by default `20`.

If Zuul is configured to fetch a list of services from the discovery server, you need to configure the same timeouts as before with the Ribbon client properties `ribbon.ReadTimeout` and `ribbon.SocketTimeout`. The maximum number of connections can be customized with `ribbon.MaxTotalConnections` and `ribbon.MaxConnectionsPerHost`.

Secure headers

You may be a little surprised if you set, for example, the `Authorization` HTTP header in the request and it isn't forwarded to the downstream service. This is because Zuul defines a default list of sensitive headers, which are removed during the routing process. These are the headers `Cookie`, `Set-Cookie`, and `Authorization`. This feature has been designed with a view to communicate with external servers. While there is no objection to sharing headers between services in the same system, it is not recommended to share them with external servers for security reasons. This approach may be customized by overriding default values for the `sensitiveHeaders` property. It may be set globally for all routes or just for a single route. The `sensitiveHeaders` are a not an empty blacklist, so to make Zuul forward all headers, you should explicitly set it to the empty list:

```
zuul:
  routes:
    accounts:
      path: /account/**
      sensitiveHeaders:
      serviceId: account-service
```

Management endpoints

Spring Cloud Netflix Zuul exposes two additional management endpoints for monitoring:

- **Routes**: Prints a list of defined routes
- **Filters**: Prints a list of implemented filters (available from version `1.4.0.RELEASE` of Spring Cloud Netflix)

To enable the managements endpoints feature, we have to include (as always) `spring-boot-starter-actuator` in the project dependencies. It's a good idea to disable endpoint security for test purposes by setting the `management.security.enabled` property to `false`. Now, you may just call the `GET /routes` method and it would print the following JSON response for our example system:

```
{
    "/api/account/**": "account-service",
    "/api/customer/**": "customer-service",
    "/api/order/**": "order-service",
    "/api/product/**": "product-service",
}
```

For more detailed information, you have to add the `?format=details` query string to the `/routes` path. That option is also available from version 1.4.0 of Spring Cloud (Edgware Release Train). There is also a `POST /route` method that would force a refresh of the currently existing routes. Additionally, you can disable the whole endpoint by setting `endpoints.routes.enabled` to `false`:

```
"/api/account/**": {
    "id": "account-service",
    "fullPath": "/api/account/**",
    "location": "account-service",
    "path": "/**",
    "prefix": "/api/account",
    "retryable": false,
    "customSensitiveHeaders": false,
    "prefixStripped": true
}
```

The response result of the `/filters` endpoint is pretty interesting. You may see how many and what types of filters are available by default on the Zuul gateway. Here's the fragment of a response with one selected filter. It contains a full class name, the order of calling, and status. For more information about filters, you can refer to the section, *Zuul filters*:

```
"route": [{
 "class":
"org.springframework.cloud.netflix.zuul.filters.route.RibbonRoutingFilter",
 "order": 10,
 "disabled": false,
 "static": true
}, {
...
]
```

Providing Hystrix fallback

We may provide a fallback response for every single route defined in Zuul's configuration, in case a circuit is opened. To do that, we should create a bean of type `ZuulFallbackProvider` (which is currently deprecated) or `FallbackProvider`. Inside that implementation, we have to specify the route ID pattern to match all the routes that should be handled by the fallback bean. The second step is to return the implementation of the `ClientHttpResponse` interface as a response in the `fallbackResponse` method.

Here's a simple fallback bean that maps every exception to the HTTP status `200 OK` and sets the `errorCode` and `errorMessage` in the JSON response. Fallback is only executed for the `account-service` route:

```
public class AccountFallbackProvider implements FallbackProvider {

    @Override
    public String getRoute() {
        return "account-service";
    }

    @Override
    public ClientHttpResponse fallbackResponse(Throwable cause) {
        return new ClientHttpResponse() {

            @Override
            public HttpHeaders getHeaders() {
                HttpHeaders headers = new HttpHeaders();
                headers.setContentType(MediaType.APPLICATION_JSON);
                return headers;
```

```
            }

            @Override
            public InputStream getBody() throws IOException {
                AccountFallbackResponse response = new
    AccountFallbackResponse("1.2", cause.getMessage());
                return new ByteArrayInputStream(new
    ObjectMapper().writeValueAsBytes(response));
            }

            @Override
            public String getStatusText() throws IOException {
                return "OK";
            }

            @Override
            public HttpStatus getStatusCode() throws IOException {
                return HttpStatus.OK;
            }

            @Override
            public int getRawStatusCode() throws IOException {
                return 200;
            }

            @Override
            public void close() {

            }
        };
    }
    // ...
}
```

Zuul filters

As I have already mentioned, Spring Cloud Zuul by default provides a couple of beans, which are the implementations of the `ZuulFilter` interface. Every built-in filter may be disabled by setting the `zuul.<SimpleClassName>.<filterType>.disable` property to `true`. For example, to disable `org.springframework.cloud.netflix.zuul.filters.post.SendResponseFilter`, you have to set `zuul.SendResponseFilter.post.disable=true`.

The HTTP filtering mechanism is probably well known to you. A filter dynamically intercepts requests and responses to transform, or just use, the information taken from the HTTP message. It may be triggered before or after an incoming request or outgoing response. We may identify a couple of types of filter provided by Zuul for Spring Cloud:

- **Pre filter**: It is used to prepare initial data in the `RequestContext` for use in filters downstream. The main responsibility is to set information required for route filters.
- **Route filter**: It is called after the pre filter and is responsible for creating requests to other services. The main reason for using it is a need to adapt a request or response to the model required by the client.
- **Post filter**: Most commonly, it manipulates the response. It may even transform the response body.
- **Error filter**: It is executed only if an exception is thrown by other filters. There is only one built-in implementation of an error filter. `SendErrorFilter` is executed if `RequestContext.getThrowable()` is not null.

Predefined filters

If you annotate the main class with `@EnableZuulProxy`, Spring Cloud Zuul loads the filter beans used by both `SimpleRouteLocator` and `DiscoveryClientRouteLocator`. This is a list of the most important implementations installed as normal Spring Beans:

- `ServletDetectionFilter`: This is a pre filter. It checks whether the request is coming through the Spring Dispatcher. Sets a Boolean with the key `FilterConstants.IS_DISPATCHER_SERVLET_REQUEST_KEY`.
- `FormBodyWrapperFilter`: This is a pre filter. It parses form data and re-encodes it for downstream requests.
- `PreDecorationFilter`: This is a pre filter. It determines where and how to route based on the supplied `RouteLocator`. It is also responsible for setting headers related to the proxy.
- `SendForwardFilter`: This is a route filter. It forwards requests using `RequestDispatcher`.
- `RibbonRoutingFilter`: This is a route filter. It uses Ribbon, Hystrix, and external HTTP clients such as Apache `HttpClient`, `OkHttpClient`, or Ribbon HTTP client to send requests. Service IDs are taken from the request context.

- `SimpleHostRoutingFilter`: This is a route filter. It sends requests to URLs via an Apache HTTP client. URLs are found in the request context.
- `SendResponseFilter`: This is a post filter. It writes responses from proxied requests to the current response.

Custom implementations

In addition to the filters installed by default, we may create our custom implementations. Each of them has to implement the `ZuulFilter` interface and its four methods. These methods are responsible for setting the type of filter (`filterType`), determining the order of filter execution between other filtering with the same type (`filterOrder`), enabling or disabling the filter (`shouldFilter`) and finally the filter logic implementation (`run`). Here's an example implementation that adds the `X-Response-ID` header to the response:

```
public class AddResponseIDHeaderFilter extends ZuulFilter {

    private int id = 1;

    @Override
    public String filterType() {
        return "post";
    }

    @Override
    public int filterOrder() {
        return 10;
    }

    @Override
    public boolean shouldFilter() {
        return true;
    }

    @Override
    public Object run() {
        RequestContext context = RequestContext.getCurrentContext();
        HttpServletResponse servletResponse = context.getResponse();
        servletResponse.addHeader("X-Response-ID",
         String.valueOf(id++));
        return null;
    }

}
```

That's not all that has to be done. The custom filter implementation should also be declared as an `@Bean` in the main class or Spring configuration class:

```
@Bean
AddResponseIDHeaderFilter filter() {
    return new AddResponseIDHeaderFilter();
}
```

Using Spring Cloud Gateway

There are three basic concepts around Spring Cloud Gateway:

- **Route**: That is the basic building block of the gateway. It consists of a unique ID for identifying a route, a destination URI, a list of predicates, and a list of filters. A route is matched only if all the predicates have been fulfilled.
- **Predicates**: These are the logic that is executed before processing each request. It is responsible for detecting whether the different attributes of the HTTP request, such as headers and parameters, match the defined criteria. The implementation is based on the Java 8 interface `java.util.function.Predicate<T>`. The input type is in turn based on Spring's `org.springframework.web.server.ServerWebExchange`.
- **Filters**: They allow the modification of the incoming HTTP request or outgoing HTTP response. They may be modified before or after sending the downstream request. Route filters are scoped to a particular route. They implement Spring's `org.springframework.web.server.GatewayFilter`.

Enable Spring Cloud Gateway for a project

Spring Cloud Gateway is built on top of the Netty web container and Reactor framework. The Reactor project and Spring Web Flux may be used together with version 2.0 of Spring Boot. Until now, we have used version 1.5, so there is a different declaration of parent project version. Currently, Spring Boot 2.0 is still at the milestone stage. Here's the fragment from Maven `pom.xml` that inherits from the `spring-boot-starter-parent` project.

```
<parent>
    <groupId>org.springframework.boot</groupId>
    <artifactId>spring-boot-starter-parent</artifactId>
    <version>2.0.0.M7</version>
</parent>
```

We also need to change the release train of Spring Cloud in comparison with the previous examples. The newest available milestone version is `Finchley.M5`:

```
<properties>
    <project.build.sourceEncoding>UTF-8</project.build.sourceEncoding>
    <project.reporting.outputEncoding>UTF-8</project.reporting.outputEncoding>
    <java.version>1.8</java.version>
    <spring-cloud.version>Finchley.M5</spring-cloud.version>
</properties>
<dependencyManagement>
    <dependencies>
        <dependency>
            <groupId>org.springframework.cloud</groupId>
            <artifactId>spring-cloud-dependencies</artifactId>
            <version>${spring-cloud.version}</version>
            <type>pom</type>
            <scope>import</scope>
        </dependency>
    </dependencies>
</dependencyManagement>
```

After setting the right versions of Spring Boot and Spring Cloud, we may finally include the `spring-cloud-starter-gateway` starter in the project dependencies:

```
<dependency>
    <groupId>org.springframework.cloud</groupId>
    <artifactId>spring-cloud-starter-gateway</artifactId>
</dependency>
```

Built-in predicates and filters

Spring Cloud Gateway includes many built-in route predicates and gateway filter factories. Every route may be defined using configuration properties in the `application.yml` file or programmatically with the Fluent Java Routes API. The list of available predicate factories is provided in the following table. Multiple factories may be combined for a single route definition with a logical `and` relation. The collection of filters may be configured in the `application.yml` file under the `spring.cloud.gateway.routes` property for each defined route under the `predicates` property:

Name	Description	Example
`After` **Route**	**It takes a date-time parameter and matches requests that happen after it**	`After=2017-11-20T...`
`Before` Route	It takes a date-time parameter and matches requests that happen before it	`Before=2017-11-20T...`
`Between` Route	It takes two date-time parameters and matches requests that happen between those dates	`Between=2017-11-20T...,` `2017-11-21T...`
`Cookie` Route	It takes a cookie name and regular expression parameters, finds the cookie in the HTTP request's header, and matches its value with the provided expression	`Cookie=SessionID, abc.`
`Header` Route	It takes the header name and regular expression parameters, finds a specific header in the HTTP request's header, and matches its value with the provided expression	`Header=X-Request-Id, \d+`
`Host` Route	It takes a hostname ANT style pattern with the `.` separator as a parameter and matches it with the `Host` header	`Host=**.example.org`
`Method` Route	It takes an HTTP method to match as a parameter	`Method=GET`
`Path` Route	It takes a pattern of request context path as a parameter	`Path=/account/{id}`

Name	Description	Example
`Query` Route	It takes two parameters—a required param and an optional regexp and matches them with query parameters	`Query=accountId, 1.`
`RemoteAddr` Route	It takes a list of IP addresses in CIDR notation, like `192.168.0.1/16`, and matches it with the remote address of a request	`RemoteAddr=192.168.0.1/16`

There are a few more built-in implementations of the gateway filter pattern. The list of available factories is also provided in the following table. The collection of filters may be configured in the `application.yml` file under the `spring.cloud.gateway.routes` property for each route defined under the `filters` property:

Name	Description	Example
`AddRequestHeader`	**Adds a header to an HTTP request with name and value provided in parameters**	`AddRequestHeader=X-Response-ID, 123`
`AddRequestParameter`	Adds a query parameter to an HTTP request with name and value provided in parameters	`AddRequestParameter=id, 123`
`AddResponseHeader`	Adds a header to an HTTP response with name and value provided in parameters	`AddResponseHeader=X-Response-ID, 123`
`Hystrix`	It takes a parameter, which is the name of the HystrixCommand	`Hystrix=account-service`

Name	Description	Example
`PrefixPath`	Adds a prefix to the HTTP request path defined in the parameter	`PrefixPath=/api`
`RequestRateLimiter`	It limits the number of processing requests per single user based on three input parameters including a maximum number of requests per second, burst capacity, and a bean that returns the user key	`RequestRateLimiter=10, 20, #{@userKeyResolver}`
`RedirectTo`	It takes an HTTP status and a redirect URL as parameters and puts it to the `Location` HTTP header in order to perform a redirect	`RedirectTo=302, http://localhost:8092`
`RemoveNonProxyHeaders`	It removes some hop-by-hop headers from forwarded requests, such as Keep-Alive, Proxy-Authenticate, or Proxy-Authorization	-
`RemoveRequestHeader`	It takes the name of the header as a parameter and removes it from the HTTP request	`RemoveRequestHeader=X-Request-Foo`

Name	Description	Example
RemoveResponseHeader	It takes the name of the header as a parameter and removes it from the HTTP response	RemoveResponseHeader=X-Response-ID
RewritePath	It takes a path regexp parameter and a replacement parameter and then rewrites the request path	RewritePath=/account/(?<path>.*), /$\{path}
SecureHeaders	It adds some secure headers to the response	-
SetPath	It takes a single parameter with a path template parameter and changes a request path	SetPath=/{segment}
SetResponseHeader	It takes name and value parameters to set a header on the HTTP response	SetResponseHeader=X-Response-ID, 123
SetStatus	It takes a single status parameter, which must be a valid HTTP status, and sets it on a response	SetStatus=401

Here's a simple example with two predicates and two filters set. Each GET /account/{id} request coming in to the gateway is forwarded to http://localhost:8080/api/account/{id} with the new HTTP header, X-Request-ID, included:

```
spring:
  cloud:
    gateway:
```

```
    routes:
    - id: example_route
      uri: http://localhost:8080
      predicates:
      - Method=GET
      - Path=/account/{id}
      filters:
      - AddRequestHeader=X-Request-ID, 123
      - PrefixPath=/api
```

The same configuration may be provided using a fluent API defined in the `Route` class. This style gives us more flexibility. While configuration with YAML may combine predicates using logical `and`, the fluent Java API allows you to use `and()`, `or()`, and `negate()` operators on the `Predicate` class. Here's the alternative route implemented using the fluent API:

```
@Bean
public RouteLocator customRouteLocator(RouteLocatorBuilder routeBuilder) {
    return routeBuilder.routes()
        .route(r -> r.method(HttpMethod.GET).and().path("/account/{id}")
            .addRequestHeader("X-Request-ID", "123").prefixPath("/api")
            .uri("http://localhost:8080"))
        .build();
}
```

Gateway for microservices

Let's get back to our example microservice-based system. We have already discussed this example in the section on API gateway configuration based on Spring Cloud Netflix Zuul. We would like to prepare the same static route definition as was already prepared for the application based on a Zuul proxy. Each service would then be available under the gateway address and specific path, for example, `http://localhost:8080/account/**`. The most suitable way to declare such a configuration with Spring Cloud Gateway is through Path Route Predicate Factory and RewritePath GatewayFilter Factory. A rewrite path mechanism changes the request path by taking part of it or adding some pattern. In our case, every incoming request path is rewritten from, for example, `account/123` to `/123`. Here's the gateway's `application.yml` file:

```
server:
 port: ${PORT:8080}

spring:
 application:
  name: gateway-service
```

```
cloud:
 gateway:
   routes:
   - id: account-service
     uri: http://localhost:8091
     predicates:
     - Path=/account/**
     filters:
     - RewritePath=/account/(?<path>.*), /$\{path}
   - id: customer-service
     uri: http://localhost:8092
     predicates:
     - Path=/customer/**
     filters:
     - RewritePath=/customer/(?<path>.*), /$\{path}
   - id: order-service
     uri: http://localhost:8090
     predicates:
     - Path=/order/**
     filters:
     - RewritePath=/order/(?<path>.*), /$\{path}
   - id: product-service
     uri: http://localhost:8093
     predicates:
     - Path=/product/**
     filters:
     - RewritePath=/product/(?<path>.*), /$\{path}
```

Surprisingly, this is all that has to be done. We don't have to provide any additional annotation compared to what we have been doing when working with other Spring Cloud components such as Eureka or Config Server. So, the main class of our gateway's application is visible in the following code fragment. You have to build the project using `mvn clean install` and launch it with `java -jar`, or just run the main class from your IDE. The example application source code is available on GitHub (`https://github.com/piomin/sample-spring-cloud-gateway.git`):

```
@SpringBootApplication
public class GatewayApplication {

    public static void main(String[] args) {
        SpringApplication.run(GatewayApplication.class, args);
    }

}
```

Integration with service discovery

The gateway may be configured to create routes based on the list of services registered in service discovery. It can integrate with those solutions that have a `DiscoveryClient` compatible service registry, such as Netflix Eureka, Consul, or Zookeeper. To enable `DiscoveryClient` Route Definition Locator, you should set the `spring.cloud.gateway.discovery.locator.enabled` property to `true` and provide a `DiscoveryClient` implementation on the classpath. We use Eureka client and server for discovery. Notice that with the newest milestone version, `Finchley.M5`, of Spring Cloud all the Netflix's artifact's names have been changed and now it is, for example, `spring-cloud-starter-netflix-eureka-client` instead of `spring-cloud-starter-eureka`:

```
<dependency>
    <groupId>org.springframework.cloud</groupId>
    <artifactId>spring-cloud-starter-netflix-eureka-client</artifactId>
</dependency>
```

The main class should be the same for the Eureka client application, annotated with `@DiscoveryClient`. Here's the `application.yml` file with routing configuration. The only change in comparison with the previous example is in the `uri` property for every defined route. Instead of providing their network address we may use its name taken from discovery server with an `lb` prefix, for example, `lb://order-service`:

```
spring:
 application:
  name: gateway-service
 cloud:
  gateway:
   discovery:
    locator:
     enabled: true
   routes:
   - id: account-service
     uri: lb://account-service
     predicates:
     - Path=/account/**
     filters:
     - RewritePath=/account/(?<path>.*), /$\{path}
   - id: customer-service
     uri: lb://customer-service
     predicates:
     - Path=/customer/**
     filters:
     - RewritePath=/customer/(?<path>.*), /$\{path}
```

```
  - id: order-service
    uri: lb://order-service
    predicates:
    - Path=/order/**
    filters:
    - RewritePath=/order/(?<path>.*), /$\{path}
  - id: product-service
    uri: lb://product-service
    predicates:
    - Path=/product/**
    filters:
    - RewritePath=/product/(?<path>.*), /$\{path}
```

Summary

With an API gateway, we have finished the discussion about the implementation of the core elements of a microservice-based architecture in Spring Cloud. After reading that part of the book, you should be able to customize and use tools such as Eureka, Spring Cloud Config, Ribbon, Feign, Hystrix, and finally a gateway based on Zuul and Spring Cloud Gateway together.

Treat this chapter as a comparison between two available solutions—the older Netflix Zuul and the newest one, Spring Cloud Gateway. The second of them is changing dynamically. Its current version, 2.0, may be used only with Spring 5 and is still not available in release version. The first of them, Netflix Zuul, is stable, but it does not support asynchronous, non-blocking connections. It is still based on Netflix Zuul 1.0, although there is a new version of Zuul that supports asynchronous communication. Regardless of the differences between them, I have described how to provide a simple and a more advanced configuration using both of these solutions. I have also presented, based on the examples from the previous chapters, an integration with a service discovery, client-side load balancer, and circuit breaker.

Distributed Logging and Tracing

9

When breaking down a monolith into microservices, we usually spend a lot of time thinking about business boundaries or the partitioning of our application logic, but we forget about the logs. From my own experience as a developer and software architect, I can say that developers do not usually pay much attention to logging. On the other hand, operation teams, which are responsible for application maintenance, are mainly dependent on logs. Regardless of one's area of expertise, it is indisputable that logging is something that all applications have to do, whether they have monolithic or microservices architecture. However, microservices force adding a whole new dimension to design and arrangement of application logs. There are many small, independent, horizontally scaled, intercommunicating services that are running on multiple machines. Requests are often processed by multiple services. We have to correlate these requests and store all the logs in a single, central place in order to make it easier to view them. Spring Cloud introduces a dedicated library that implements a distributed tracing solution, Spring Cloud Sleuth.

There is also one thing that should be discussed here. Logging is not the same as tracing! It is worth pointing out the differences between them. Tracing is following your program's data flow. It is typically used by technical support teams to diagnose where a problem occurs. You have to trace your system flow to discover performance bottlenecks or times when the error occurs. Logging is used for error reporting and detecting. It should always be enabled, in contrast to tracing. When you design a large system and you would like to have good and flexible error reporting across machines, you should definitely think about collecting log data in a centralized way. The recommended and most popular solution for this is the **ELK** stack (**Elasticsearch** + **Logstash** + **Kibana**). There is no dedicated library for this stack in Spring Cloud, but the integration may be realized with Java logging frameworks, such as Logback or Log4j. There is another tool that will be discussed in this chapter, Zipkin. It is a typical tracing tool that helps gather timing data that can be used to troubleshoot latency problems in microservice architecture.

The topics we will cover in this chapter include the following:

- The best practices for logging in microservices-based systems
- Using Spring Cloud Sleuth to append tracing information to messages and correlating events
- Integrating the Spring Boot application with Logstash
- Displaying and filtering log entries using Kibana
- Using Zipkin as a distributed tracing tool and integrating it with the application through Spring Cloud Sleuth

Best logging practices for microservices

One of the most important best practices for dealing with logging is to trace all the incoming requests and outgoing responses. Maybe it seems obvious to you, but I have seen a couple of applications that did not comply with that requirement. If you meet this demand, there is one consequence that occurs with microservices-based architecture. The overall number of logs in your system increases compared to monolithic applications, where there is no messaging. This, in turn, requires us to pay even more attention to logging than before. We should do our best to generate as little information as possible, even though this information can tell us much about the situation. How do we achieve this? First of all, it is good to have the same log message format across all the microservices. For example, let's consider how to print variables in the application logs. I suggest you use the JSON notation in view of the fact that, usually, messages exchanged between microservices are formatted with JSON. This format has a very straightforward standard, which makes your logs easily readable and parseable, as shown in the following code fragment:

```
17:11:53.712   INFO   Order received:
{"id":1,"customerId":5,"productId":10}
```

The preceding format is much easier to analyze than something like the following:

```
17:11:53.712   INFO   Order received with id 1, customerId 5 and productId
10.
```

But generally, the most important thing here is standardization. No matter which format you choose, it is crucial to use it everywhere. You should also be careful to ensure that your logs are meaningful. Try to avoid sentences that do not contain any information. For example, from the following format, it is not clear which order is being processed:

```
17:11:53.712   INFO   Processing order
```

However, if you really want this kind of log entry format, try to assign it to different log levels. It is really a bad practice to log everything with the same level of INFO. Some kinds of information are more important than others, so the one difficulty here is to decide what level the log entry should be logged at. Here are some suggestions:

- TRACE: This is for very detailed information, intended only for development. You might keep it for a short period of time, just after deployment to a production environment, but treat it as a temporary file.
- DEBUG: At this level, log anything that happens in the program. This is mostly used for debugging or troubleshooting by developers. The distinction between DEBUG and TRACE is probably the most difficult.
- INFO: At this level, you should log the most important information during the operation. These messages have to be easily understandable, not just for developers, but also for administrators or advanced users, to let them quickly find out what the application is doing.
- WARN: At this level, log all events that could potentially become errors. Such a process may be continued, but you should take extra caution with it.
- ERROR: Usually, you print exceptions at this level. The important thing here is not to throw exceptions everywhere if, for example, only one business logic execution has not succeeded.
- FATAL: This Java logging level designates very severe error events that will probably cause the application to stop.

There are other good logging practices, but I have mentioned the most important ones for use in microservices-based systems. It is also worth mentioning one more aspect of logging, normalization. If you would like to easily understand and interpret your logs, you should definitely know how and when they were collected, what they contain, and why they were emitted. There are some especially important characteristics that should be normalized across all microservices, such as Time (when), Hostname (where), and AppName (who). As you will see in the next part of this chapter, this kind of normalization is very useful when a centralized method of collecting logs is implemented in your system.

Logging with Spring Boot

Spring Boot uses Apache Commons Logging for internal logging, but if you are including dependencies with starters, Logback will be used by default in your application. It doesn't inhibit the possibility of using other logging frameworks in any way. The default configurations are also provided for Java Util Logging, Log4J2, and SLF4J. Logging settings may be configured in the `application.yml` file with `logging.*` properties. The default log output contains the date and time in milliseconds, log level, process ID, thread name, the full name of the class that has emitted the entry, and the message. It may be overridden by using the `logging.pattern.console` and `logging.pattern.file` properties respectively for the console and file appenders.

By default, Spring Boot only logs on to a console. In order to allow the writing of log files in addition to a console output, you should set a `logging.file` or `logging.path` property. If you specify the `logging.file` property, the logs would be written to the file at an exact location or a location relative to the current directory. If you set `logging.path`, it creates a `spring.log` file in the specified directory. Log files will be rotated after reaching 10 MB.

The last thing that can be customized in the `application.yml` settings file is the log levels. By default, Spring Boot writes messages with ERROR, WARN, and INFO levels. We may override this setting for every single package or class with `logging.level.*` properties. The root logger can also be configured using `logging.level.root`. Here's an example configuration in the `application.yml` file, which changes the default pattern format, as well as a few log levels, and sets the location of the logging file:

```
logging:
 file: logs/order.log
 level:
  com.netflix: DEBUG
  org.springframework.web.filter.CommonsRequestLoggingFilter: DEBUG
 pattern:
  console: "%d{HH:mm:ss.SSS} %-5level %msg%n"
  file: "%d{HH:mm:ss.SSS} %-5level %msg%n"
```

As you can see in the preceding example, such a configuration is pretty simple, but, in some cases, it is not enough. If you would like to define additional appenders or filters, you should definitely include the configuration for one of the available logging systems—Logback (`logback-spring.xml`), Log4j2 (`log4j2-spring.xml`), or Java Util Logging (`logging.properties`). As I have mentioned earlier, by default, Spring Boot uses Logback for the application logs. If you provide the `logback-spring.xml` file in the root of the classpath, it will override all settings defined in `application.yml`. For example, you may create file appenders that rotate logs daily and retain a maximum history of 10 days. This feature is very commonly used in applications. In the next section of this chapter, you will also learn that a custom appender is required to integrate your microservice with Logstash. Here's an example Logback configuration file's fragment that sets a daily rolling policy for the `logs/order.log` file:

```
<configuration>
 <appender name="FILE"
class="ch.qos.logback.core.rolling.RollingFileAppender">
   <file>logs/order.log</file>
   <rollingPolicy
class="ch.qos.logback.core.rolling.TimeBasedRollingPolicy">
    <fileNamePattern>order.%d{yyyy-MM-dd}.log</fileNamePattern>
    <maxHistory>10</maxHistory>
    <totalSizeCap>1GB</totalSizeCap>
   </rollingPolicy>
   <encoder>
    <pattern>%d{HH:mm:ss.SSS} %-5level %msg%n</pattern>
   </encoder>
 </appender>
 <root level="DEBUG">
  <appender-ref ref="FILE" />
 </root>
</configuration>
```

It is also worth mentioning that Spring recommends using `logback-spring.xml` for Logback instead of the default `logback.xml`. Spring Boot includes a couple of extensions to Logback that may be helpful for an advanced configuration. They cannot be used in the standard `logback.xml`, but only with `logback-spring.xml`. We have listed some of these extensions that will allow you to define profile-specific configurations or surface properties from the Spring Environment:

```
<springProperty scope="context" name="springAppName"
source="spring.application.name" />
<property name="LOG_FILE" value="${BUILD_FOLDER:-build}/${springAppName}"/>

<springProfile name="development">
```

```
...
</springProfile>

<springProfile name="production">
 <appender name="flatfile"
class="ch.qos.logback.core.rolling.RollingFileAppender">
   <file>${LOG_FILE}</file>
   <rollingPolicy
class="ch.qos.logback.core.rolling.TimeBasedRollingPolicy">
     <fileNamePattern>${LOG_FILE}.%d{yyyy-MM-dd}.gz</fileNamePattern>
     <maxHistory>7</maxHistory>
   </rollingPolicy>
   <encoder>
     <pattern>${CONSOLE_LOG_PATTERN}</pattern>
     <charset>utf8</charset>
   </encoder>
 </appender>
 ...
</springProfile>
```

Centralizing logs with ELK Stack

ELK is the acronym for three open source tools—Elasticsearch, Logstash, and Kibana. It is also called **Elastic Stack**. The heart of this system is **Elasticsearch**, a search engine based on another open source project written in Java, Apache Lucene. This library is especially suitable for applications that require full-text searches in cross-platform environments. The main reason for the popularity of Elasticsearch is its performance. Of course, it has some other advantages, such as scalability, flexibility, and easy integration by providing a RESTful, JSON-based API for searching stored data. It has a large community and many use cases, but the most interesting one for us is its ability to store and search logs generated by applications. Logging is the main reason for including Logstash in ELK Stack. This open source data-processing pipeline allows us to collect, process, and input data into Elasticsearch.

Logstash supports many inputs that pull events from external sources. What is interesting is that it has many outputs, and Elasticsearch is only one of them. For example, it can write events to Apache Kafka, RabbitMQ, or MongoDB, and it can write metrics to InfluxDB or Graphite. It not only receives and forwards data to their destinations, but can also parse and transform it on the fly.

Kibana is the last element of ELK Stack. It is an open source, data-visualization plugin for Elasticsearch. It allows you to visualize, explore, and discover data from Elasticsearch. We may easily display and filter all the logs collected from our application by creating search queries. On this basis, we can export data to PDF or CSV formats to provide reports.

Setting up ELK Stack on the machine

Before we try to send any logs from our application to Logstash, we have to configure ELK Stack on the local machine. The most suitable way to run it is through Docker containers. All the products in the stack are available as Docker images. There is a dedicated Docker registry hosted by Elastic Stack's vendor. A full list of published images and tags can be found at www.docker.elastic.co. All of them use centos:7 as the base image.

We will begin from the Elasticsearch instance. Its development can be started with the following command:

```
docker run -d --name es -p 9200:9200 -p 9300:9300 -e
"discovery.type=single-node"
docker.elastic.co/elasticsearch/elasticsearch:6.1.1
```

Running Elasticsearch in development mode is the most convenient way of running it because we don't have to provide any additional configuration. If you would like to launch it in production mode, the vm.max_map_count Linux kernel setting needs to be set to at least 262144. The procedure for modifying it is different depending on the OS platform. For Windows with Docker Toolbox, it must be set via docker-machine:

```
docker-machine ssh
sudo sysctl -w vm.max_map_count=262144
```

The next step is to run a container with Logstash. In addition to launching a container with Logstash, we should also define an input and output. The output is obvious—Elasticsearch, which is now available under the default Docker machine address, 192.168.99.100. As an input, we define the simple TCP plugin logstash-input-tcp, which is compatible with LogstashTcpSocketAppender used as a logging appender in our sample application. All the logs from our microservices will be sent in JSON format. For now, it is important to set the json codec for that plugin. Each microservice will be indexed in Elasticsearch with its name and micro prefix. Here's the Logstash configuration file, logstash.conf:

```
input {
  tcp {
    port => 5000
    codec => json
```

```
    }
  }

  output {
    elasticsearch {
      hosts => ["http://192.168.99.100:9200"]
      index => "micro-%{appName}"
    }
  }
```

Here's the command that runs Logstash and exposes it on port 5000. It also copies the file with the preceding settings to the container and overrides the default location of the Logstash configuration file:

```
docker run -d --name logstash -p 5000:5000 -v ~/logstash.conf:/config-
dir/logstash.conf docker.elastic.co/logstash/logstash-oss:6.1.1 -f /config-
dir/logstash.conf
```

Finally, we can run the last element of the stack, Kibana. By default, this is exposed on port 5601 and connects to the Elasticsearch API available on port 9200 in order to be able to load data from there:

```
docker run -d --name kibana -e
"ELASTICSEARCH_URL=http://192.168.99.100:9200" -p 5601:5601
docker.elastic.co/kibana/kibana:6.1.1
```

If you would like to run all Elastic Stack products on your Docker machine on Windows, you would probably have to increase the default RAM memory for your Linux virtual image to a minimum of 2 GB. After launching all containers, you may finally access the Kibana dashboard available under http://192.168.99.100:5601 and then proceed to integrate your application with Logstash.

Integrating an application with ELK Stack

There are many ways of integrating Java applications with ELK Stack via Logstash. One of the methods involves using Filebeat, which is a log data shipper for local files. This approach requires a beats (logstash-input-beats) input configured for the instance of Logstash, which is, in fact, the default option. You should also install and launch a Filebeat daemon on the server machine. It is responsible for the delivery of the logs to Logstash.

Personally, I prefer a configuration based on Logback and dedicated appenders. It seems to be simpler than using a Filebeat agent. Besides having to deploy an additional service, Filebeat requires us to play with a parsing expression, such as the Grok filter. When using a Logback appender, you don't require any log shippers. This appender is available within the project Logstash JSON encoder. You may enable it for your application by declaring the `net.logstash.logback.appender.LogstashSocketAppender` appender inside the `logback-spring.xml` file.

We will also discuss an alternative approach for sending data to Logstash, using a message broker. In the example that we will shortly examine, I'm going to show you how to use Spring `AMQPAppender` to publish logging events to a RabbitMQ exchange. In this case, Logstash subscribes to the exchange and consumes published messages.

Using LogstashTCPAppender

The library `logstash-logback-encoder` provides three types of appenders—UDP, TCP, and async. The TCP appender is most commonly used. What is worth mentioning is that TCP appenders are asynchronous, and all the encoding and communication is delegated to a single thread. In addition to appenders, the library also provides some encoders and layouts to enable you to log in the JSON format. Because Spring Boot includes a Logback library by default, as well as `spring-boot-starter-web`, we only have to add one dependency to Maven `pom.xml`:

```
<dependency>
 <groupId>net.logstash.logback</groupId>
 <artifactId>logstash-logback-encoder</artifactId>
 <version>4.11</version>
</dependency>
```

The next step is to define the appender with the `LogstashTCPAppender` class in the Logback configuration file. Every TCP appender requires you to configure an encoder. You may choose between `LogstashEncoder` and `LoggingEventCompositeJsonEncoder`. `LoggingEventCompositeJsonEncoder` gives you more flexibility. It is composed of one or more JSON providers that are mapped to the JSON output. By default, there are no providers configured. It doesn't work that way with `LogstashTCPAppender`. By default, it includes several standard fields, such as timestamp, version, logger name, and stack trace. It also adds all entries from the **mapped diagnostic context** (**MDC**) and the context, unless you disable it by setting one of the `includeMdc` or `includeContext` properties to `false`:

```
<appender name="STASH"
class="net.logstash.logback.appender.LogstashTcpSocketAppender">
 <destination>192.168.99.100:5000</destination>
```

```
  <encoder
class="net.logstash.logback.encoder.LoggingEventCompositeJsonEncoder">
    <providers>
     <mdc />
     <context />
     <logLevel />
     <loggerName />
     <pattern>
      <pattern>
      {
      "appName": "order-service"
      }
      </pattern>
     </pattern>
     <threadName />
     <message />
     <logstashMarkers />
     <stackTrace />
    </providers>
   </encoder>
  </appender>
```

Now, I would like to come back for a moment to our sample system. We are still in the same Git repository (`https://github.com/piomin/sample-spring-cloud-comm.git`) and `feign_with_discovery` branch (`https://github.com/piomin/sample-spring-cloud-comm/tree/feign_with_discovery`). I have added some logging entries in the source code in accordance with the recommendations described in the *Best logging practices for microservices* section. Here's the current version of the `POST` method inside `order-service`. I have used Logback over SLF4J as a logger by calling the `getLogger` method from `org.slf4j.LoggerFactory`:

```
@PostMapping
public Order prepare(@RequestBody Order order) throws
JsonProcessingException {
    int price = 0;
    List<Product> products =
productClient.findByIds(order.getProductIds());
    LOGGER.info("Products found: {}", mapper.writeValueAsString(products));
    Customer customer =
customerClient.findByIdWithAccounts(order.getCustomerId());
    LOGGER.info("Customer found: {}", mapper.writeValueAsString(customer));
    for (Product product : products)
        price += product.getPrice();
    final int priceDiscounted = priceDiscount(price, customer);
    LOGGER.info("Discounted price: {}",
mapper.writeValueAsString(Collections.singletonMap("price",
```

```
priceDiscounted)));
    Optional<Account> account = customer.getAccounts().stream().filter(a ->
(a.getBalance() > priceDiscounted)).findFirst();
    if (account.isPresent()) {
        order.setAccountId(account.get().getId());
        order.setStatus(OrderStatus.ACCEPTED);
        order.setPrice(priceDiscounted);
        LOGGER.info("Account found: {}",
mapper.writeValueAsString(account.get()));
    } else {
        order.setStatus(OrderStatus.REJECTED);
        LOGGER.info("Account not found: {}",
mapper.writeValueAsString(customer.getAccounts()));
    }

    return repository.add(order);
}
```

Let's take a look at the Kibana dashboard. It is available
at http://192.168.99.100:5601. The application logs may be easily discovered and
analyzed there. You can select the required index name in the menu on the left side of the
page (labeled **1** in the following screenshot). Log statistics are presented on the timeline
graph (**2**). You can narrow down the time taken as search parameter by clicking a concrete
bar or choosing a group of bars. All logs for a given period of time are displayed on the
panel present below the graph (**3**):

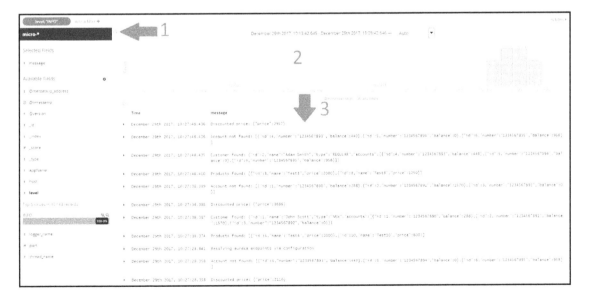

Each entry can be expanded to look at its details. In the detailed table view, we can see, for example, the name of the Elasticsearch index (_index) and the level or name of the microservice (appName). Most of those fields have been set by LoggingEventCompositeJsonEncoder. I have only defined one application-specific field, appName:

Kibana gives us a great ability to search for particular entries. We may define filters just by clicking on the selected entries in order to define a set of search criteria. In the preceding screenshot, you can see how I filtered out all the entries with incoming HTTP requests. As you probably remember, the `org.springframework.web.filter.CommonsRequestLoggingFilter` class is responsible for logging them. I have just defined the filter whose name is equal to a fully-qualified logger class name. Here's the screen from my Kibana dashboard, which displays the logs generated only by `CommonsRequestLoggingFilter`:

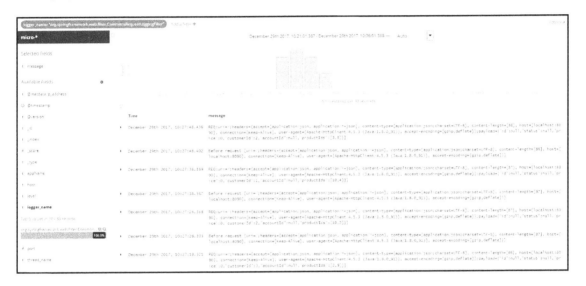

Using AMQP appender and a message broker

The configuration with the Spring AMQP appender and message broker is a little bit more complicated than the method that uses the simple TCP appender. First, you need to launch a message broker on your local machine. I have described this process in `Chapter 5`, *Distributed Configuration with Spring Cloud Config*, where I introduced RabbitMQ for dynamic configuration reloading with Spring Cloud Bus. Assuming you have started an instance of RabbitMQ locally or as a Docker container, you can proceed to configuration. We have to create a queue for publishing incoming events and then bind it to the exchange. To achieve this, you should log in to the Rabbit management console and then go to the **Queues** section. I have created the queue with the name `q_logstash`. I defined the new exchange with the name `ex_logstash`, which is visible in the following screenshot. The queue has been bound to the exchange with routing keys for all the example microservices:

After we have launched and configured the instance of RabbitMQ, we may start integrating on the application side. First, you have to include `spring-boot-starter-amqp` in the project dependencies to provide implementations of the AMQP client and AMQP appender:

```
<dependency>
    <groupId>org.springframework.boot</groupId>
    <artifactId>spring-boot-starter-amqp</artifactId>
</dependency>
```

Then, the only thing you have to do is to define the appender with the `org.springframework.amqp.rabbit.logback.AmqpAppender` class in the Logback configuration file. The most important properties that need to be set are the RabbitMQ network address (`host`, `port`), the name of the declared exchange (`exchangeName`), and the routing key (`routingKeyPattern`), which has to match one of the keys declared for the exchange bindings. In comparison with the TCP appender, a disadvantage of this approach is the need to prepare a JSON message sent to Logstash by yourself. Here's a fragment of the Logback configuration for `order-service`:

```
<appender name="AMQP"
 class="org.springframework.amqp.rabbit.logback.AmqpAppender">
 <layout>
  <pattern>
  {
  "time": "%date{ISO8601}",
  "thread": "%thread",
  "level": "%level",
  "class": "%logger{36}",
  "message": "%message"
  }
  </pattern>
 </layout>
 <host>192.168.99.100</host>
 <port>5672</port>
 <username>guest</username>
 <password>guest</password>
 <applicationId>order-service</applicationId>
 <routingKeyPattern>order-service</routingKeyPattern>
 <declareExchange>true</declareExchange>
 <exchangeType>direct</exchangeType>
 <exchangeName>ex_logstash</exchangeName>
 <generateId>true</generateId>
 <charset>UTF-8</charset>
 <durable>true</durable>
 <deliveryMode>PERSISTENT</deliveryMode>
</appender>
```

Logstash may be easily integrated with RabbitMQ by declaring the `rabbitmq` (`logstash-input-rabbitmq`) input:

```
input {
  rabbitmq {
    host => "192.168.99.100"
    port => 5672
    durable => true
    exchange => "ex_logstash"
  }
}

output {
  elasticsearch {
    hosts => ["http://192.168.99.100:9200"]
  }
}
```

Spring Cloud Sleuth

Spring Cloud Sleuth is a rather small, simple project, which nevertheless provides some useful features for logging and tracing. If you refer to the example discussed in the *Using LogstashTCPAppender* section, you can easily see that there is no possibility to filter all the logs related to single request. In a microservices-based environment, it is also very important to correlate messages exchanged by the applications when handling requests that are coming into the system. This is the main motivation in creating the Spring Cloud Sleuth project.

If Spring Cloud Sleuth is enabled for the application, it adds some HTTP headers to the requests, which allows you to link requests with the responses and the messages exchanged by independent applications, for example, through RESTful API. It defines two basic units of work—span and trace. Each of these is identified by a unique 64 bit ID. The value of the trace ID is equal to the initial value of the span ID. Span refers to a single exchange, where the response is sent as a reaction to the request. Trace is something that is usually called **correlation IT**, and it helps us to link all the logs from different applications generated during the processing of requests coming into the system.

Every trace and span ID is added to the Slf4J **MDC** (**mapped diagnostic context**), so you will able to extract all the logs with a given trace or span in a log aggregator. MDC is just a map that stores the context data of the current thread. Every client request coming to the server is handled by a different thread. Thanks to this, each thread can have access to the values of its MDC within the thread lifecycle. As well as `spanId` and `traceId`, Spring Cloud Sleuth also adds the following two spans to the MDC:

- `appName`: The name of the application that has generated the log entry
- `exportable`: This specifies whether the log should be exported to Zipkin or not

In addition to the preceding features, Spring Cloud Sleuth also provides:

- An abstraction over common distributed tracing data models, which allows integrating with Zipkin.
- Records timing information in order to aid it in latency analysis. It also includes different sampling policies to manage the volume of data exported to Zipkin.
- Integrates with common Spring components taking part in communication like servlet filter, asynchronous endpoints, RestTemplate, message channels, Zuul filters and Feign client.

Integrating Sleuth with an application

In order to enable Spring Cloud Sleuth features for the application, just add the `spring-cloud-starter-sleuth` starter to the dependencies:

```
<dependency>
    <groupId>org.springframework.cloud</groupId>
    <artifactId>spring-cloud-starter-sleuth</artifactId>
</dependency>
```

After including this dependency, the format of the log entries generated by the application has been changed. You can see this as follows:

```
2017-12-30 00:21:31.639 INFO [order-
service,9a3fef0169864e80,9a3fef0169864e80,false] 49212 --- [nio-8090-
exec-6] p.p.s.order.controller.OrderController : Products found:
[{"id":2,"name":"Test2","price":1500},{"id":9,"name":"Test9","price":2450}]
2017-12-30 00:21:31.683 INFO [order-
service,9a3fef0169864e80,9a3fef0169864e80,false] 49212 --- [nio-8090-
exec-6] p.p.s.order.controller.OrderController : Customer found:
{"id":2,"name":"Adam
Smith","type":"REGULAR","accounts":[{"id":4,"number":"1234567893","balance"
:5000},{"id":5,"number":"1234567894","balance":0},{"id":6,"number":"1234567
```

```
895","balance":5000}]}
2017-12-30 00:21:31.684 INFO [order-
service,9a3fef0169864e80,9a3fef0169864e80,false] 49212 --- [nio-8090-
exec-6] p.p.s.order.controller.OrderController : Discounted price:
{"price":3752}
2017-12-30 00:21:31.684 INFO [order-
service,9a3fef0169864e80,9a3fef0169864e80,false] 49212 --- [nio-8090-
exec-6] p.p.s.order.controller.OrderController : Account found:
{"id":4,"number":"1234567893","balance":5000}
2017-12-30 00:21:31.711 INFO [order-
service,58b06c4c412c76cc,58b06c4c412c76cc,false] 49212 --- [nio-8090-
exec-7] p.p.s.order.controller.OrderController : Order found:
{"id":4,"status":"ACCEPTED","price":3752,"customerId":2,"accountId":4,"prod
uctIds":[9,2]}
2017-12-30 00:21:31.722 INFO [order-
service,58b06c4c412c76cc,58b06c4c412c76cc,false] 49212 --- [nio-8090-
exec-7] p.p.s.order.controller.OrderController : Account modified:
{"accountId":4,"price":3752}
2017-12-30 00:21:31.723 INFO [order-
service,58b06c4c412c76cc,58b06c4c412c76cc,false] 49212 --- [nio-8090-
exec-7] p.p.s.order.controller.OrderController : Order status changed:
{"status":"DONE"}
```

Searching events using Kibana

Spring Cloud Sleuth automatically adds HTTP headers `X-B3-SpanId` and `X-B3-TraceId` to all the requests and responses. These fields are also included to the MDC as `spanId` and `traceId`. But before moving to the Kibana dashboard, I would like you to take a look at the following figure. This is a sequence diagram that illustrates the communication flow between sample microservices:

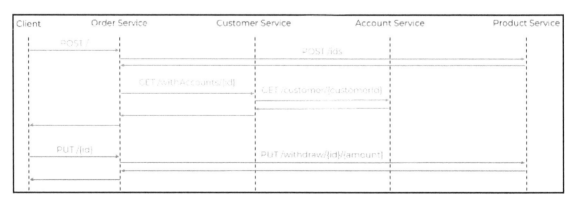

There are two available methods that are exposed by `order-service`. The first is for creating a new order and the second is for confirming it. The first `POST /` method, in fact, calls endpoints from all other services directly from `customer-service`, `product-service`, and `account-service` through `customer-service`. The second `PUT /{id}` method integrates with only one endpoint from `account-service`.

The flow described previously may now be mapped by the log entries stored in ELK Stack. When using Kibana as a log aggregator, together with fields generated by Spring Cloud Sleuth, we may easily find entries by filtering them using trace or span IDs. Here's an example, where we have discovered all the events related to a call of the `POST /` endpoint from `order-service` with the `X-B3-TraceId` field equal to `103ec949877519c2`:

Here's an example similar to the previous one, but where all events stored during the processing request are sent to the `PUT /{id}` endpoint. These entries have been also filtered out by the `X-B3-TraceId` field, the value of which is equal to `7070b90bfb36c961`:

Here, you can see the full list of fields, which has been sent to Logstash by the microservice application. The fields with the X- prefix have been included in the message by the Spring Cloud Sleuth library:

```
▼   December 29th 2017, 15:39:43.029   Account found: {"id":9,"number":"1234567898","balance":5000,"customerId":3}


    Table    JSON

t   @metdata.ip_address   Q Q ▥ ✱ 192.168.99.1

⊘   @timestamp            Q Q ▥ ✱ December 29th 2017, 15:39:43.029

t   @version              Q Q ▥ ✱ 1

?   X-B3-ParentSpanId       ▥ ✱ ⚠ 7079b90bfb36c961

?   X-B3-SpanId             ▥ ✱ ⚠ 2db3a2acca189c51

?   X-B3-TraceId            ▥ ✱ ⚠ 7079b90bfb36c961

?   X-Span-Export           ▥ ✱ ⚠ false

t   _id                   Q Q ▥   1CK2omABfCW_oGSV42bG

t   _index                Q Q ▥   micro-account-service

#   _score                    ▥   -

t   _type                 Q Q ▥   doc

t   appName               Q Q ▥ ✱ account-service

t   host                  Q Q ▥ ✱ 192.168.99.1

t   level                 Q Q ▥ ✱ INFO

t   logger_name           Q Q ▥ ✱ pl.piomin.services.account.controller.AccountController

t   message               Q Q ▥ ✱ Account found: {"id":9,"number":"1234567898","balance":5000,"customerId":3}

#   port                  Q Q ▥ ✱ 57,684

t   thread_name           Q Q ▥ ✱ http-nio-8091-exec-2
```

Integrating Sleuth with Zipkin

Zipkin is a popular, open source, distributed tracing system, which helps in gathering timing data needed to analyze latency problems in microservices-based architecture. It is able to collect, look up, and visualize data using a UI web console. The Zipkin UI provides a dependency diagram showing how many traced requests were processed by all applications within the system. Zipkin consists of four elements. I have already mentioned one of them, Web UI. The second one is Zipkin collector, which is responsible for validating, storing, and indexing all incoming trace data. Zipkin uses Cassandra as a default backend store. It also natively supports Elasticsearch and MySQL. The last element is query service, which provides a simple JSON API for finding and retrieving traces. It is mostly consumed by Web UI.

Running the Zipkin server

We may run the Zipkin server locally in several ways. One of these ways involves using a Docker container. The following command launches an in-memory server instance:

```
docker run -d --name zipkin -p 9411:9411 openzipkin/zipkin
```

After running the Docker container, the Zipkin API is available at `http://192.168.99.100:9411`. Alternatively, you can start it using Java libraries and the Spring Boot application. To enable Zipkin for your application, you should include the following dependencies to your Maven `pom.xml` file, as shown in the following code fragment. The default versions are managed by `spring-cloud-dependencies`. For our example application, I have used `Edgware.RELEASE` Spring Cloud Release Train:

```
<dependency>
    <groupId>io.zipkin.java</groupId>
    <artifactId>zipkin-server</artifactId>
</dependency>
<dependency>
    <groupId>io.zipkin.java</groupId>
    <artifactId>zipkin-autoconfigure-ui</artifactId>
</dependency>
```

I have added a new `zipkin-service` module to our example system. It is really simple. The only thing that has to be implemented is the application main class, which is annotated with `@EnableZipkinServer`. Thanks to this, the Zipkin instance is embedded in the Spring Boot application:

```
@SpringBootApplication
@EnableZipkinServer
public class ZipkinApplication {

    public static void main(String[] args) {
        new
SpringApplicationBuilder(ZipkinApplication.class).web(true).run(args);
    }

}
```

In order to launch the Zipkin instance on its default port, we have to override the default server port in the `application.yml` file. After launching the application, the Zipkin API is available at `http://localhost:9411`:

```
spring:
 application:
  name: zipkin-service

server:
 port: ${PORT:9411}
```

Building the client application

If you would like to use both Spring Cloud Sleuth and Zipkin in your project, just add starter `spring-cloud-starter-zipkin` to the dependencies. It enables integration with Zipkin via the HTTP API. If you have started the Zipkin server as an embedded instance inside the Spring Boot application, you don't have to provide any additional configuration containing connection address. If you use the Docker container, you should override the default URL in `application.yml`:

```
spring:
 zipkin:
  baseUrl: http://192.168.99.100:9411/
```

You can always take advantage of integration with service discovery. If you have the discovery client enabled through `@EnableDiscoveryClient` for your application with the embedded Zipkin server, you may just set the property `spring.zipkin.locator.discovery.enabled` to `true`. In that case, even if it is not available under the default port, all applications will be able to localize it through the registered name. You should also override the default Zipkin application name with the `spring.zipkin.baseUrl` property:

```
spring:
  zipkin:
    baseUrl: http://zipkin-service/
```

By default, Spring Cloud Sleuth sends only a few selected incoming requests. It is determined by the property `spring.sleuth.sampler.percentage`, the value of which needs to be a double between 0.0 and 1.0. The sampling solution has been implemented because data volumes exchanged between distributed systems can be sometimes very high. Spring Cloud Sleuth provides sampler interface that can be implemented to take control over the sampling algorithm. The default implementation is available in class `PercentageBasedSampler`. If you would like to trace all the requests exchanged by your applications, just declare `AlwaysSampler` bean. It may be useful for the test purposes:

```
@Bean
public Sampler defaultSampler() {
    return new AlwaysSampler();
}
```

Analyze data with the Zipkin UI

Let's go back for a moment to our example system. As I have mentioned before, the new `zipkin-service` module has been added. I have also enabled Zipkin tracing for all the microservices, including `gateway-service`. By default, Sleuth takes the value `spring.application.name` as a span's service name. You may override that name with the `spring.zipkin.service.name` property.

To successfully test our system with Zipkin, we have to start the microservices, gateway, discovery, and Zipkin servers. To generate and send some test data, you could just run the JUnit test implemented by the `pl.piomin.services.gateway.GatewayControllerTest` class. It sends 100 messages to `order-service` via `gateway-service`, available at `http://localhost:8080/api/order/**`.

Let's analyze the data collected from all the services by Zipkin. You may easily check it out using its UI web console. All the traces are tagged with the service's name spans. If there are five spans for the entry, it means that the request coming into the system has been processed by five different services. You can see this in the following screenshot:

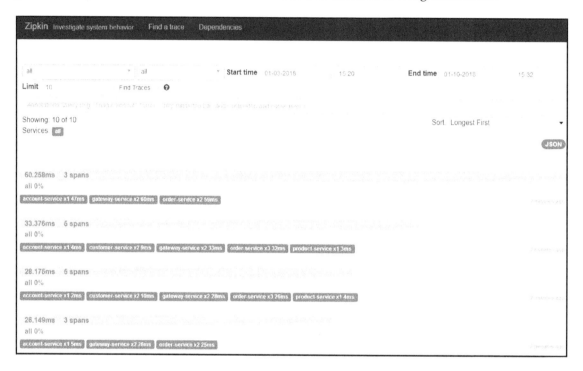

You may filter the entries with different criteria, such as the service name, span name, trace ID, request time, or duration. Zipkin also visualizes failed requests and sorts them by duration, in descending or ascending order:

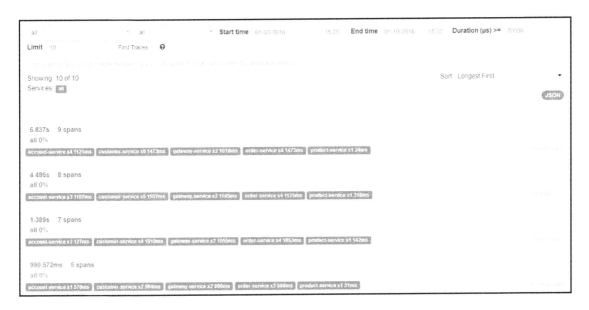

You can take a look at the details of every entry. Zipkin visualizes the flow between all the microservices taking part in communication. It is considering timing the data of every incoming request. You may uncover the reasons for latency in your system:

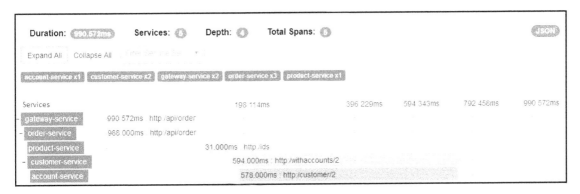

Zipkin provides some additional interesting features. One of these is the ability to visualize dependencies between applications. The following screenshot illustrates the communication flow of our sample system:

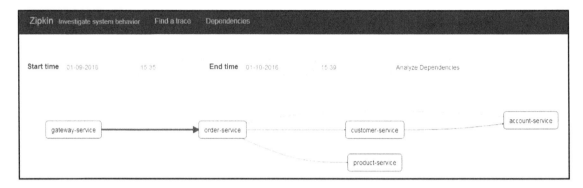

You may check out how many messages have been exchanged between services just by clicking on the relevant element:

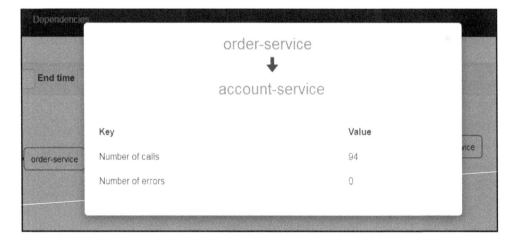

Integration via message broker

Integration with Zipkin via HTTP is not the only option. As is usual with Spring Cloud, we may use a message broker as a proxy. There are two available brokers—RabbitMQ and Kafka. The first of these can be included in the project by using the `spring-rabbit` dependency, while the second can be included with `spring-kafka`. The default destination name for both of these brokers is `zipkin`:

```
<dependency>
  <groupId>org.springframework.cloud</groupId>
  <artifactId>spring-cloud-starter-zipkin</artifactId>
</dependency>
<dependency>
  <groupId>org.springframework.amqp</groupId>
  <artifactId>spring-rabbit</artifactId>
</dependency>
```

This feature also requires changes on the Zipkin server side. We have configured a consumer that is listening for the data coming into the RabbitMQ or Kafka queue. To achieve this, just include the following dependencies in your project. You still need to have the `zipkin-server` and `zipkin-autoconfigure-ui` artifacts in the classpath:

```
<dependency>
  <groupId>org.springframework.cloud</groupId>
  <artifactId>spring-cloud-sleuth-zipkin-stream</artifactId>
</dependency>
<dependency>
  <groupId>org.springframework.cloud</groupId>
  <artifactId>spring-cloud-starter-stream-rabbit</artifactId>
</dependency>
```

You should annotate the main application class with @EnableZipkinStreamServer instead of @EnableZipkinServer. Fortunately, @EnableZipkinStreamServer is also annotated with @EnableZipkinServer, which means that you may also use the standard Zipkin server endpoints for collecting spans over HTTP, and for searching them with the UI web console:

```
@SpringBootApplication
@EnableZipkinStreamServer
public class ZipkinApplication {

    public static void main(String[] args) {
        new
SpringApplicationBuilder(ZipkinApplication.class).web(true).run(args);
    }

}
```

Summary

Logging and tracing are usually not very important during development, but these are the key features that are used in the maintenance of the system. In this chapter, I have placed emphasis on the fields of development and operations. I have shown you how to integrate a Spring Boot microservice application with Logstash and Zipkin in several ways. I have also shown you some examples to illustrate how to enable Spring Cloud Sleuth features for an application in order to make it easier to monitor calls between many microservices. After reading this chapter, you should also be able to effectively use Kibana as a log aggregator tool and Zipkin as a tracing tool for discovering bottlenecks in communication inside your system.

Spring Cloud Sleuth, in conjunction with Elastic Stack and Zipkin, seems to be a very powerful ecosystem, which removes any doubts you might have about problems with monitoring systems that consist of many independent microservices.

10
Additional Configuration and Discovery Features

We talked a great deal about service discovery and distributed configuration in `Chapter 4`, *Service Discovery*, and `Chapter 5`, *Distributed Configuration with Spring Cloud Config*. We discussed two solutions in detail. The first of them, Eureka, is provided by Netflix OSS and has been adopted by Spring Cloud for service discovery. The second was the Spring Cloud Config project dedicated only to a distributed configuration. However, there are some interesting solutions on the market effectively combining both of these features. Currently, Spring Cloud supports two of them:

- **Consul**: This product is built by HashiCorp. It is a highly available, distributed solution designed to connect and configure applications across dynamic, distributed infrastructure. Consul is a rather complex product, and has multiple components, but its main functionality is discovering and configuring services across any infrastructure.
- **Zookeeper**: This product is built by Apache Software Foundation. It is a distributed, hierarchical key/value storage written in Java. It is designed to maintain configuration information, naming, and distributed synchronization. In contrast to Consul, it is more of a primitive key/value storage than a modern service discovery tool. However, Zookeeper is still very popular, especially for solutions based on the Apache Software stack.

Support for two other popular products from that area is still in the development stage. The following projects have still not been added to the official Spring Cloud Release Train:

- **Kubernetes**: This is an open-source solution designed for automating deployment, scaling, and management of containerized applications, originally created by Google. This tool is enjoying great popularity right now. Recently, the Docker platform has started supporting Kubernetes.
- **Etcd**: This is a distributed reliable key/value storage for the most critical data of a distributed system written in Go. It is used in production by many companies and other software products, for example, Kubernetes.

In this chapter, I'm going to introduce only officially supported solutions, namely Consul and Zookeeper. Kubernetes, which is much more than only a key/value storage or a service registry, will be discussed in Chapter 14, *Docker Support*.

Using Spring Cloud Consul

The Spring Cloud Consul project provides integration for Consul and Spring Boot applications through auto-configuration. By using the well-known Spring Framework annotation style, we may enable and configure common patterns within microservice-based environments. These patterns include service discovery using Consul agent, distributed configuration using Consul key/value store, distributed events with Spring Cloud Bus, and Consul Events. The project also supports a client-side load balancer based on Netflix's Ribbon and an API gateway based on Netflix's Zuul. Before we start to discuss these features, we first have to run and configure Consul agent.

Running Consul agent

We will begin with the simplest way of starting Consul agent on our local machines. The standalone development mode may be easily set up with the Docker container. Here's the command, which will start the Consul container from the official Hashicorp's image available on Docker Hub:

```
docker run -d --name consul -p 8500:8500 consul
```

After launching, Consul is available under the address `http://192.168.99.100:8500`. It exposes RESTful HTTP API, that is, the main interface. All the API routes are prefixed with `/v1/`. Of course, it is not required to use the API directly. There are some programming libraries that can be used to consume the API more conveniently. One of them is `consul-api`, the client written in Java and also used by Spring Cloud Consul internally. There is also the web UI dashboard provided by Consul available under the same address as the HTTP API, but on a different context path, `/ui/`. It allows for viewing all registered services and nodes, viewing all health checks and their current status, and reading and setting key/value data.

As I mentioned in the preface to this section, we are going to use three different features of Consul—agent, events, and KV store. Each of them is represented by the group of endpoints, respectively `/agent`, `/event`, and `/kv`. The most interesting agent endpoints are those related with service registration. Here's a list of these endpoints:

Method	Path	Description
GET	`/agent/services`	It returns a list of the services registered with the local agent. If Consul is run in a clustered mode, that list may be different than the list reported by the `/catalog` endpoint before synchronization performed between cluster members.
PUT	`/agent/service/register`	It adds a new service to the local agent. The agent is responsible for managing local services, and for sending updates to the servers to perform synchronization for the global catalog.
PUT	`/agent/service/deregister/:service_id`	It removes a service with `service_id` from the local agent. The agent takes care of de-registering the service with the global catalog.

The `/kv` endpoints are dedicated to managing simple key/value store, which is especially useful for storing service configuration or other metadata. It is worth noting that each data center has its own KV store, so in order to share it across multiple nodes, we should have configured the Consul replicate daemon. Anyway, here's a list of the three endpoints for managing the key/value store:

Method	Path	Description
GET	/kv/:key	It returns the value for the given key name. If the requested key does not exist, HTTP status 404 is returned as a response.
PUT	/kv/:key	It is used for adding a new key to the store, or just to update the existing one with a key name.
DELETE	/kv/:key	It is the last CRUD method that is used for deleting a single key, or all keys, with the same prefix.

Spring Cloud uses Consul Events for providing a dynamic configuration reload. There are two simple API methods. The first of them, `PUT /event/fire/:name`, triggers a new event. The second, `GET /event/list`, returns a list of events, which might be filtered by name, tag, node, or service name.

Integration on the client side

To activate Consul service discovery in your project, you should include the starter `spring-cloud-starter-consul-discovery` to the dependencies. If you would like to enable distributed configuration with Consul, just include `spring-cloud-starter-consul-config`. In some cases, you would probably use both these features in your client-side application. Then, you should declare a dependency to the `spring-cloud-starter-consul-all` artifact:

```xml
<dependency>
    <groupId>org.springframework.cloud</groupId>
    <artifactId>spring-cloud-starter-consul-all</artifactId>
</dependency>
```

By default, the Consul agent is expected to be available under the address
`localhost:8500`. If it is different for your application, you should provide the appropriate
address in the `application.yml` or `bootstrap.yml` file:

```
spring:
  cloud:
    consul:
      host: 192.168.99.100
      port: 18500
```

Service discovery

Discovery with Consul is enabled for the application by annotating the main class with the
generic Spring Cloud `@EnableDiscoveryClient`. You should remember that from
`Chapter 4`, *Service Discovery*, because there is no difference in comparison with Eureka. The
default service name is also taken from the `${spring.application.name}` property.
Sample microservices that use Consul as a discovery server are available on GitHub in the
`https://github.com/piomin/sample-spring-cloud-consul.git` repository. The
architecture of the system is the same as for examples in some previous chapters. There are
four microservices, `order-service`, `product-service`, `customer-service`,
and `account-service`, and the API gateway is implemented in the module `gateway-
service`. For inter-service communication, we use the Feign client together with the
Ribbon load balancer:

```
@SpringBootApplication
@EnableDiscoveryClient
@EnableFeignClients
public class CustomerApplication {

    public static void main(String[] args) {
        new
SpringApplicationBuilder(CustomerApplication.class).web(true).run(args);
    }

}
```

By default, the Spring Boot application is registered in Consul with the instance ID generated as a concatenation of values taken from the properties `spring.application.name`, `spring.profiles.active`, `server.port`. In most cases, it is enough to be sure that the ID is unique, but if the custom pattern is required, it may be easily set with the `spring.cloud.consul.discovery.instanceId` property:

```
spring:
 cloud:
  consul:
   discovery:
    instanceId:
${spring.application.name}:${vcap.application.instance_id:${spring.applicat
ion.instance_id:${random.value}}}
```

After launching all the sample microservices, take a look at the Consul UI dashboard. You should see there are four different services registered, like in the following screenshot:

Alternatively, you may check out a list of registered services using the RESTful HTTP API endpoint `GET /v1/agent/services`. Here's the fragment of the JSON response:

```
"customer-service-zone1-8092": {
 "ID": "customer-service-zone1-8092",
 "Service": "customer-service",
 "Tags": [],
 "Address": "minkowp-l.p4.org",
 "Port": 8092,
 "EnableTagOverride": false,
 "CreateIndex": 0,
 "ModifyIndex": 0
},
"order-service-zone1-8090": {
 "ID": "order-service-zone1-8090",
 "Service": "order-service",
 "Tags": [],
```

```
  "Address": "minkowp-l.p4.org",
  "Port": 8090,
  "EnableTagOverride": false,
  "CreateIndex": 0,
  "ModifyIndex": 0
}
```

Now, you may easily test the whole system by sending some test requests to `order-service` using the `pl.piomin.services.order.OrderControllerTest` JUnit test class. Everything should work fine, and the same as for discovery with Eureka.

Health check

Consul checks out the health status of every registered instance by calling the `/health` endpoint. If you do not wish to provide the Spring Boot Actuator library in the classpath, or there are some problems with your service, it will be visible on the web dashboard:

If the health check endpoint is available under a different context path for any reason, you may override that path with the `spring.cloud.consul.discovery.healthCheckPath` property. There is also the possibility to change the status refresh interval by defining `healthCheckInterval` with a pattern, such as, for example, `10s` for seconds or `2m` for minutes.

```
spring:
  cloud:
    consul:
      discovery:
        healthCheckPath: admin/health
        healthCheckInterval: 20s
```

Zones

I assume you remember our discussion about zoning mechanisms available for discovery with Eureka in `Chapter 4`, *Service Discovery*. It is useful when the hosts are placed in a different location, and you would prefer communication between instances registered in the same zone. The official documentation of the Spring Cloud Consul (`http://cloud.spring.io/spring-cloud-static/spring-cloud-consul/1.2.3.RELEASE/single/spring-cloud-consul.html`) says nothing about such a solution, which fortunately doesn't mean it is not implemented. Spring Cloud provides a zoning mechanism based on Consul tags. The default zone for the application may be configured with the `spring.cloud.consul.discovery.instanceZone` property. It sets the tag configured in the `spring.cloud.consul.discovery.defaultZoneMetadataName` property with the passed value. The default metadata tag name is `zone`.

Let's go back to the sample applications. I have extended all the configuration files with two profiles, `zone1` and `zone2`. Here's the `bootstrap.yml` file for `order-service`:

```
spring:
 application:
  name: order-service
 cloud:
  consul:
   host: 192.168.99.100
   port: 8500

---
spring:
 profiles: zone1
 cloud:
  consul:
   discovery:
    instanceZone: zone1
server:
 port: ${PORT:8090}

---
spring:
 profiles: zone2
  cloud:
   consul:
    discovery:
     instanceZone: zone2
server:
 port: ${PORT:9090}
```

There are two running instances of every microservice registered in two different zones. After building the whole project with the `mvn clean install` command, you should launch the Spring Boot application with the active profile `zone1` or `zone2`, for example, `java -jar --spring.profiles.active=zone1 target/order-service-1.0-SNAPSHOT.jar`. You can see the full list of registered instances tagged with the zone in the **Nodes** section. The view from the Consul dashboard is visible in the following screenshot:

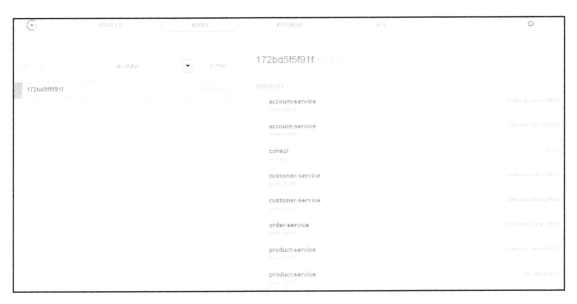

The last element of our architecture is an API gateway based on Zuul. We also run two instances of `gateway-service` in different zones. We would like to omit registration in Consul and allow only a configuration to be fetched, which is used by the Ribbon client while performing load balancing. Here's the fragment of the `bootstrap.yml` file of `gateway-service`. Registration has been disabled by setting the properties `spring.cloud.consul.discovery.register` and `spring.cloud.consul.discovery.registerHealthCheck` to `false`:

```
---
spring:
 profiles: zone1
 cloud:
 consul:
 discovery:
 instanceZone: zone1
 register: false
 registerHealthCheck: false
```

```
server:
 port: ${PORT:8080}

---
spring:
 profiles: zone2
 cloud:
 consul:
 discovery:
 instanceZone: zone2
 register: false
 registerHealthCheck: false
server:
 port: ${PORT:9080}
```

Client settings customization

The Spring Cloud Consul client may be customized through the properties in the configuration file. Some of those settings have already been introduced in the previous sections in this chapter. Other useful settings have been listed in the following table. All of them are prefixed with `spring.cloud.consul.discovery`:

Property	Default value	Description
enabled	true	It sets whether Consul discovery is enabled or disabled for an application
failFast	true	It throws exceptions during service registration if `true`; otherwise, it logs warnings
hostname	-	It sets the hostname of the instance when registering in Consul
preferIpAddress	false	It forces an application to send its IP address instead of the hostname during registration
scheme	http	It sets whether the service is available under HTTP or HTTPS protocol
serverListQueryTags	-	It allows filtering services by a single tag
serviceName	-	It overrides the service name, which by default takes from the property `spring.application.name`

| tags | - | It sets the list tags with values to use when registering the service |

Running in clustered mode

Until now, we were always launching a single, standalone instance of Consul. As far as this is a suitable solution in development mode, it is not enough for a production. There, we would like to have a scalable, production-grade service discovery infrastructure, consisting of some nodes working together inside the cluster. Consul provides support for clustering based on a gossip protocol used for communication between members and a Raft consensus protocol for a leadership election. I wouldn't like to go into the details of that process, but some basics about Consul architecture should be clarified.

We have already talked about Consul agent, but what it is exactly and what is its role weren't explained. An agent is the long-running daemon on every member of the Consul cluster. It may be run in either client or server mode. All agents are responsible for running checks and keeping services registered, in different nodes and in sync, globally.

Our main goal in this section is to set up and configure the Consul cluster using its Docker image. First, we will start the container, which acts as a leader of the cluster. There is only one difference in the currently used Docker command than for the standalone Consul server. We have set the environment variable CONSUL_BIND_INTERFACE=eth0 in order to change the network address of the cluster agent from 127.0.0.1 to the one available for other member containers. My Consul server is now running at the internal address 172.17.0.2. To check out what your address is (it should be the same) you may run the command docker logs consul. The appropriate information is logged just after container startup:

```
docker run -d --name consul-1 -p 8500:8500 -e CONSUL_BIND_INTERFACE=eth0
consul
```

Knowledge of that address is very important, since now we have to pass it to every member container startup command as a cluster join parameter. We also bind it to all interfaces by setting 0.0.0.0 as a client address. Now, we may easily expose the client agent API outside the container using the -p parameter:

```
docker run -d --name consul-2 -p 8501:8500 consul agent -server -
client=0.0.0.0 -join=172.17.0.2
docker run -d --name consul-3 -p 8502:8500 consul agent -server -
client=0.0.0.0 -join=172.17.0.2
```

After running two containers with Consul agent, you may check out the full list of cluster members by executing the following command on the leader's container:

```
$ docker exec -t consul-1 consul members
Node           Address            Status  Type    Build  Protocol  DC   Segment
4b3c3c84dd96   172.17.0.3:8301    alive   server  0.9.3  2         dc1  <all>
7b4c661849ed   172.17.0.2:8301    alive   server  0.9.3  2         dc1  <all>
8429a8226624   172.17.0.4:8301    alive   server  0.9.3  2         dc1  <all>
```

The Consul server agent is exposed on the 8500 port, while member agents on ports 8501 and 8502. Even if the microservice instance registers itself to a member agent, it is visible to all members of a cluster:

We may easily change the default Consul agent address for the Spring Boot application by changing the configuration properties:

```
spring:
 application:
  name: customer-service
 cloud:
  consul:
   host: 192.168.99.100
   port: 8501
```

Distributed configuration

An application with Spring Cloud Consul Config library in the classpath fetches configuration from the Consul key/value store during the bootstrap phase. That is, by default, stored in the `/config` folder. When we are creating a new key first, we have to set a folder path. That path is then used for identifying the key and assigning it to the application. Spring Cloud Config tries to resolve properties stored in the folder based on the application name and active profiles. Assuming we have the `spring.application.name` property set to `order-service` in the `bootstrap.yml` file and the `spring.profiles.active` running argument set to `zone1`, it tries to locate the property sources in the following order: `config/order-service,zone1/`, `config/order-service/`, `config/application,zone1/`, `config/application/`. All folders with the prefix `config/application` are the default configuration dedicated to all the applications that do not have service-specific property sources.

Managing properties in Consul

The most comfortable way to add a single key to Consul is through its web dashboard. The other way is by using the `/kv` HTTP endpoint, which has been already described at the beginning of this chapter. When using a web console, you have to go to the section **KEY/VALUE**. Then, you may view all the currently existing keys and also create a new one by providing its full path and value, in any format. That feature is visualized in the following screenshot:

Every single key may be updated or deleted:

To access a sample application that uses a property source stored in Consul, you should switch to the branch configuration in the same repository as the previous sample. I have created keys, `server.port` and `spring.cloud.consul.discovery.instanceZone`, for every microservice instead of defining it in the `application.yml` or `bootstrap.yml` files.

Client customization

The Consul Config client may be customized with the following properties, which are prefixed with `spring.cloud.consul.config`:

- `enabled`: By setting this property to `false`, you may disable Consul Config. It is useful if you include `spring-cloud-starter-consul-all`, which enables both discovery and distributed configuration.
- `fail-fast`: This sets whether to throw exceptions during configuration lookup or log warnings in case of connection failure. Setting it to `true` allows the application to continue startup normally.
- `prefix`: This sets the base folder for all the configuration values. By default, it is `/config`.
- `defaultContext`: This sets the folder name used by all applications that do not have a specific configuration. By default, it is `/application`. For example, if you override it to `app`, the properties should be searched in the folder `/config/apps`

- `profileSeparator`: By default, a profile is separated with an application name using a comma. That property allows you to override the value of that separator. For example, if you set it to `::`, you should create the folder `/config/order-service::zone1/`. Here's an example:

```
spring:
  cloud:
    consul:
      config:
        enabled: true
        prefix: props
        defaultContext: app
        profileSeparator: '::'
```

Sometimes, you would like to store a blob of properties created in a YAML or Properties format, in contrast to individual key/value pairs. In that case, you should set the `spring.cloud.consul.config.format` property to `YAML` or `PROPERTIES`. Then, the application would look for configuration properties located inside a folder with the data key, for example, `config/order-service,zone1/data`, `config/order-service/data`, `config/application,zone1/data`, or `config/application/data`. The default data key may be changed using the `spring.cloud.consul.config.data-key` property.

Watching configuration changes

The sample that has been discussed in the previous section loads the configuration on startup of the application. If you would like that configuration to be reloaded, you should send an HTTP `POST` to the `/refresh` endpoint. In order to examine how such a refresh would work for our application, we modify the fragment of application code responsible for creating some test data. Until now, it has been provided as a repository, `@Bean`, with some hardcoded in-memory objects. Take a look at the following code:

```
@Bean
CustomerRepository repository() {
    CustomerRepository repository = new CustomerRepository();
    repository.add(new Customer("John Scott", CustomerType.NEW));
    repository.add(new Customer("Adam Smith", CustomerType.REGULAR));
    repository.add(new Customer("Jacob Ryan", CustomerType.VIP));
    return repository;
}
```

Our goal is to move the code visible here to the configuration store using the Consul key/value feature. To achieve this, we have to create three keys per object, with names id, name, and type. The configuration is loaded from the properties with the repository prefix:

```
@RefreshScope
@Repository
@ConfigurationProperties(prefix = "repository")
public class CustomerRepository {

    private List<Customer> customers = new ArrayList<>();

    public List<Customer> getCustomers() {
        return customers;
    }

    public void setCustomers(List<Customer> customers) {
        this.customers = customers;
    }
    // ...
}
```

The next step is to define the appropriate keys for each service using the Consul web dashboard. Here's the sample configuration for the list consisting of Customer objects. The list is initialized on application startup:

You may change the value of each property. The update event would be automatically sent to application thanks to Consul's ability to watch a key prefix. If there is a new configuration data, the refresh event is published to the queue. All queues and exchanges are created on application startup by Spring Cloud Bus, which is included in the project as a dependency of `spring-cloud-starter-consul-all`. If your application receives such an event, it prints the following information in logs:

```
Refresh keys changed: [repository.customers[1].name]
```

Using Spring Cloud Zookeeper

Spring Cloud supports various products used as a part of the microservices architecture. You can find this out when reading this chapter where Consul has been compared with Eureka as a discovery tool, and with Spring Cloud Config as a distributed configuration tool. Zookeeper is another solution that might serve as an alternative choice to those listed previously. As with Consul, it can be used for both service discovery and distributed configuration. To enable Spring Cloud Zookeeper in the project, you should include the `spring-cloud-starter-zookeeper-discovery` starter for the service discovery feature, or `spring-cloud-starter-zookeeper-config` for the configuration server feature. Alternatively, you may declare a `spring-cloud-starter-zookeeper-all` dependency that activates all functionalities for the application. Don't forget to include `spring-boot-starter-web`, which is still required to provide web functionality:

```xml
<dependency>
    <groupId>org.springframework.cloud</groupId>
    <artifactId>spring-cloud-starter-zookeeper-all</artifactId>
</dependency>
<dependency>
    <groupId>org.springframework.boot</groupId>
    <artifactId>spring-boot-starter-web</artifactId>
</dependency>
```

Zookeeper connection settings are auto-configured. By default, the client tries to connect to `localhost:2181`. In order to override it, you should define the `spring.cloud.zookeeper.connect-string` property with the current server network address:

```yaml
spring:
 cloud:
  zookeeper:
   connect-string: 192.168.99.100:2181
```

As with Spring Cloud Consul, Zookeeper supports all the most popular communication libraries provided by Spring Cloud Netflix, such as Feign, Ribbon, Zuul, or Hystrix. Before we start working on the sample implementation, first we have to start the Zookeeper instance.

Running Zookeeper

As you probably guessed, I'm going to launch Zookeeper on the local machine using its Docker image. The following command starts the Zookeeper server instance. Since it *fails fast*, the best approach is to always restart it:

```
docker run -d --name zookeeper --restart always -p 2181:2181 zookeeper
```

In contrast to previously discussed solutions in this area, such as Consul or Eureka, Zookeeper doesn't provide a simple RESTful API or a web management console that allows us to easily manage it. It has an official API binding for Java and C. We may also use its command line interface, which can be easily started within the Docker container. The command visible here starts the container with the command line client, and links it to the Zookeeper server container:

```
docker run -it --rm --link zookeeper:zookeeper zookeeper zkCli.sh -server
zookeeper
```

Zookeeper CLI allows for performing some useful operations, such as the following:

- **Creating znodes**: To create a znode with the given path, use the command `create /path /data`.
- **Getting data**: The command `get /path` returns the data and metadata associated with the znode.
- **Watching znode for changes**: This shows a notification if znode or znode's children data changes. Watching can only be set with the `get` command.
- **Setting data**: To set znode data, use the command `set /path /data`.
- **Creating children of a znode**: This command is similar to that used for creating a single znode. The only difference is that the path of the child znode includes the parent path `create /parent/path/subnode/path /data`.
- **Listing children of a znode**: This may be displayed using the `ls /path` command.
- **Checking status**: This may be checked out with the command `stat /path`. Status describes the metadata of a specified znode, like timestamp or version number.

- **Removing/deleting a znode**: The command `rmr /path` removes the znode with all its children.

In that fragment, the term *znode* has appeared for the first time. When storing data, Zookeeper uses a tree structure, where each node is called a **znode**. The names of those znodes are based on the path taken from the root node. Each node has a name. It can be accessed using the absolute path that begins from the root node. This concept is similar to Consul folders, and has been used for creating keys in the key/value store.

Service discovery

The most popular Java client library for Apache Zookeeper is Apache Curator. It provides an API framework and utilities to make using Apache Zookeeper much easier. It also includes recipes for common-use cases and extensions, such as service discovery or Java 8 asynchronous DSL. Spring Cloud Zookeeper leverages one such extension for service discovery implementation. The usage of the Curator library by Spring Cloud Zookeeper is completely transparent for the developer, so I wouldn't like to describe it in more detail here.

Client implementation

The usage on the client side is the same as for other Spring Cloud projects related to service discovery. The application main class, or `@Configuration` class, should be annotated with `@EnableDiscoveryClient`. The default service name, instance ID, and port are taken from `spring.application.name`, the Spring Context ID, and `server.port`, respectively. Sample application source code is available in the GitHub repository at `https://github.com/piomin/sample-spring-cloud-zookeeper.git`. Fundamentally, it is no different than the sample system introduced for Consul, other than the dependency on Spring Cloud Zookeeper Discovery. It still consists of four microservices, which communicate with each other. Now, after cloning the repository, build it with the `mvn clean install` command. Then, run every service with an active profile name using `java -jar` command, for example, `java -jar --spring.profiles.active=zone1 order-service/target/order-service-1.0-SNAPSHOT.jar`.

You may see the list of registered services and instances by using the CLI commands `ls` and `get`. Spring Cloud Zookeeper, by default, registers all instances in the `/services` root folder. It may be overridden with the `spring.cloud.zookeeper.discovery.root` property. You may check out a list of currently registered services by using the Docker container with the command-line client:

```
[zk: zookeeper(CONNECTED) 13] ls /services
[product-service, order-service, account-service, customer-service]
[zk: zookeeper(CONNECTED) 14] ls /services/order-service
[987ae9bd-6e80-41ad-899d-1ab68709717b, 1c5dcd1a-423c-487f-a006-de3d1caee224]
[zk: zookeeper(CONNECTED) 15] get /services/order-service/987ae9bd-6e80-41ad-899d-1ab68709717b
{"name":"order-service","id":"987ae9bd-6e80-41ad-899d-1ab68709717b","address":"minkowp-1.p4.org","port":9090,"sslPort":null,"payload":{"@class":"org.springframework.cloud.zookeeper
.discovery.ZookeeperInstance","id":"order-service:zone2:9090","name":"order-service","metadata":{"instance_status":"UP"}},"registrationTimeUTC":1515075800204,"serviceType":"DYNAMIC
","uriSpec":{"parts":[{"value":"scheme","variable":true},{"value":"://","variable":false},{"value":"address","variable":true},{"value":":","variable":false},{"value":"port","variab
le":true}]}}
cZxid = 0xb
ctime = Thu Jan 04 14:23:20 GMT 2018
mZxid = 0xb
mtime = Thu Jan 04 14:23:20 GMT 2018
pZxid = 0xb
cversion = 0
dataVersion = 0
aclVersion = 0
ephemeralOwner = 0x10000081d640002
dataLength = 552
numChildren = 0
```

Zookeeper dependencies

Spring Cloud Zookeeper has one additional feature, called **Zookeeper dependencies**. Dependencies are to be understood as the other applications registered in Zookeeper, which are called via the Feign client or the Spring `RestTemplate`. These dependencies may be provided as properties of the application. The functionality is enabled through auto-configuration after you include the `spring-cloud-starter-zookeeper-discovery` starter to the project. It may be disabled by setting the `spring.cloud.zookeeper.dependency.enabled` property to `false`.

The configuration of the Zookeeper Dependency mechanism is provided with `spring.cloud.zookeeper.dependencies.*` properties. Here's the fragment of the `bootstrap.yml` file from `order-service`. This service integrates with all other available services:

```yaml
spring:
 application:
  name: order-service
 cloud:
  zookeeper:
   connect-string: 192.168.99.100:2181
  dependency:
   resttemplate:
    enabled: false
  dependencies:
   account:
    path: account-service
```

```
      loadBalancerType: ROUND_ROBIN
      required: true
    customer:
     path: customer-service
     loadBalancerType: ROUND_ROBIN
     required: true
    product:
     path: product-service
     loadBalancerType: ROUND_ROBIN
     required: true
```

Let's take a closer look at the preceding configuration. The root property of every called service is the alias, which may then be used as the service name by the Feign client or `@LoadBalanced RestTemplate`:

```
@FeignClient(name = "customer")
public interface CustomerClient {

    @GetMapping("/withAccounts/{customerId}")
    Customer findByIdWithAccounts(@PathVariable("customerId") Long
customerId);

}
```

The next very important field in the configuration is the path. It sets the path under which the dependency is registered in Zookeeper. So, if that property has the value `customer-service`, it means Spring Cloud Zookeeper tries to look up the appropriate service znode under the path `/services/customer-service`. There are some other properties that may customize the behavior of the client. One of them is `loadBalancerType`, used for applying the load balancing strategy. We can choose between three available strategies—ROUND_ROBIN, RANDOM, and STICKY. I also set the `required` property to `true` for every service mapping. Now, if your application can't detect the required dependency during boot time, it fails to start. Spring Cloud Zookeeper dependencies also allow managing API versions (the properties `contentTypeTemplate` and `versions`), and request headers (the `headers` property).

By default, Spring Cloud Zookeeper enables `RestTemplate` for communication with dependencies. In the sample application available in branch dependencies (`https://github.com/piomin/sample-spring-cloud-zookeeper/tree/dependencies`), we use the Feign client instead of `@LoadBalanced RestTemplate`. In order to disable that feature, we should set the property `spring.cloud.zookeeper.dependency.resttemplate.enabled` to `false`.

Distributed configuration

Configuration management with Zookeeper is pretty similar to that described for Spring Cloud Consul Config. By default, all the property sources are stored in the `/config` folder (or znode in Zookeeper nomenclature). Let me point it out one more time. Assuming we have the `spring.application.name` property set to `order-service` in the `bootstrap.yml` file, and the `spring.profiles.active` running argument set to `zone1`, it tries to locate the property sources in the following order: `config/order-service,zone1/`, `config/order-service/`, `config/application,zone1/`, `config/application/`. Properties stored in the folder with the prefix `config/application` in the namespace are available for all applications that use Zookeeper for distributed configuration.

To access the sample application, you need to switch to the branch configuration in the `https://github.com/piomin/sample-spring-cloud-zookeeper.git` repository. The configuration defined in the local `application.yml` or `bootstrap.yml` file, visible here, has now been moved to Zookeeper:

```
---
spring:
 profiles: zone1
server:
 port: ${PORT:8090}

---
spring:
 profiles: zone2
server:
 port: ${PORT:9090}
```

The required znodes have to be created using CLI. Here's the list of Zookeeper commands that create znodes with the given path. I have used the `create /path /data` command:

```
[zk: zookeeper(CONNECTED) 11] create /config ""
Created /config
[zk: zookeeper(CONNECTED) 12] create /config/order-service,zone1 ""
Created /config/order-service,zone1
[zk: zookeeper(CONNECTED) 13] create /config/order-service,zone1/server.port 8090
Created /config/order-service,zone1/server.port
[zk: zookeeper(CONNECTED) 14] create /config/order-service,zone2/server.port 9090
Node does not exist: /config/order-service,zone2/server.port
[zk: zookeeper(CONNECTED) 15] create /config/order-service,zone2 ""
Created /config/order-service,zone2
[zk: zookeeper(CONNECTED) 16] create /config/order-service,zone2/server.port 9090
Created /config/order-service,zone2/server.port
[zk: zookeeper(CONNECTED) 17] ls /config
[order-service,zone1, order-service,zone2]
```

Summary

In this chapter, I have guided you through the main features of two Spring Cloud projects—Consul and Zookeeper. I haven't focused only on Spring Cloud functionalities, but have also given you the instructions on how to start, configure, and maintain instances of its tools. We have discussed even more advanced scenarios, such as setting up a cluster consisting of numerous members using Docker. There, you had a chance to see the true power of Docker as a development tool. It allowed us to initialize a cluster that consists of three members just by using three simple commands, without any additional configuration.

Consul seems to be an important alternative to Eureka as a discovery server when using Spring Cloud. I cannot say the same about Zookeeper. As you have probably noticed, I have written much more about Consul than Zookeeper. Also, Spring Cloud treats Zookeeper as a second choice. It still does not have a zoning mechanism or watching capability for configuration changes that are implemented, in contrast to Spring Cloud Consul. You shouldn't be surprised by this. Consul is a modern solution designed in order to meet needs of the newest architectures, such as microservices-based systems, while Zookeeper is a key/value store adopted as a service discovery tool for applications running in a distributed environment. However, it is worth considering this tool if you use an Apache Foundation stack in your system. Thanks to that, you may take advantage of integration between Zookeeper and other Apache components, such as Camel or Karaf, and easily discover services created using the Spring Cloud framework.

To conclude, after reading this chapter, you should be able to use the main features of Spring Cloud Consul and Spring Cloud Zookeeper in your microservice-based architecture. You should also know the major advantages and disadvantages of all available discovery and configuration tools within Spring Cloud, in order to choose the most appropriate solution for your system.

Message-Driven Microservices

11

We have already discussed many features around microservice-based architecture provided by Spring Cloud. However, we have always been considering synchronous, RESTful-based inter-service communication. As you probably remember from `Chapter 1`, *Introduction to Microservices*, there are some other popular communication styles, such as publish/subscribe or asynchronous, event-driven point-to-point messaging. In this chapter, I would like to introduce a different approach to microservices than that presented in previous chapters. We will talk in more detail about how you can work with Spring Cloud Stream in order to build message-driven microservices.

Topics we will cover in this chapter include:

- The main terms and concepts related to Spring Cloud Stream
- Using RabbitMQ and Apache Kafka message brokers as binders
- The Spring Cloud Stream programming model
- Advanced configurations of binding, producers, and consumers
- Implementation of scaling, grouping, and partitioning mechanisms
- Multiple binder support

Learning about Spring Cloud Stream

Spring Cloud Stream is built on top of Spring Boot. It allows us to create standalone, production-grade Spring applications and uses Spring Integration that helps in implementing communication with message brokers. Every application created with Spring Cloud Stream integrates with other microservices through input and output channels. Those channels are connected to external message brokers via middleware-specific binder implementations. There are two built-in binder implementations available—Kafka and Rabbit MQ.

Spring Integration extends the Spring programming model to support the well-known **Enterprise Integration Patterns** (**EIP**). EIP defines a number of components that are typically used for orchestration in distributed systems. You have probably heard about patterns such as message channels, routers, aggregators, or endpoints. A primary goal of the Spring Integration framework is to provide a simple model for building Spring applications based on EIP. If you are interested in more details about EIP, please refer to the website at `http://www.enterpriseintegrationpatterns.com/patterns/messaging/toc.html`.

Building a messaging system

I think that the most suitable way to introduce main Spring Cloud Stream features is through the sample microservices-based system. We will lightly modify an architecture of the system that has been discussed in the previous chapters. Let me provide a short recall of that architecture. Our system is responsible for processing orders. It consists of four independent microservices. The `order-service` microservice first communicates with `product-service` in order to collect the details of the selected products, and then with `customer-service` to retrieve information about the customer and his accounts. Now, the orders sent to `order-service` will be processed asynchronously. There is still an exposed RESTful HTTP API endpoint for submitting new orders by the clients, but they are not processed by the application. It only saves new orders, sends it to a message broker, and then responds to the client that the order has been approved for processing. The main goal of the currently discussed example is to show a point-to-point communication, so the messages would be received by only one application, `account-service`. Here's a diagram that illustrates the sample system architecture:

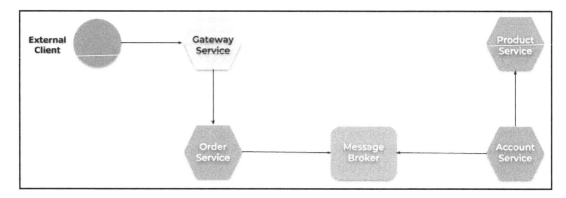

After receiving a new message, `account-service` calls the method exposed by `product-service` in order to find out its price. It withdraws money from the account and then sends back the response to `order-service` with the current order status. That message is also sent through the message broker. The `order-service` microservice receives the message and updates the order status. If the external client would like to check the current status order, it may call the endpoint exposing the `find` method with the order details. The sample application's source code is available on GitHub (`https://github.com/piomin/sample-spring-cloud-messaging.git`).

Enabling Spring Cloud Stream

The recommended way to include Spring Cloud Stream in the project is with a dependency management system. Spring Cloud Stream has an independent release trains management in relation to the whole Spring Cloud framework. However, if we have declared `spring-cloud-dependencies` in the `Edgware.RELEASE` version in the `dependencyManagement` section, we wouldn't have to declare anything else in `pom.xml`. If you prefer to use only the Spring Cloud Stream project, you should define the following section:

```
<dependencyManagement>
 <dependencies>
  <dependency>
   <groupId>org.springframework.cloud</groupId>
   <artifactId>spring-cloud-stream-dependencies</artifactId>
   <version>Ditmars.SR2</version>
   <type>pom</type>
   <scope>import</scope>
  </dependency>
 </dependencies>
</dependencyManagement>
```

The next step is to add `spring-cloud-stream` to the project dependencies. I also recommend you include at least the `spring-cloud-sleuth` library to provide sending messaging with the same `traceId` as the source request incoming to `order-service` via the Zuul gateway:

```
<dependency>
 <groupId>org.springframework.cloud</groupId>
 <artifactId>spring-cloud-stream</artifactId>
</dependency>
<dependency>
 <groupId>org.springframework.cloud</groupId>
 <artifactId>spring-cloud-sleuth</artifactId>
</dependency>
```

To enable connectivity to a message broker for your application, annotate the main class with `@EnableBinding`. The `@EnableBinding` annotation takes one or more interfaces as parameters. You may choose between three interfaces provided by Spring Cloud Stream:

- `Sink`: This is used for marking a service that receives messages from the inbound channel.
- `Source`: This is used for sending messages to the outbound channel.
- `Processor`: This can be used in case you need both an inbound channel and an outbound channel, as it extends the `Source` and `Sink` interfaces. Because `order-service` sends messages, as well as receives them, its main class has been annotated with `@EnableBinding(Processor.class)`.

Here's the main class of `order-service` that enables Spring Cloud Stream binding:

```
@SpringBootApplication
@EnableDiscoveryClient
@EnableBinding(Processor.class)
public class OrderApplication {

    public static void main(String[] args) {
        new
SpringApplicationBuilder(OrderApplication.class).web(true).run(args);
    }

}
```

Declaring and binding channels

Thanks to the use of Spring Integration, the application is independent from a message broker implementation included in the project. Spring Cloud Stream automatically detects and uses a binder found on the classpath. It means we may choose different types of middleware, and use it with the same code. All the middleware-specific settings can be overridden through external configuration properties in the form supported by Spring Boot, such as application arguments, environment variables, or just the `application.yml` file. As I have mentioned before, Spring Cloud Stream provides binder implementations for Kafka and Rabbit MQ. To include support for Kafka, you add the following dependency to the project:

```
<dependency>
  <groupId>org.springframework.cloud</groupId>
  <artifactId>spring-cloud-starter-stream-kafka</artifactId>
</dependency>
```

Personally, I prefer RabbitMQ, but in this chapter, we will create a sample for both RabbitMQ and Kafka. Since we have already discussed RabbitMQ's features, I'll begin with the samples based on RabbitMQ:

```
<dependency>
  <groupId>org.springframework.cloud</groupId>
  <artifactId>spring-cloud-starter-stream-rabbit</artifactId>
</dependency>
```

After enabling Spring Cloud Stream and including the binder implementation, we may create senders and listeners. Let's begin with the producer responsible for sending new order messages to the broker. This is implemented by `OrderSender` in `order-service`, which uses the `Output` bean for sending messages:

```
@Service
public class OrderSender {

    @Autowired
    private Source source;

    public boolean send(Order order) {
        return
this.source.output().send(MessageBuilder.withPayload(order).build());
    }

}
```

That bean is called by the controller, which exposes the HTTP method that allows submitting new orders:

```
@RestController
public class OrderController {

    private static final Logger LOGGER =
LoggerFactory.getLogger(OrderController.class);
    private ObjectMapper mapper = new ObjectMapper();

    @Autowired
    OrderRepository repository;
    @Autowired
    OrderSender sender;

    @PostMapping
    public Order process(@RequestBody Order order) throws
JsonProcessingException {
        Order o = repository.add(order);
        LOGGER.info("Order saved: {}", mapper.writeValueAsString(order));
```

```
        boolean isSent = sender.send(o);
        LOGGER.info("Order sent: {}",
mapper.writeValueAsString(Collections.singletonMap("isSent", isSent)));
        return o;
    }

}
```

The message with information about the order has been sent to message broker. Now, it should be received by `account-service`. To make this happen, we have to declare the receiver, which is listening for messages incoming to the queue created on the message broker. To receive the message with the order data, we just have to annotate the method that takes the `Order` object as a parameter with `@StreamListener`:

```
@SpringBootApplication
@EnableDiscoveryClient
@EnableBinding(Processor.class)
public class AccountApplication {

    @Autowired
    AccountService service;

    public static void main(String[] args) {
        new
SpringApplicationBuilder(AccountApplication.class).web(true).run(args);
    }

    @Bean
    @StreamListener(Processor.INPUT)
    public void receiveOrder(Order order) throws JsonProcessingException {
        service.process(order);
    }

}
```

Now you may launch the sample applications. But, there is one important detail that has not yet been mentioned. Both those applications try to connect with RabbitMQ running on localhost, and both of them treat the same exchanges as an input or output. It is a problem, since `order-service` sends the message to the output exchange, while `account-service` listens for messages incoming to its input exchange. These are different exchanges, but first things first. Let's begin with running a message broker.

Customizing connectivity with the RabbitMQ broker

We have already started the RabbitMQ broker using its Docker image in the previous chapters, so it is worth reminding ourselves of that command. It starts a standalone Docker container with RabbitMQ, available under port `5672`, and its UI web console, available under port `15672`:

```
docker run -d --name rabbit -p 15672:15672 -p 5672:5672 rabbitmq:management
```

The default RabbitMQ address should be overridden with the `spring.rabbit.*` properties inside the `application.yml` file:

```
spring:
  rabbitmq:
    host: 192.168.99.100
    port: 5672
```

By default, Spring Cloud Stream creates a topic exchange for communication. This type of exchange better suits the publish/subscribe interaction model. We may override it with the `exchangeType` property, as in the fragment of `application.yml`, as shown here:

```
spring:
  cloud:
    stream:
      rabbit:
        bindings:
          output:
            producer:
              exchangeType: direct
          input:
            consumer:
              exchangeType: direct
```

The same configuration settings should be provided for both `order-service` and `account-service`. You don't have to create any exchange manually. If it does not exist, it is automatically created by the application during startup. Otherwise, the application just binds to that exchange. By default, it creates exchanges with names input for the `@Input` channel, and output for the `@Output` channel. These names may be overridden with the `spring.cloud.stream.bindings.output.destination` and `spring.cloud.stream.bindings.input.destination` properties, where input and output are the names of the channels. This configuration option is not just a nice addition to the Spring Cloud Stream features, but the key setting used for correlating the input and output destinations in inter-service communication. The explanation for why that happens is very simple. In our example, `order-service` is the message source application, so it sends messages to the output channel. Then, on the other hand, `account-service` listens for incoming messages on the input channel. If the `order-service` output channel and `account-service` input channel do not refer to the same destination on the broker, the communication between them would fail. In conclusion, I decided to use a destination with the names `orders-out` and `orders-in`, and I have provided the following configuration for `order-service`:

```
spring:
 cloud:
  stream:
   bindings:
    output:
     destination: orders-out
    input:
     destination: orders-in
```

The similar configuration settings for `account-service` are reversed:

```
spring:
 cloud:
  stream:
   bindings:
    output:
     destination: orders-in
    input:
     destination: orders-out
```

After both applications start up, you may easily check out the list of exchanges declared on the RabbitMQ broker using its web management console, available at `http://192.168.99.100:15672` (`quest/guest`). The following the implicitly created exchanges, and you may see our two destinations created for the test purpose:

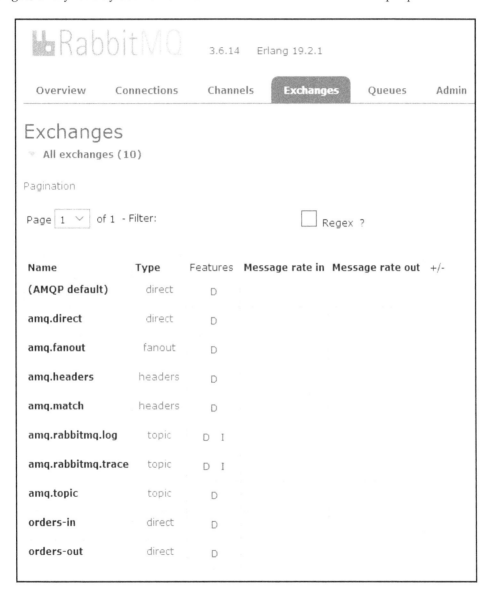

By default, Spring Cloud Stream provides one input and one output message channel. We may imagine a situation where our system would need more than one destination for each type of message channel. Let's move back to the sample system architecture for a moment, and consider the situation where every order is asynchronously processed by two other microservices. Until now, only `account-service` has been listening for incoming events from `order-service`. In the current sample, `product-service` would be the receiver of incoming orders. Its main goal in that scenario is to manage the number of available products and decrease them on the basis of order details. It requires us to define two input and output message channels inside `order-service`, because we still have point-to-point communication based on a direct RabbitMQ exchange, where each message may be processed by exactly one consumer.

In that case, we should declare two interfaces with `@Input` and `@Output` methods. Every method has to return a `channel` object. Spring Cloud Stream provides two bindable message components—`MessageChannel` for an outbound communication, and its extension, `SubscribableChannel`, for an inbound communication. Here's the interface definition for interaction with `product-service`. The analogous interface has been created for messaging with `account-service`:

```
public interface ProductOrder {

    @Input
    SubscribableChannel productOrdersIn();

    @Output
    MessageChannel productOrdersOut();
}
```

The next step is to activate the declared components for the application by annotating its main class with `@EnableBinding(value={AccountOrder.class, ProductOrder.class}`. Now, you may refer to these channels in the configuration properties using their names, for example, `spring.cloud.stream.bindings.productOrdersOut.destination=product-orders-in`. Each channel name may be customized by specifying a channel name when using the `@Input` and `@Output` annotations, as shown in the following example:

```
public interface ProductOrder {

    @Input("productOrdersIn")
    SubscribableChannel ordersIn();

    @Output("productOrdersOut")
    MessageChannel ordersOut();
```

```
}
```

Based on the custom interfaces declaration, Spring Cloud Stream will generate a bean that implements that interface. However, it still has to be accessed in the bean responsible for sending the message. In comparison with the previous sample, it would be more comfortable to inject bound channels directly. Here's the current product order sender's bean implementation. There is also a similar implementation of the bean, which sends messages to `account-service`:

```
@Service
public class ProductOrderSender {

    @Autowired
    private MessageChannel output;
    @Autowired
    public SendingBean(@Qualifier("productOrdersOut") MessageChannel
output) {
        this.output = output;
    }

    public boolean send(Order order) {
        return this.output.send(MessageBuilder.withPayload(order).build());
    }

}
```

Every message-channel custom interface should also be provided for the target service. The listener should be bound to the right message channel and the destination on the message broker:

```
@StreamListener(ProductOrder.INPUT)
public void receiveOrder(Order order) throws JsonProcessingException {
    service.process(order);
}
```

Integration with other Spring Cloud projects

You have probably noticed that the sample system mixes different styles of inter-service communication. There are some microservices that use typical RESTful HTTP API, and some others that use the message broker. There are also no objections to mixing different styles of communication inside a single application. You may, for example, include `spring-cloud-starter-feign` to the project with Spring Cloud Stream, and enable it with the `@EnableFeignClients` annotation. In our sample system, those two different styles of communication combine `account-service`, which integrates with `order-service` via the message broker, and with `product-service` through the REST API. Here's the Feign client's `product-service` implementation inside the `account-service` module:

```
@FeignClient(name = "product-service")
public interface ProductClient {
    @PostMapping("/ids")
    List<Product> findByIds(@RequestBody List<Long> ids);
}
```

There is other good news. Thanks to Spring Cloud Sleuth, all the messages exchanged during a single request incoming to the system via a gateway have the same `traceId`. Whether it is synchronous REST communication, or asynchronous messaging, you may easily track and correlate the logs between microservices using standard log files, or log aggregator tools such as Elastic Stack.

I think now is a good time to run and test our sample system. First, we have to build the whole project with the `mvn clean install` command. To access the code sample with two microservices listening for messages on two different exchanges, you should switch to the `advanced` branch (`https://github.com/piomin/sample-spring-cloud-messaging/tree/advanced`). You should launch all the applications available there—gateway, discovery, and the three microservices (`account-service`, `order-service`, `product-service`). The currently discussed case assumes we have also started RabbitMQ, Logstash, Elasticsearch, and Kibana using its Docker container. For detailed instructions on how to run Elastic Stack locally using Docker images, refer to Chapter 9, *Distributed Logging and Tracing*. The following diagram shows the architecture of the system in detail:

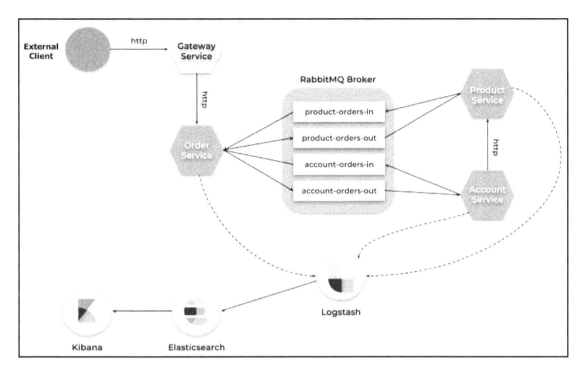

After running all the required applications and tools, we may proceed to the tests. Here's the sample request, which can be sent to the order-service via the API gateway:

```
curl -H "Content-Type: application/json" -X POST -d
'{"customerId":1,"productIds":[1,3,4],"status":"NEW"}'
http://localhost:8080/api/order
```

When I run the test for the first time with the applications configured following the description in the previous sections, it doesn't work. I can understand that some of you may be confused a little, because generally it was tested on the default settings. To make it run properly, I also have to add the following property in `application.yml`: `spring.cloud.stream.rabbit.bindings.output.producer.routingKeyExpression: '"#"'`. It sets the default producer's routing key to conform with the exchange's routing key automatically created during the application boot. In the following screenshot, you may see one of the output exchange definitions:

After the modification described previously, the test should be concluded successfully. The logs printed by the microservices are correlated with each other by `traceId`. I modified the default Sleuth logging format in `logback-spring.xml` a little, and that's how it is configured now—`%d{HH:mm:ss.SSS} %-5level [%X{X-B3-TraceId:-},%X{X-B3-SpanId:-}] %msg%n`. After sending the test request `order-service` test request, log the following information:

```
12:34:48.696 INFO [68038cdd653f7b0b, 68038cdd653f7b0b] Order saved:
{"id":1,"status":"NEW","price":0,"customerId":1,"accountId":null,"productId
s":[1,3,4]}
12:34:49.821 INFO [68038cdd653f7b0b, 68038cdd653f7b0b] Order sent:
{"isSent":true}
```

As you can see, `account-service` also uses the same logging format and prints the same `traceId` as `order-service`:

```
12:34:50.079 INFO [68038cdd653f7b0b, 23432d962ec92f7a] Order processed:
{"id":1,"status":"NEW","price":0,"customerId":1,"accountId":null,"productId
s":[1,3,4]}
12:34:50.332 INFO [68038cdd653f7b0b, 23432d962ec92f7a] Account found:
{"id":1,"number":"1234567890","balance":50000,"customerId":1}
12:34:52.344 INFO [68038cdd653f7b0b, 23432d962ec92f7a] Products found:
[{"id":1,"name":"Test1","price":1000},{"id":3,"name":"Test3","price":2000},
{"id":4,"name":"Test4","price":3000}]
```

All the logs generated during the single transaction can be aggregated using Elastic Stack. You may filter the entries by the `X-B3-TraceId` field, for example, `9da1e5c83094390d`:

The publish/subscribe model

The main motivation for creating a Spring Cloud Stream project is, in fact, support for a persistent publish/subscribe model. In the previous sections, we have discussed point-to-point communication between microservices, which is just an additional feature. However, the programming model is still the same, irrespective of whether we decided to use a point-to-point or publish/subscribe model.

In publish/subscribe communication, the data is broadcast through shared topics. It reduces the complexity of both the producer and the consumer, and allows new applications to be easily added to the existing topology without any changes in flow. This can be clearly seen in the last-presented sample of the system, where we decided to add the second application that has consumed events produced by the source microservice. In comparison to the initial architecture, we had to define custom message channels dedicated for each of the target applications. With direct communication through queues, the message can be consumed by only one application instance, so as such, the solution was necessary. The uses of the publish/subscribe model simplify that architecture.

Running a sample system

The development of the sample application is simpler for the publish/subscribe model than for point-to-point communication. We don't have to override any default message channels to enable interaction with more than one receiver. In comparison with the initial sample that has illustrated messaging to a single target application (`account-service`), we only need to modify configuration settings a little. Because Spring Cloud Stream, by default, binds to the topic, we don't have to override `exchangeType` for the input message channel. As you may see in the configuration fragment that follows, we still use point-to-point communication when sending the response to `order-service`. If we really think about it, that makes sense. The `order-service` microservice sends the message that has to be received by both `account-service` and `product-service`, while the response from them is addressed only to `order-service`:

```
spring:
  application:
    name: product-service
  rabbitmq:
    host: 192.168.99.100
    port: 5672
  cloud:
    stream:
      bindings:
```

```
  output:
    destination: orders-in
  input:
    destination: orders-out
rabbit:
  bindings:
    output:
      producer:
        exchangeType: direct
        routingKeyExpression: '"#"'
```

The logic of the main processing method of product-service is really simple. It just has to find all the productIds from the received order, change the number of stored products for every one of them, and then send the response to order-service:

```
@Autowired
ProductRepository productRepository;
@Autowired
OrderSender orderSender;

public void process(final Order order) throws JsonProcessingException {
  LOGGER.info("Order processed: {}", mapper.writeValueAsString(order));
  for (Long productId : order.getProductIds()) {
      Product product = productRepository.findById(productId);
      if (product.getCount() == 0) {
          order.setStatus(OrderStatus.REJECTED);
          break;
      }
      product.setCount(product.getCount() - 1);
      productRepository.update(product);
      LOGGER.info("Product updated: {}",
mapper.writeValueAsString(product));
  }
  if (order.getStatus() != OrderStatus.REJECTED) {
      order.setStatus(OrderStatus.ACCEPTED);
  }
  LOGGER.info("Order response sent: {}",
mapper.writeValueAsString(Collections.singletonMap("status",
order.getStatus())));
  orderSender.send(order);
}
```

To access the current sample, you just have to switch to the `publish_subscribe` branch, available at `https://github.com/piomin/sample-spring-cloud-messaging/tree/publish_subscribe`. Then, you should build the parent project and run all the services as for the previous sample. If you would like to test it all works fine until you have only one running instance of `account-service` and `product-service`. Let's discuss that problem.

Scaling and grouping

When talking about microservice-based architecture, scalability is always presented as one of its main advantages. The ability to scale up the system by creating multiple instances of a given application is very important. When doing this, different instances of an application are placed in a competing consumer relationship, where only one of the instances is expected to handle a given message. For point-to-point communication, it is not a problem, but in a publish-subscribe model, where the message is consumed by all the receivers, it may be a challenge.

Running multiple instances

Availability for scaling up the number of microservice's instances is one of the main concepts around Spring Cloud Stream. However, there is no magic behind this idea. Running multiple instances of an application is very easy with Spring Cloud Stream. One of the reasons for this is native support from message brokers, which is designed to handle many consumers and huge amounts of traffic.

In our case, all the messaging microservices also expose the RESTful HTTP API, so first, we have to customize the server port per instance. We have performed such operations before. We may also consider setting two Spring Cloud Stream properties, `spring.cloud.stream.instanceCount` and `spring.cloud.stream.instanceIndex`. Thanks to them, every instance of the microservice is able to receive information about how many other examples of the same application are started and what is its own instance index. The correct configuration of these properties is required only if you would like to enable the partitioning feature. I'll talk about this mechanism more in a moment. Now, let's take a look at the configuration settings of the scaled-up applications. Both `account-service` and `product-service` define two profiles for the purpose of running multiple instances of the application. We have customized there an HTTP port of the server, number, and an index of the instance:

```
---
spring:
 profiles: instance1
```

```
cloud:
  stream:
    instanceCount: 2
    instanceIndex: 0
server:
  port: ${PORT:8091}

---

spring:
  profiles: instance2
  cloud:
    stream:
      instanceCount: 2
      instanceIndex: 1
server:
  port: ${PORT:9091}
```

After building the parent project, you may run two instances of the application. Each of them is initialized with properties assigned to the right profile passed during startup, for example, `java -jar --spring.profiles.active=instance1 target/account-service-1.0-SNAPSHOT.jar`. If you send a test request to the `order-service` endpoint `POST /`, the new order would be forwarded to the RabbitMQ topic exchange in order to be received by both the `account-service` and `product-service`, which are connected to that exchange. The problem is that the message is received by all the instances of each service, which is not exactly what we wanted to achieve. Here, a grouping mechanism comes with help.

Consumer groups

Our purpose is clear. We have many microservices that consume messages from the same topic. Different instances of an application are placed in a competing consumer relationship, but only one of them should handle a given message. Spring Cloud Stream introduces the concept of a consumer group that models this behavior. To activate such a behavior, we should set a property called `spring.cloud.stream.bindings.<channelName>.group`, with a group name. After setting it, all groups that subscribe to a given destination receive a copy of the published data, but only one member of each group receives and handles a message from that destination. In our case, there are two groups. First, for all the `account-service` instances with a name account, and second, for a `product-service` with a name product.

Here's the current binding configuration for `account-service`. The `orders-in` destination is a queue created for direct communication with `order-service`, so only `orders-out` is grouped by service name. An analogous configuration has been prepared for `product-service`:

```
spring:
  cloud:
    stream:
      bindings:
        output:
          destination: orders-in
        input:
          destination: orders-out
          group: account
```

The first difference is visible in the names of queues automatically created for the RabbitMQ exchange. Now, it is not a randomly generated name, such as `orders-in.anonymous.qNxjzDq5Qra-yqHLUv50PQ`, but a determined string consisting of the destination and group name. The following screenshot shows all the queues currently existing on RabbitMQ:

Overview			Messages			Message rates		
Name	Features	State	Ready	Unacked	Total	incoming	deliver / get	ack
orders-in.anonymous.qNxjzDq5Qra-yqHLUv50PQ	AD Excl	idle	24	1	25	2.6/s	0.20/s	0.00/s
orders-out.account	D	running	11	2	13	0.20/s	2.4/s	2.4/s
orders-out.product	D	idle	0	0	0	0.20/s	0.20/s	0.20/s

You may perform the retest by yourself to verify if the message is received by only one application in the same group. However, you have no confidence which instance would handle the incoming message. In order to determine this, you can use a partitioning mechanism.

Partitioning

Spring Cloud Stream provides support for partitioning data between multiple instances of an application. In the typical use case, the destination is viewed as being divided into different partitions. Each producer, when sending messages received by multiple consumer instances, ensures that data is identified by configured fields to force processing by the same consumer instance.

To enable the partitioning feature for your application, you have to define the `partitionKeyExpression` or `partitionKeyExtractorClass` properties, and `partitionCount` in the producer configuration settings. Here's the sample configuration that may be provided for your application:

```
spring.cloud.stream.bindings.output.producer.partitionKeyExpression=payload
.customerId
spring.cloud.stream.bindings.output.producer.partitionCount=2
```

Partitioning mechanisms also require setting of the `spring.cloud.stream.instanceCount` and `spring.cloud.stream.instanceIndex` properties on the consumer side. It also has to be explicitly enabled with the `spring.cloud.stream.bindings.input.consumer.partitioned` property set to `true`. The instance index is responsible for identifying the unique partition from which a particular instance receives data. Generally, `partitionCount` on the producer side and `instanceCount` on the consumer side should be equal.

Let me familiarize you with the partitioning mechanism provided by Spring Cloud Stream. First, it calculates a partition key based on `partitionKeyExpression`, which is evaluated against the outbound message or implementation of the `PartitionKeyExtractorStrategy` interface, which defines the algorithm for extracting the key for the message. Once the message key is calculated, the target partition is determined as a value between zero and `partitionCount` - `1`. The default calculation formula is `key.hashCode()` % `partitionCount`. It can be customized with the `partitionSelectorExpression` property, or by creating an implementation of the `org.springframework.cloud.stream.binder.PartitionSelectorStrategy` interface. The calculated key is matched with `instanceIndex` on the consumer side.

I think that the main concept around partitioning has been explained. Let's proceed to the sample. Here's the current configuration of the input channel for `product-service` (the same as with the account group name set for `account-service`):

```
spring:
  cloud:
    stream:
      bindings:
        input:
          consumer:
            partitioned: true
          destination: orders-out
          group: product
```

We have two running instances of each microservice that consumes data from the topic exchange. There are also two partitions set for the producer within `order-service`. The message key is calculated based on the `customerId` field from the `Order` object. The partition with index `0` is dedicated for orders having an even number in the `customerId` field, while the partition with index `1` is for odd numbers in the `customerId` field.

In fact, RabbitMQ does not have native support for partitioning. It is interesting how Spring Cloud Stream implements the partitioning process with RabbitMQ. Here's a screenshot that illustrates the list of bindings for exchanges created in RabbitMQ. As you may see, there are two routing keys that have been defined for the exchange—`orders-out-0` and `orders-out-1`:

If you send an order with `customerId` equal to 1 in a JSON message, for example, `{"customerId": 1,"productIds": [4],"status": "NEW"}`, it would always be processed by an instance with `instanceIndex=1`. It may be checked out in the application logs or by using the RabbitMQ web console. Here's a diagram with the message rates for each queue, where the message with `customerId=1` has been sent several times:

Overview			Messages			Message rates		
Name	Features	State	Ready	Unacked	Total	incoming	deliver / get	ack
orders-in.anonymous.IoLFDyEMTZCsMI2R7-ac9Q	AD Excl	running	44	1	45	8.8/s	0.40/s	0.00/s
orders-out.account-0	D	idle	0	0	0			
orders-out.account-1	D	running	0	0	0	4.4/s	4.4/s	4.4/s
orders-out.product-0	D	idle	0	0	0			
orders-out.product-1	D	running	0	0	0	4.4/s	4.4/s	4.4/s

Configuration options

Spring Cloud Stream configuration settings may be overridden using any mechanism supported by Spring Boot, such as application arguments, environment variables, and YAML or property files. It defines a number of generic configuration options that may be applied to all binders. However, there are also some additional properties specific for a particular message broker used by the application.

Spring Cloud Stream properties

The current group of properties applies to the whole Spring Cloud Stream application. All the following properties are prefixed with `spring.cloud.stream`:

Name	Default value	Description
`instanceCount`	1	**The number of running instances of an application. For more details, refer to the** *Scaling and grouping* **section.**
`instanceIndex`	0	The index of the instance of the application. For more details, also refer to the *Scaling and grouping* section.

Name	Default value	Description
`dynamicDestinations`	-	A list of destinations that can be bound dynamically.
`defaultBinder`	-	The default binder in case there are multiple binders defined. For more details, also refer to the *Multiple binders* section.
`overrideCloudConnectors`	false	This is used only if the cloud is active and Spring Cloud Connectors is found on the classpath. When it is set to `true`, binders completely ignore the bound services and rely on the `spring.rabbitmq.*` or `spring.kafka.*` Spring Boot properties.

Binding properties

The next group of properties is related to a message channel. In Spring Cloud nomenclature, these are binding properties. They may be assigned only to a consumer, a producer, or to both simultaneously. Here is a list of the properties, along with their default value and a description:

Name	Default value	Description
`destination`	-	The target destination name on the broker configured for the message channel. It can be specified as a comma-separated list of destinations if the channel is used by only one consumer.
`group`	null	The consumer group of the channel. See the *Scaling and grouping* section for more details.
`contentType`	null	The content type of messages exchanged via a given channel. We may set it, for example, to `application/json`. Then all the objects sent from that application would be automatically converted to a JSON string.
`binder`	null	The default binder used by the channel. See the *Multiple binders* section for more details.

The consumer

The following list of properties is available for input bindings only, and must be prefixed with `spring.cloud.stream.bindings.<channelName>.consumer`. I'll indicate just the most important of them:

Name	Default value	Description
concurrency	1	**Number of consumers per single input channel**
partitioned	false	It enables receiving data from a partitioned producer
headerMode	embeddedHeaders	If it is set to `raw`, header parsing on input is disabled
maxAttempts	3	Number of retries if message processing fails. Setting this option to 1 disables the retry mechanism

The producer

The following binding properties are available for output bindings only, and must be prefixed with `spring.cloud.stream.bindings.<channelName>.producer`. I'll also indicate only the most important of them:

Name	Default value	Description
requiredGroups	-	A comma-separated list of groups that must be created on the message broker
headerMode	embeddedHeaders	If it is set to `raw`, header parsing on input is disabled
useNativeEncoding	false	If it is set to `true`, the outbound message is serialized directly by the client library
errorChannelEnabled	false	If it is set to `true`, failure messages are sent to the error channel for the destination

The advanced programming model

The basics around the Spring Cloud Stream programming model have been presented together with samples of point-to-point and publish/subscribe communication. Let's discuss some more advanced example features.

Producing messages

In all the samples presented in this chapter, we have sent orders through RESTful API for testing purposes. However, we may easily create some test data by defining the message source inside the application. Here's a bean that generates one message per second using `@Poller` and sends it to the output channel:

```
@Bean
@InboundChannelAdapter(value = Source.OUTPUT, poller = @Poller(fixedDelay =
"1000", maxMessagesPerPoll = "1"))
public MessageSource<Order> ordersSource() {
    Random r = new Random();
    return () -> new GenericMessage<>(new Order(OrderStatus.NEW, (long)
r.nextInt(5), Collections.singletonList((long) r.nextInt(10))));
}
```

Transformation

As you probably remember, `account-service` and `product-service` have been receiving events from `order-service` and then sending back the response message. We have created the `OrderSender` bean, which was responsible for preparing the response payload and sending it to the output channel. It turns out that the implementation may be simpler if we return the response object in method and annotate it with `@SentTo`:

```
@StreamListener(Processor.INPUT)
@SendTo(Processor.OUTPUT)
public Order receiveAndSendOrder(Order order) throws
JsonProcessingException {
    LOGGER.info("Order received: {}", mapper.writeValueAsString(order));
    return service.process(order);
}
```

We can even imagine such an implementation, such as the following, without using `@StreamListener`. The transformer pattern is responsible for changing the object's form. In that case, it modifies two `order` fields—`status` and `price`:

```
@EnableBinding(Processor.class)
public class OrderProcessor {

    @Transformer(inputChannel = Processor.INPUT, outputChannel =
Processor.OUTPUT)
    public Order process(final Order order) throws JsonProcessingException
{
        LOGGER.info("Order processed: {}",
```

```
mapper.writeValueAsString(order));
        // ...
        products.forEach(p -> order.setPrice(order.getPrice() +
p.getPrice()));
        if (order.getPrice() <= account.getBalance()) {
            order.setStatus(OrderStatus.ACCEPTED);
            account.setBalance(account.getBalance() - order.getPrice());
        } else {
            order.setStatus(OrderStatus.REJECTED);
        }
        return order;
    }

}
```

Consuming messages conditionally

Assuming we would like to treat messages incoming to the same message channel differently, we may use conditional dispatching. Spring Cloud Stream supports dispatching messages to multiple `@StreamListener` methods registered on an input channel, based on a condition. That condition is a **Spring Expression Language (SpEL)** expression defined in the `condition` attribute of the `@StreamListener` annotation:

```
public boolean send(Order order) {
    Message<Order> orderMessage =
MessageBuilder.withPayload(order).build();
    orderMessage.getHeaders().put("processor", "account");
    return this.source.output().send(orderMessage);
}
```

Here's the sample implementation that defines two methods annotated with `@StreamListener` that listen on the same topic. One of them is dedicated only for messages incoming from `account-service`, while the second is dedicated only for `product-service`. The incoming message is dispatched, based on its header with the `processor` name:

```
@SpringBootApplication
@EnableDiscoveryClient
@EnableBinding(Processor.class)
public class OrderApplication {

    @StreamListener(target = Processor.INPUT, condition =
"headers['processor']=='account'")
    public void receiveOrder(Order order) throws JsonProcessingException {
```

```
        LOGGER.info("Order received from account: {}",
    mapper.writeValueAsString(order));
        // ...
    }

    @StreamListener(target = Processor.INPUT, condition =
    "headers['processor']=='product'")
    public void receiveOrder(Order order) throws JsonProcessingException {
        LOGGER.info("Order received from product: {}",
    mapper.writeValueAsString(order));
        // ...
    }

}
```

Using Apache Kafka

I have mentioned Apache Kafka a couple of times when discussing Spring Cloud integration with message brokers. However, until now, we haven't run any samples based on that platform. The fact is that RabbitMQ tends to be the preferred choice when working with Spring Cloud projects, but Kafka is also worthy of our attention. One of its advantages over RabbitMQ is native support for partitioning, which is one of the most important features of Spring Cloud Stream.

Kafka is not a typical message broker. It is rather a distributed streaming platform. Its main feature is to allow you to publish and subscribe to streams of records. It is especially useful for real-time streaming applications that transform or react to streams of data. It is usually run as a cluster consisting of one or more servers, and stores streams of records in topics.

Running Kafka

Unfortunately, there is no official Docker image with Apache Kafka. However, we may use one that is unofficial, for example, that shared by Spotify. In comparison to other available Kafka docker images, this one runs both Zookeeper and Kafka in the same container. Here's the Docker command that launches Kafka and exposes it on port 9092. Zookeeper is also available outside on port 2181:

```
docker run -d --name kafka -p 2181:2181 -p 9092:9092 --env
ADVERTISED_HOST=192.168.99.100 --env ADVERTISED_PORT=9092 spotify/kafka
```

Customizing application settings

To enable Apache Kafka for the application, include the `spring-cloud-starter-stream-kafka` starter to the dependencies. Our current sample is very similar to to the sample of publish/subscribe using with RabbitMQ publish/subscribe with grouping and partitioning presented in *The publish/subscribe model*, section. The only difference is in the dependencies and configuration settings.

Spring Cloud Stream automatically detects and uses a binder found on the classpath. The connection settings may be overridden with `spring.kafka.*` properties. In our case, we just need to change the auto-configured Kafka client address to the Docker machine address `192.168.99.100`. The same modification should be performed for Zookeeper, which is used by the Kafka client:

```
spring:
 application:
  name: order-service
  kafka:
   bootstrap-servers: 192.168.99.100:9092
 cloud:
  stream:
   bindings:
    output:
     destination: orders-out
     producer:
      partitionKeyExpression: payload.customerId
      partitionCount: 2
    input:
     destination: orders-in
   kafka:
    binder:
     zkNodes: 192.168.99.100
```

After starting discovery, gateway, and all the required instances of microservices, you can perform the same tests as for the previous samples. If everything is configured correctly, you should see the following fragment in the logs during your application boot. The result of the tests is exactly the same as for the sample based on RabbitMQ:

```
16:58:30.008 INFO [,] Discovered coordinator 192.168.99.100:9092 (id:
2147483647 rack: null) for group account.
16:58:30.038 INFO [,] Successfully joined group account with generation 1
16:58:30.039 INFO [,] Setting newly assigned partitions [orders-out-0,
orders-out-1] for group account
16:58:30.081 INFO [,] partitions assigned:[orders-out-0, orders-out-1]
```

Kafka Streams API support

Spring Cloud Stream Kafka provides a binder specially designed for Kafka Streams binding. With this binder, the application can leverage the Kafka Streams API. To enable such a feature for your application, include the following dependency to your project:

```
<dependency>
 <groupId>org.springframework.cloud</groupId>
 <artifactId>spring-cloud-stream-binder-kstream</artifactId>
</dependency>
```

The Kafka Streams API provides high-level stream DSL. It may be accessed by declaring the `@StreamListener` method that takes the `KStream` interface as a parameter. KStream provides some useful methods for stream manipulation, well-known from other streaming APIs such as `map`, `flatMap`, `join`, or `filter`. There are also some other methods specific to Kafka Stream, such as `to(...)` (for sending streams to a topic) or `through(...)` (same as `to`, but also creates a new instance of `KStream` from the topic):

```
@SpringBootApplication
@EnableBinding(KStreamProcessor.class)
public class AccountApplication {

    @StreamListener("input")
    @SendTo("output")
    public KStream<?, Order> process(KStream<?, Order> input) {
        // ..
    }

    public static void main(String[] args) {
        SpringApplication.run(AccountApplication.class, args);
    }

}
```

Configuration properties

Some of the Spring Cloud configuration settings for Kafka have been presented before when discussing the implementation of the sample application. Here's a table with the most important properties, which can be set for customizing the Apache Kafka binder. All these properties are prefixed by `spring.cloud.stream.kafka.binder`:

Name	Default value	Description
brokers	localhost	**A comma-separated list of brokers with or without port information.**
defaultBrokerPort	9092	It sets the default port if no port is defined using the brokers property.
zkNodes	localhost	A comma-separated list of ZooKeeper nodes with or without port information.
defaultZkPort	2181	It sets the default ZooKeeper port if no port is defined using the zkNodes property.
configuration	-	A Key/Value map of Kafka client properties. It applies to all the clients created by the binder.
headers	-	The list of custom headers that will be forwarded by the binder.
autoCreateTopics	true	If set to true, the binder creates new topics automatically.
autoAddPartitions	false	If set to true, the binder creates new partitions automatically.

Multiple binders

In Spring Cloud Stream nomenclature, the interface that may be implemented to provide connection to physical destinations at the external middleware is called **binder**. Currently, there are two available built-in binder implementations—Kafka and RabbitMQ. In case you would like to provide a custom binder library, the key interface that is an abstraction for a strategy for connecting inputs and outputs to external middleware is Binder, having two methods—bindConsumer and bindProducer. For more details, you may refer to the Spring Cloud Stream specifications.

The important thing for us is an ability to use multiple binders in a single application. You can even mix different implementations, for example, RabbitMQ with Kafka. Spring Cloud Stream relies on Spring Boot's auto-configuration in the binding process. The implementation available on the classpath is used automatically. In case you would like to use both the default Binders, include the following dependencies to the project:

```
<dependency>
  <groupId>org.springframework.cloud</groupId>
  <artifactId>spring-cloud-stream-binder-rabbit</artifactId>
```

```
</dependency>
<dependency>
 <groupId>org.springframework.cloud</groupId>
 <artifactId>spring-cloud-stream-binder-kafka</artifactId>
</dependency>
```

If more than one binder has been found in the classpath, the application must detect which of them should be used for the particular channel binding. We may configure the default binder globally with the `spring.cloud.stream.defaultBinder` property, or individually per each channel with the `spring.cloud.stream.bindings.<channelName>.binder` property. Now, we go back for a moment to our sample to configure multiple binders there. We define RabbitMQ for direct communication between `account-service` and `order-service`, and Kafka for the publish/subscribe model between `order-service` and other microservices.

Here's the equivalent configuration to that provided for `account-service` in the `publish_subscribe` branch (`https://github.com/piomin/sample-spring-cloud-messaging/tree/publish_subscribe`), but based on two different binders:

```
spring:
 cloud:
  stream:
   bindings:
    output:
     destination: orders-in
     binder: rabbit1
    input:
     consumer:
      partitioned: true
     destination: orders-out
     binder: kafka1
     group: account
   rabbit:
    bindings:
     output:
      producer:
       exchangeType: direct
       routingKeyExpression: '"#"'
   binders:
    rabbit1:
     type: rabbit
     environment:
      spring:
       rabbitmq:
        host: 192.168.99.100
    kafka1:
```

```
type: kafka
environment:
 spring:
  kafka:
   bootstrap-servers: 192.168.99.100:9092
```

Summary

Spring Cloud Stream can be treated as a separate category in comparison to all the other Spring Cloud projects. It is often being associated with other projects, and which are currently strongly promoted by Pivotal Spring Cloud Data Flow. That is a toolkit for building data integration and real-time data processing pipelines. However, it is a huge subject and rather a topic of discussion for a separate book.

More to the point, Spring Cloud Stream provides support for asynchronous messaging, which may be easily implemented using a Spring annotation style. I think that for some of you, that style of inter-service communication is not as obvious as the RESTful API model. Therefore, I have focused on showing you the examples of point-to-point and publish/subscribe communication using Spring Cloud Stream. I have also described the differences between those two styles of messaging.

The publish/subscribe model is nothing new, but thanks to Spring Cloud Stream, it may be easily included to the microservice-based system. Some of the key concepts, such as consumer groups or partitioning, have also been described in this chapter. After reading it, you should be able to implement microservices based on the messaging model, and integrate them with other Spring Cloud libraries in order to provide logging, tracing, or just deploying them as part of the existing, REST-based microservices system.

12
Securing an API

Security is one of the most commonly discussed problems related to microservices-based architecture. There is always one main problem for all security concerns—a network. With microservices, where typically there is much more communication over the network than there is for monolithic applications, the approach to authentication and authorization should be reconsidered. Traditional systems are usually secured at the border and then allow the frontend service full access to the backend components. The migration to microservices forces us to change this approach to delegated-access management.

How does Spring Framework address the security concerns of microservices-based architecture? It provides several projects that implement different patterns regarding authentication and authorization. The first of these is Spring Security, which is a de facto standard for secure Spring-based Java applications. It consists of a few submodules that help you get started with SAML, OAuth2, or Kerberos. There is also the Spring Cloud Security project. It provides several components that allow you to integrate basic Spring Security features with the main elements of microservices architecture, such as gateways, load balancers, and REST HTTP clients.

In this chapter, I'm going to show you how to secure all the main components of your microservices-based system. I will describe the particular elements relevant to the topic in the order of the chapters that compose the second part of this book. So, we would begin from service discovery with Eureka, then move on to the Spring Cloud Config Server and inter-service communication, and then finally discuss API gateway security.

Here's what we will look at in this chapter:

- Configuring a secure connection for a single Spring Boot application
- Enabling HTTPS communication for the most important elements of microservice-based architecture
- Encrypting and decrypting property values in configuration files stored on Config Server

- Simple in-memory based authentication with OAuth2 for microservices
- More advanced OAuth2 configuration with JDBC backend store and JWT tokens
- Using OAuth2 authorization in inter-service communication with Feign client

But first, let's begin with the basics. I'll show you how to create your first secure microservice that exposes an API over HTTPS.

Enabling HTTPS for Spring Boot

If you want to use SSL and serve your RESTful APIs over HTTPS, you will need to generate a certificate. The fastest way to achieve this is through a self-signed certificate, which is enough for development mode. JRE provides a simple tool for certificate management—`keytool`. It is available under your `JRE_HOME\bin` directory. The command in the following code generates a self-signed certificate and puts it into the PKCS12 KeyStore. Besides KeyStore's type, you will also have to set its validity, alias, and the name of the file. Before starting the generation process, `keytool` will ask you for your password and some additional information, as follows:

```
keytool -genkeypair -alias account-key -keyalg RSA -keysize 2048 -storetype
PKCS12 -keystore account-key.p12 -validity 3650

Enter keystore password:
Re-enter new password:
What is your first and last name?
 [Unknown]: localhost
What is the name of your organizational unit?
 [Unknown]: =
What is the name of your organization?
 [Unknown]: piomin
What is the name of your City or Locality?
 [Unknown]: Warsaw
What is the name of your State or Province?
 [Unknown]: mazowieckie
What is the two-letter country code for this unit?
 [Unknown]: PL
Is CN=localhost, OU=Unknown, O=piomin, L=Warsaw, ST=mazowieckie, C=PL
correct?
 [no]: yes
```

I have copied the generated certificate into the `src/main/resources` directory inside the Spring Boot application. After building and running the application, it will be available on the classpath. To enable SSL, we have to provide some configuration settings in the `application.yml` file. SSL can be customized for Spring by setting the various `server.ssl.*` properties:

```
server:
 port: ${PORT:8090}

ssl:
 key-store: classpath:account-key.p12
 key-store-password: 123456
 key-store-type: PKCS12
 key-alias: account-key

security:
 require-ssl: true
```

Secure discovery

As you can see, the configuration of SSL for a microservice application is not a very hard task. However, it is time to increase the difficulty level. We have already launched a single microservice that serves a RESTful API over HTTPS. Now we want that microservice to integrate with the discovery server. There are two problems that arise from this. The first of these is the need to publish information about the secure microservice's instance in Eureka. The second of these concerns exposing Eureka over HTTPS and forcing the discovery client to authenticate against a discovery server using a private key. Let's discuss these issues in detail.

Registering a secure application

If your application is exposed over a secure SSL port, you should change two flags from the `EurekaInstanceConfig`—`nonSecurePortEnabled` to `false` and `securePortEnabled` to `true`. This forces Eureka to publish instance information that shows an explicit preference for secure communication. The Spring Cloud `DiscoveryClient` will always return a URL starting with HTTPS for a service that is configured this way, and the Eureka instance information will have a secure health check URL:

```
eureka:
 instance:
  nonSecurePortEnabled: false
```

```
securePortEnabled: true
securePort: ${PORT:8091}
statusPageUrl: https://localhost:${eureka.instance.securePort}/info
healthCheckUrl: https://localhost:${eureka.instance.securePort}/health
homePageUrl: https://localhost:${eureka.instance.securePort}
```

Serving Eureka over HTTPS

When the Eureka server starts with Spring Boot, it is deployed on an embedded Tomcat container, so the SSL configuration is the same as for the standard microservice. The difference is that we must take account of the client-side application, which establishes a secure connection with a discovery server over HTTPS. The discovery client should authenticate itself against the Eureka server and it should also verify the server's certificate. That communication process between client and server is called **two-way SSL** or **mutual authentication**. There is also one-way authentication, which is in fact the default option, where only the client validates the server's public key. Java applications use KeyStore and trustStore for storing private keys and certificates corresponding to public keys. The only difference between trustStore and KeyStore is what they store and for what purpose. When an SSL handshake between client and server is performed, a trustStore is used to verify the credentials, while a KeyStore is used to provide credentials. So in other words, a KeyStore keeps a private key and certificate for a given application, while a trustStore keeps the certificates that are used to identify it from the third party. Developers often do not pay much attention to those terms when configuring a secure connection, but a proper understanding of them helps you to easily understand what will happen next.

In a typical microservices-based architecture, there are plenty of independent applications and a single discovery server. Every application has its own private key stored in a KeyStore and a certificate corresponding to a discovery server's public key in a trustStore. On the other hand, the server keeps all the certificates generated for the client-side applications. That's enough theory for now. Let's take a look at the following figure. It illustrates the current situation of our system that was used as an example in the previous chapters:

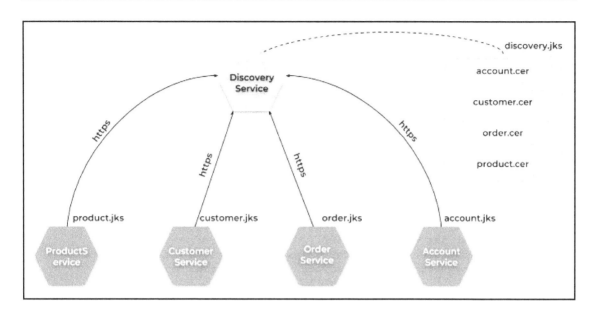

Keystore generation

After discussing the basics regarding security in Java, we may proceed to the generation of private and public keys for our microservices. Just like before, we will use the command-line tool provided under JRE—`keytool`. Let's begin with a well-known command for generating a `keystore` file with a key pair. One KeyStore is generated for a discovery server, and a second for the one selected microservice, in this particular case, for `account-service`:

```
keytool -genkey -alias account -store  type JKS -keyalg RSA -keysize 2048 -
keystore account.jks -validity 3650
keytool -genkey -alias discovery -storetype JKS -keyalg RSA -keysize 2048 -
keystore discovery.jks -validity 3650
```

Then, the self-signed certificate has to be exported from a KeyStore to a file—for example, with a `.cer` or `.crt` extension. You will then be prompted for the password you provided during the KeyStore's generation:

```
keytool -exportcert -alias account -keystore account.jks -file account.cer
keytool -exportcert -alias discovery -keystore discovery.jks -file
discovery.cer
```

The certificate corresponding to the public key has been extracted from the KeyStore, so now it can be distributed to all interested parties. The public certificate from `account-service` should be included in the discovery server's trustStore and vice-versa:

```
keytool -importcert -alias discovery -keystore account.jks -file
discovery.cer
keytool -importcert -alias account -keystore discovery.jks -file
account.cer
```

The same steps that were performed for `account-service` have to be repeated for each subsequent microservice that registers itself in the Eureka server. Here are the keytool's commands used for generating SSL keys and certificates for `order-service`:

```
keytool -genkey -alias order -storetype JKS -keyalg RSA -keysize 2048 -
keystore order.jks -validity 3650
keytool -exportcert -alias order -keystore order.jks -file order.cer
keytool -importcert -alias discovery -keystore order.jks -file
discovery.cer
keytool -importcert -alias order -keystore discovery.jks -file order.cer
```

Configurating SSL for microservices and Eureka server

Each `keystore` file has been placed in the `src/main/resources` directory of every secure microservice and service discovery. The SSL configuration settings of every microservice are very similar to those from the example in the section titled *Enabling HTTPS for Spring Boot*. The only difference is the type of currently used KeyStore, which is now JKS instead of PKCS12. However, there are more differences between the earlier sample and the service discovery configuration. First, I have enabled client certificate authentication by setting the `server.ssl.client-auth` property to `need`. This in turn requires us to provide a trustStore with the `server.ssl.trust-store` property. Here are the current SSL configuration settings in `application.yml` for `discovery-service`:

```
server:
 port: ${PORT:8761}
 ssl:
  enabled: true
  client-auth: need
  key-store: classpath:discovery.jks
  key-store-password: 123456
  trust-store: classpath:discovery.jks
  trust-store-password: 123456
  key-alias: discovery
```

If you run the Eureka application with the preceding configuration and then try to visit its web dashboard available under `https://localhost:8761/`, you will probably get an error code like `SSL_ERROR_BAD_CERT_ALERT`. This error occurs because there is no trusted certificate imported to your web browser. For this purpose, we may import one of the client's application KeyStores, from `account-service`, for example. But first, we need to convert it from JKS format to another format supported by a web browser, such as PKCS12. Here's the `keytool` command for the conversion of KeyStore from JKS to PKCS12 format:

```
keytool -importkeystore -srckeystore account.jks -srcstoretype JKS -
deststoretype PKCS12 -destkeystore account.p12
```

PKCS12 is supported by all the most popular web browsers, such as Google Chrome and Mozilla Firefox. You can import a PKCS12 KeyStore to Google Chrome by navigating to the section **Settings** | **Show advanced settings...** | **HTTPS/SSL** | **Manage certificates**. If you try to visit the Eureka web dashboard one more time, you should be authenticated successfully, and you will be able to see the list of registered services. However, there will be no application registered there. In order to provide secure communication between the discovery clients and the server, we need to create a `@Bean` of a `DiscoveryClientOptionalArgs` type for every microservice, which overwrites the discovery client's implementation. What is interesting is that Eureka uses Jersey as a REST client. With `EurekaJerseyClientBuilder`, we may easily build a new client implementation and pass the `keystore` and `truststore` file's location. The following is the code fragment from `account-service`, where we create a new `EurekaJerseyClient` object and set it as an argument of `DiscoveryClientOptionalArgs`:

```
@Bean
public DiscoveryClient.DiscoveryClientOptionalArgs
discoveryClientOptionalArgs() throws NoSuchAlgorithmException {
  DiscoveryClient.DiscoveryClientOptionalArgs args = new
DiscoveryClient.DiscoveryClientOptionalArgs();
  System.setProperty("javax.net.ssl.keyStore",
    "src/main/resources/account.jks");
  System.setProperty("javax.net.ssl.keyStorePassword", "123456");
  System.setProperty("javax.net.ssl.trustStore",
    "src/main/resources/account.jks");
  System.setProperty("javax.net.ssl.trustStorePassword", "123456");
  EurekaJerseyClientBuilder builder = new EurekaJerseyClientBuilder();
  builder.withClientName("account-client");
  builder.withSystemSSLConfiguration();
  builder.withMaxTotalConnections(10);
  builder.withMaxConnectionsPerHost(10);
  args.setEurekaJerseyClient(builder.build());
  return args;
}
```

A similar implementation should be provided for every microservice in our sample system. A sample application source code is available on GitHub (`https://github.com/piomin/sample-spring-cloud-security.git`). You may clone it and run all the Spring Boot applications with your IDE. If everything works, you should see the same list of registered services in the Eureka dashboard as you can see in the following screenshot. In case of any problem with the SSL connection, try and set the `-Djava.net.debug=ssl` VM argument during the boot of the application to be able to check out the full logs from the SSL handshake process:

Instances currently registered with Eureka

Application	AMIs	Availability Zones	Status
ACCOUNT-SERVICE	n/a (1)	(1)	UP (1) - minkowp-l.p4.org:account-service:8091
CUSTOMER-SERVICE	n/a (1)	(1)	UP (1) - minkowp-l.p4.org:customer-service:8092
ORDER-SERVICE	n/a (1)	(1)	UP (1) - minkowp-l.p4.org:order-service:8090
PRODUCT-SERVICE	n/a (1)	(1)	UP (1) - minkowp-l.p4.org:product-service:8093

Secure configuration server

There is one other key element in our architecture that should be considered during our discussion about security—the Spring Cloud Config Server. I would say that it is even more important to protect the config server than the discovery service. Why? Because we usually store their authentication credentials to the external systems, along with other data that should be hidden from unauthorized access and usage. There are several ways to properly secure your config server. You may configure an HTTP basic authentication, a secure SSL connection, encrypt/decrypt sensitive data, or use third-party tools such as those already described in `Chapter 5`, Distributed Configuration with Spring Cloud Config. Let's take a closer look at some of them.

Encryption and decryption

Before we begin, we have to download and install the **Java Cryptography Extension** (**JCE**) provided by Oracle. It consists of two JAR files (`local_policy.jar` and `US_export_policy.jar`), which need to override the existing policy files in the JRE lib/security directory.

If the remote property sources stored on the config server contain encrypted data, their values should be prefixed with {cipher} and wrapped in quotes to designate it as a YAML file. Wrapping in quotes is not necessary for .properties files. If such a value cannot be decrypted, it is replaced by an additional value (usually <n/a>) under the same key prefixed with invalid.

In our last sample, we stored the passphrase used for protecting the keystore file in the application configuration settings. Keeping it there as a plain text file may not be the best idea, so it is the first candidate for encryption. The question is, how do we encrypt it? Fortunately, Spring Boot provides two RESTful endpoints that can help with that.

Let's see how it works. First, we need to start a config server instance. The simplest way for this is to activate the --spring.profiles.active=native profile, which launches the server with the property sources from the local classpath or filesystem. Now we may call two POST endpoints /encrypt and /decrypt. The /encrypt method takes our plain-text password as an argument. The result can be checked out using an inverse operation, /decrypt, which takes an encrypted password as a parameter:

```
$ curl http://localhost:8888/encrypt -d 123456
AQAzI8jv26K3n6ff+iFzQA9DUpWmg79emWu4ndEXyvjYnKFSG7rBmJP0oFTb8RzjZbTwt4ehRiK
Wqu5qXkH8SAv/8mr2kdwB28kfVvPj/Lb5hdUkH1TVrylcnpZaKaQYBaxlsa0RWAKQDk8MQKRw1n
J5HM4LY9yjda0YQFNYAy0/KRnwUFihiV5xDk5lMOiG4b77AVLmz+9aSAODKLO57wOQUzM1tSA7l
O9HyDQW2Hzl1q93uOCaP5VQLCJAjmHcHvhlvM442bU3B29JNjH+2nFS0RhEyUvpUqzo+PBi4RoA
KJH9XZ8G7RaTOeWIcJhentKRf0U/EgWIVW21NpsE29BHwf4F2JZiWY2+WqcHuHk367X21vk11AV
19tJk9aUVNRk=
```

The encryption is done with the public key, while the decryption is done with the private key. Therefore, you need to provide only the public key in the server if you perform just the encryption. For testing purposes, we can create the KeyStore using keytool. We have already created some KeyStores before, so you will not have any problems with that. The generated file should be placed in the classpath and then in the config-service configuration settings using encrypt.keyStore.* properties:

```
encrypt:
  keyStore:
    location: classpath:/config.jks
    password: 123456
    alias: config
    secret: 123456
```

Now, if you move the configuration settings of each microservice to the config server, you can encrypt every password, as shown in the following sample fragment:

```
server:
 port: ${PORT:8091}
 ssl:
 enabled: true
 key-store: classpath:account.jks
 key-store-password:
 '{cipher}AQAzI8jv26K3n6ff+iFzQA9DUpWmg79emWu4ndEXyvjYnKFSG7rBmJP0oFTb8RzjZb
 Twt4ehRiKWqu5qXkH8SAv/8mr2kdwB28kfVvPj/Lb5hdUkH1TVrylcnpZaKaQYBaxlsa0RWAKQD
 k8MQKRw1nJ5HM4LY9yjda0YQFNYAy0/KRnwUFihiV5xDk5lMOiG4b77AVLmz+9aSAODKLO57wOQ
 UzM1tSA7lO9HyDQW2Hzl1q93uOCaP5VQLCJAjmHcHvhlvM442bU3B29JNjH+2nFS0RhEyUvpUqz
 o+PBi4RoAKJH9XZ8G7RaTOeWIcJhentKRf0U/EgWIVW21NpsE29BHwf4F2JZiWY2+WqcHuHk367
 X21vk11AVl9tJk9aUVNRk='
 key-alias: account
```

Configuring authentication for a client and a server

The implementation of authentication for Spring Cloud Config Server looks exactly the same as for the Eureka server. We can use an HTTP basic authentication basing on standard Spring security mechanisms. First, we need to make sure that the `spring-security` artifact is on the classpath. Then we should enable security with `security.basic.enabled` set to `true` and define a username and password. The sample configuration settings are visible in the following code fragment:

```
security:
 basic:
  enabled: true
 user:
  name: admin
  password: admin123
```

The basic authentication must also be enabled on the client side. It can be realized in two different ways. The first of these is via the config server URL:

```
spring:
 cloud:
  config:
   uri: http://admin:admin123@localhost:8888
```

The second approach is based on separate `username` and `password` properties:

```
spring:
 cloud:
  config:
   uri: http://localhost:8888
   username: admin
   password: admin123
```

If you would like to set up SSL authentication, you need to follow the steps described in the section titled *Secure discovery*. After generating the KeyStores with private keys and certificates and setting the proper configuration, we may run the config server. Now, it is exposing its RESTful API over HTTPS. The only difference is in the implementation on the client side. This is because Spring Cloud Config uses a different HTTP client than Spring Cloud Netflix Eureka. As you may probably guess, it leverages `RestTemplate`, as it is entirely created within the Spring Cloud project.

To force the client-side application to use two-way SSL authentication instead of a standard, nonsecure HTTP connection, first we should create a `@Configuration` bean implementing the `PropertySourceLocator` interface. There, we may build a custom `RestTemplate` that uses a secure HTTP connection factory:

```
@Configuration
public class SSLConfigServiceBootstrapConfiguration {

    @Autowired
    ConfigClientProperties properties;

    @Bean
    public ConfigServicePropertySourceLocator
configServicePropertySourceLocator() throws Exception {
        final char[] password = "123456".toCharArray();
        final File keyStoreFile = new
File("src/main/resources/discovery.jks");
        SSLContext sslContext = SSLContexts.custom()
                .loadKeyMaterial(keyStoreFile, password, password)
                .loadTrustMaterial(keyStoreFile).build();
        CloseableHttpClient httpClient =
HttpClients.custom().setSSLContext(sslContext).build();
        HttpComponentsClientHttpRequestFactory requestFactory = new
HttpComponentsClientHttpRequestFactory(httpClient);
        ConfigServicePropertySourceLocator
configServicePropertySourceLocator = new
ConfigServicePropertySourceLocator(properties);
        configServicePropertySourceLocator.setRestTemplate(new
RestTemplate(requestFactory));
```

```
            return configServicePropertySourceLocator;
    }

}
```

However, by default, this bean would not be created before the application tries to establish a connection with the config server. To change this behavior, we should also create the `spring.factories` file in `/src/main/resources/META-INF` and specify the custom bootstrap configuration class:

```
org.springframework.cloud.bootstrap.BootstrapConfiguration =
pl.piomin.services.account.SSLConfigServiceBootstrapConfiguration
```

Authorization with OAuth2

We have already discussed some concepts and solutions related to authentication in a microservices environment. I have shown you the examples of basic and SSL authentication between microservices and a service discovery, and also between microservices and a config server. In inter-service communication, authorization seems to be more important then authentication, which is instead implemented on the edge of the system. It's worth understanding the difference between authentication and authorization. Simply put, authentication verifies who you are, while authorization verifies what you are authorized to do.

Currently the most popular authorization methods for RESTful HTTP APIs are OAuth2 and **Java Web Tokens** (**JWT**). They may be mixed together as they are rather more complementary than other solutions. Spring provides support for OAuth providers and consumers. With Spring Boot and Spring Security OAuth2, we may quickly implement common security patterns, such as single sign-on, token relay, or token exchange. But before we dive into the details regarding those projects, as well as other development details, we need to acquire a basic knowledge of the preceding solution.

Introduction to OAuth2

OAuth2 is the standard currently used by almost all major websites that allow you to access their resources through a shared API. It delegates user authentication to an independent service that stores user credentials and authorizes third-party applications to access shared information about users' accounts. OAuth2 is used for giving your users access to data while protecting their account credentials. It provides flows for web, desktop, and mobile applications. The following are some basic terms and roles related to OAuth2:

- **Resource owner**: This role governs access to the resource. This access is limited by the scope of the granted authorization.
- **Authorization grant**: This grants permission for access. There are various ways you may choose to confirm access—authorization code, implicit, resource-owner password credentials, and client credentials.
- **Resource server**: This is a server that stores the owner's resources that can be shared using a special token.
- **Authorization server**: This manages the allocation of keys, tokens, and other temporary resource access codes. It also has to ensure that access is granted to the relevant user.
- **Access token**: This is a key that allows access to a resource.

In order to better understand what these terms and roles are in practice, take a look at the following diagram. It visualizes a typical flow of the authorization process using the OAuth protocol:

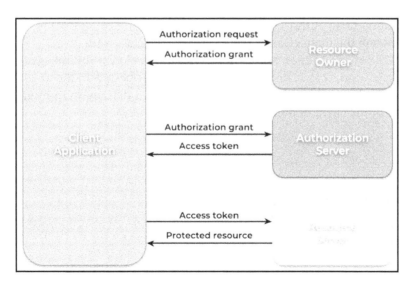

Let's run through the further steps of interaction between the individual components listed previously. The application requests authorization from the resource owner in order to be able to access the requested service. The resource sends an authorization grant as the response, which is then sent by the application, together with its own identity, to the authorization server. The authorization server verifies the application identity's credentials and authorization grant, and then sends an access token back. The application requests the resource from the resource server using a received access token. Finally, if the access token is valid, the application is able to invoke the request service.

Building an authorization server

After moving from monolithic applications to microservices, the obvious solution seems to be the centralization of the authorization effort by creating an authorization service. With Spring Boot and Spring Security, you may easily create, configure, and launch an authorization server. First, we need to include the following `starters` to the project dependencies:

```
<dependency>
    <groupId>org.springframework.cloud</groupId>
    <artifactId>spring-cloud-starter-oauth2</artifactId>
</dependency>
<dependency>
    <groupId>org.springframework.cloud</groupId>
    <artifactId>spring-cloud-starter-security</artifactId>
</dependency>
```

The implementation of an authorization server pattern with Spring Boot is very easy. We just have to annotate the main class or the configuration class with `@EnableAuthorizationServer` and then provide `security.oauth2.client.client-id` and `security.oauth2.client.client-secret` properties in the `application.yml` file. Of course, this variant is as simple as possible, since it defines an in-memory implementation of the client details service.

A sample application is available in the same repository as the previous samples in this chapter (`https://github.com/piomin/sample-spring-cloud-security.git`), but in a different branch, `oauth2` (`https://github.com/piomin/sample-spring-cloud-security/tree/oauth2`). The authorization server is available under the `auth-service` module. Here's the main class of `auth-service`:

```
@SpringBootApplication
@EnableAuthorizationServer
public class AuthApplication {

    public static void main(String[] args) {
        new
SpringApplicationBuilder(AuthApplication.class).web(true).run(args);
    }

}
```

Here is the fragment of the application's configuration settings. In addition to the client's ID and secret, I have also set its default scope and enabled basic security for the whole project:

```
security:
  user:
    name: root
    password: password
  oauth2:
    client:
      client-id: piotr.minkowski
      client-secret: 123456
      scope: read
```

After running our authorization service, we may perform some tests. For example, we may call the `POST /oauth/token` method in order to create an access token using resource owner password credentials, just like in the following command:

```
$ curl piotr.minkowski:123456@localhost:9999/oauth/token -d
grant_type=password -d username=root -d password=password
```

We may also use an authorization code grant type by calling the `GET /oauth/authorize` endpoint from your web browser:

```
http://localhost:9999/oauth/authorize?response_type=token&client_id=piotr.m
inkowski&redirect_uri=http://example.com&scope=read
```

After that, you will be redirected to the approval page. You may confirm the action and finally get your access token. It will be sent to the callback URL passed in the `redirect_uri` parameter of the initial request. Here's the sample response that I received after my test:

```
http://example.com/#access_token=dd736a4a-1408-4f3f-b3ca-43dcc05e6df0&token
_type=bearer&expires_in=43200.
```

The same OAuth2 configuration that was provided within the `application.yml` file can be also implemented programatically. In order to achieve this, we should declare any `@Beans` that implements `AuthorizationServerConfigurer`. One of these is the `AuthorizationServerConfigurerAdapter` adapter, which provides empty methods, allowing you to create custom definitions of the following separated configurers:

- `ClientDetailsServiceConfigurer`: This defines the client details service. Client details can be initialized, or you can just refer to an existing store.
- `AuthorizationServerSecurityConfigurer`: This defines the security constraints on the token endpoints `/oauth/token_key` and `/oauth/check_token`.
- `AuthorizationServerEndpointsConfigurer`: This defines the authorization and token endpoints and the token services.

This approach to the authorization server implementation gives us many more opportunities. For example, we may define more than one client with an ID and a secret, as shown in the following code fragment. I'll show you some more advanced samples in the next part of this chapter:

```
@Configuration
@EnableAuthorizationServer
public class AuthServerConfig extends AuthorizationServerConfigurerAdapter
{
```

```
    @Override
    public void configure(AuthorizationServerSecurityConfigurer
oauthServer) throws      Exception {
       oauthServer
         .tokenKeyAccess("permitAll()")
         .checkTokenAccess("isAuthenticated()");
    }

    @Override
    public void configure(ClientDetailsServiceConfigurer clients) throws
Exception {
        clients.inMemory()
            .withClient("piotr.minkowski").secret("123456")
                .scopes("read")
                .authorities("ROLE_CLIENT")
                .authorizedGrantTypes("authorization_code",
 "refresh_token", "implicit")
                .autoApprove(true)
            .and()
            .withClient("john.smith").secret("123456")
                .scopes("read", "write")
                .authorities("ROLE_CLIENT")
                .authorizedGrantTypes("authorization_code",
 "refresh_token", "implicit")
                .autoApprove(true);
    }
}
```

The last thing that has to be configured for our authorization server is web security. In the class extending WebSecurityConfigurerAdapter, we have defined an in-memory user credentials store and permissions to access specific resources, such as a login page:

```
@Configuration
public class SecurityConfig extends WebSecurityConfigurerAdapter {

    @Autowired
    private AuthenticationManager authenticationManager;

    @Override
    protected void configure(HttpSecurity http) throws Exception {
        http.requestMatchers()
          .antMatchers("/login", "/oauth/authorize")
          .and()
          .authorizeRequests()
          .anyRequest().authenticated()
          .and()
          .formLogin().permitAll();
```

```
        }

        @Override
        protected void configure(AuthenticationManagerBuilder auth) throws
    Exception {
            auth.parentAuthenticationManager(authenticationManager)
                .inMemoryAuthentication()
                .withUser("piotr.minkowski").password("123456").roles("USERS");
        }

    }
```

Client configuration

Your application can use the OAuth2 client that is configured in two different ways. The first of these ways is through the `@EnableOAuth2Client` annotation, which creates a filter bean with an ID of `oauth2ClientContextFilter` that is responsible for storing the request and context. It also manages communication between your application and an authorization server. However, we will be looking at the second approach to OAuth2's client-side implementation, through `@EnableOAuth2Sso`. **Single sign-on** (**SSO**) is a well-known security pattern that allows a user to use one set of login credentials to access multiple applications. There are two features provided by this annotation—the OAuth2 client and the authentication. The authentication piece aligns your application with the typical Spring Security mechanisms, such as a form login. The client piece has the same functionality as that provided by `@EnableOAuth2Client`. So, we may think of `@EnableOAuth2Sso` as just a higher level annotation than `@EnableOAuth2Client`.

In the following sample code fragment, I have annotated the class that extends `WebSecurityConfigurerAdapter` with `@EnableOAuth2Sso`. Thanks to this extension, Spring Boot configures the security filter chain that carries the OAuth2 authentication processor. In this case, requests to the `/login` page are permitted, while all other requests require authentication. The form login page path may be overridden with the `security.oauth2.sso.login-path` property. After overriding it there, we should also remember to change the path pattern inside `WebSecurityConfig`:

```
@Configuration
@EnableOAuth2Sso
public class WebSecurityConfig extends WebSecurityConfigurerAdapter {

    @Override
    protected void configure(HttpSecurity http) throws Exception {
        http.antMatcher("/**")
```

```
                    .authorizeRequests()
                    .antMatchers("/login**")
                        .permitAll()
                    .anyRequest()
                        .authenticated();
        }

    }
```

There are also some configuration settings that need to be set. First, we should disable basic authentication, because we use the form login method enabled together with the `@EnableOAuth2Sso` annotation. Then, we have to provide some basic OAuth2 client properties, such as client credentials and the addresses of the HTTP API endpoints exposed by the authorization server:

```
security:
 basic:
   enabled: false
 oauth2:
  client:
    clientId: piotr.minkowski
    clientSecret: 123456
    accessTokenUri: http://localhost:9999/oauth/token
    userAuthorizationUri: http://localhost:9999/oauth/authorize
  resource:
    userInfoUri: http://localhost:9999/user
```

The last property from the fragment of the `application.yml` file is `security.oauth2.resource.userInfoUri`, which requires an additional endpoint on the server side. The endpoint implemented by `UserController` returns the `java.security.Principal` object, indicating the currently authenticated user:

```
@RestController
public class UserController {

    @RequestMapping("/user")
    public Principal user(Principal user) {
        return user;
    }

}
```

Now, if you invoke any endpoint exposed by one of our microservices, you will be automatically redirected to the login page. Since we set an `autoApprove` option for our in-memory clients' details store, the authorization grant and access token are generated automatically without any interaction from the user. After providing your credentials in the login page, you should get the response from the requested resource.

Using the JDBC backend store

In the previous sections, we configured an authentication server and client application, which grants access to the resources protected by the resource server. However, the whole authorization server configuration has been provided inside in-memory storage. Such a solution meets our needs during development, but it is not the most desirable approach in production mode. The target solution should store all the authentication credentials and tokens in the database. We may choose between many relational databases supported by Spring. In this case, I have decided to use MySQL.

So, the first step is to start the MySQL database locally. The most comfortable way to achieve this is through a Docker container. In addition to starting the database, the following command also creates a schema and a user called `oauth2`:

```
docker run -d --name mysql -e MYSQL_DATABASE=oauth2 -e MYSQL_USER=oauth2 -e
MYSQL_PASSWORD=oauth2 -e MYSQL_ALLOW_EMPTY_PASSWORD=yes -p 33306:3306 mysql
```

Once we have started MySQL, we now have to provide the connection settings on the client side. MySQL is available under the host address `192.168.99.100` if you run Docker on a Windows machine and on port `33306`. Data source properties should be set in the `application.yml` of `auth-service`. Spring Boot is also able to run some SQL scripts on the selected data source on the application's startup. It's good news for us because we have to create some tables on the schema dedicated for our OAuth2 process:

```yaml
spring:
 application:
  name: auth-service
 datasource:
  url: jdbc:mysql://192.168.99.100:33306/oauth2?useSSL=false
  username: oauth2
  password: oauth2
  driver-class-name: com.mysql.jdbc.Driver
  schema: classpath:/script/schema.sql
  data: classpath:/script/data.sql
```

The created schema contains some tables used for storing OAuth2 credentials and tokens—oauth_client_details, oauth_client_token, oauth_access_token, oauth_refresh_token, oauth_code, and oauth_approvals. The full script with SQL - creation commands is available inside /src/main/resources/script/schema.sql. There is also a second SQL script, /src/main/resources/script/data.sql, with some insert commands for test purposes. The most important thing is to add some client ID/client secret pairs:

```
INSERT INTO `oauth_client_details` (`client_id`, `client_secret`, `scope`,
`authorized_grant_types`, `access_token_validity`,
`additional_information`) VALUES ('piotr.minkowski', '123456', 'read',
'authorization_code,password,refresh_token,implicit', '900', '{}');
INSERT INTO `oauth_client_details` (`client_id`, `client_secret`, `scope`,
`authorized_grant_types`, `access_token_validity`,
`additional_information`) VALUES ('john.smith', '123456', 'write',
'authorization_code,password,refresh_token,implicit', '900', '{}');
```

There are some differences in implementation between the current version of the authentication server and the version described in the basic example. The first important thing here is to set the default token storage to a database by providing a JdbcTokenStore bean with the default data source as a parameter. Although all tokens are now stored in a database, we still want to generate them in JWT format. That's why the second bean, JwtAccessTokenConverter, has to be provided in that class. By overriding different configure methods inherited from the base class, we can set a default storage for OAuth2 client details and configure the authorization server to always verify the API key submitted in HTTP headers:

```
@Configuration
@EnableAuthorizationServer
public class OAuth2Config extends AuthorizationServerConfigurerAdapter {

    @Autowired
    private DataSource dataSource;
    @Autowired
    private AuthenticationManager authenticationManager;

    @Override
    public void configure(AuthorizationServerEndpointsConfigurer endpoints)
throws Exception {
        endpoints.authenticationManager(this.authenticationManager)
            .tokenStore(tokenStore())
            .accessTokenConverter(accessTokenConverter());
    }

    @Override
```

```
    public void configure(AuthorizationServerSecurityConfigurer
oauthServer) throws Exception {
        oauthServer.checkTokenAccess("permitAll()");
    }

    @Bean
    public JwtAccessTokenConverter accessTokenConverter() {
        return new JwtAccessTokenConverter();
    }

    @Override
    public void configure(ClientDetailsServiceConfigurer clients) throws
Exception {
        clients.jdbc(dataSource);
    }

    @Bean
    public JdbcTokenStore tokenStore() {
        return new JdbcTokenStore(dataSource);
    }

}
```

The Spring application provides a custom authentication mechanism. To use it in the application, we must implement the UserDetailsService interface and override its loadUserByUsername method. In our example application, user credentials and authorities are also stored in the database, so we inject the UserRepository bean to the custom UserDetailsService class:

```
@Component("userDetailsService")
public class UserDetailsServiceImpl implements UserDetailsService {

    private final Logger log =
LoggerFactory.getLogger(UserDetailsServiceImpl.class);

    @Autowired
    private UserRepository userRepository;

    @Override
    @Transactional
    public UserDetails loadUserByUsername(final String login) {
        log.debug("Authenticating {}", login);
        String lowercaseLogin = login.toLowerCase();
        User userFromDatabase;
        if(lowercaseLogin.contains("@")) {
            userFromDatabase = userRepository.findByEmail(lowercaseLogin);
        } else {
```

```
                userFromDatabase =
userRepository.findByUsernameCaseInsensitive(lowercaseLogin);
        }
        if (userFromDatabase == null) {
            throw new UsernameNotFoundException("User " + lowercaseLogin +
" was not found in the database");
        } else if (!userFromDatabase.isActivated()) {
            throw new UserNotActivatedException("User " + lowercaseLogin +
" is not activated");
        }
        Collection<GrantedAuthority> grantedAuthorities = new
ArrayList<>();
        for (Authority authority : userFromDatabase.getAuthorities()) {
            GrantedAuthority grantedAuthority = new
SimpleGrantedAuthority(authority.getName());
            grantedAuthorities.add(grantedAuthority);
        }
        return new
org.springframework.security.core.userdetails.User(userFromDatabase.getUser
name(), userFromDatabase.getPassword(), grantedAuthorities);
    }

}
```

Inter-service authorization

Inter-service communication in our sample is realized using Feign clients. Here's one of the chosen implementations—in this case, from `order-service`—which calls the endpoint from `customer-service`:

```
@FeignClient(name = "customer-service")
public interface CustomerClient {

    @GetMapping("/withAccounts/{customerId}")
    Customer findByIdWithAccounts(@PathVariable("customerId") Long
customerId);

}
```

In the same way as with the other services, all the available methods from `customer-service` are protected by the preauthorization mechanism based on the OAuth token scope. It allows us to annotate every method with `@PreAuthorize`, defining the required scope:

```
@PreAuthorize("#oauth2.hasScope('write')")
@PutMapping
public Customer update(@RequestBody Customer customer) {
    return repository.update(customer);
}

@PreAuthorize("#oauth2.hasScope('read')")
@GetMapping("/withAccounts/{id}")
public Customer findByIdWithAccounts(@PathVariable("id") Long id) throws
JsonProcessingException {
    List<Account> accounts = accountClient.findByCustomer(id);
    LOGGER.info("Accounts found: {}", mapper.writeValueAsString(accounts));
    Customer c = repository.findById(id);
    c.setAccounts(accounts);
    return c;
}
```

Preauthorization is disabled by default. To enable it for API methods, we should use the `@EnableGlobalMethodSecurity` annotation. We should also indicate that such a preauthorization will be based on the OAuth2 token scope:

```
@Configuration
@EnableResourceServer
@EnableGlobalMethodSecurity(prePostEnabled = true)
public class OAuth2ResourceServerConfig extends
GlobalMethodSecurityConfiguration {

    @Override
    protected MethodSecurityExpressionHandler createExpressionHandler() {
        return new OAuth2MethodSecurityExpressionHandler();
    }

}
```

If you call the account service endpoint via the Feign client, you get the following exception:

```
feign.FeignException: status 401 reading
CustomerClient#findByIdWithAccounts();
content:{"error":"unauthorized","error_description":"Full authentication is
required to access this resource"}
```

Why does such an exception occur? Of course, `customer-service` is protected with a OAuth2 token authorization, but the Feign client does not send an authorization token in the request header. That approach may be customized by defining a custom configuration class for the Feign client. It allows us to declare a request interceptor. In that case, we can use an implementation for OAuth2 provided by `OAuth2FeignRequestInterceptor` from the Spring Cloud OAuth2 library. For test purposes, I decided to use a resource owner password grant type:

```
public class CustomerClientConfiguration {

    @Value("${security.oauth2.client.access-token-uri}")
    private String accessTokenUri;
    @Value("${security.oauth2.client.client-id}")
    private String clientId;
    @Value("${security.oauth2.client.client-secret}")
    private String clientSecret;
    @Value("${security.oauth2.client.scope}")
    private String scope;

    @Bean
    RequestInterceptor oauth2FeignRequestInterceptor() {
        return new OAuth2FeignRequestInterceptor(new
DefaultOAuth2ClientContext(), resource());
    }

    @Bean
    Logger.Level feignLoggerLevel() {
        return Logger.Level.FULL;
    }

    private OAuth2ProtectedResourceDetails resource() {
        ResourceOwnerPasswordResourceDetails resourceDetails = new
ResourceOwnerPasswordResourceDetails();
        resourceDetails.setUsername("root");
        resourceDetails.setPassword("password");
        resourceDetails.setAccessTokenUri(accessTokenUri);
        resourceDetails.setClientId(clientId);
        resourceDetails.setClientSecret(clientSecret);
        resourceDetails.setGrantType("password");
        resourceDetails.setScope(Arrays.asList(scope));
        return resourceDetails;
    }

}
```

Finally, we may test the implemented solution. This time, we will create a JUnit automated test instead of clicking it in a web browser or sending requests using other tools. The test method is shown in the following code snippet. We use `OAuth2RestTemplate` with `ResourceOwnerPasswordResourceDetails` to perform a resource owner credentials grant operation and call the `POST` / API method from `order-service` with an OAuth2 token sent in the request header. Of course, before running that test, you have to start all the microservices, as well as the discovery and authorization server:

```
@Test
public void testClient() {
    ResourceOwnerPasswordResourceDetails resourceDetails = new
ResourceOwnerPasswordResourceDetails();
    resourceDetails.setUsername("root");
    resourceDetails.setPassword("password");
    resourceDetails.setAccessTokenUri("http://localhost:9999/oauth/token");
    resourceDetails.setClientId("piotr.minkowski");
    resourceDetails.setClientSecret("123456");
    resourceDetails.setGrantType("password");
    resourceDetails.setScope(Arrays.asList("read"));
    DefaultOAuth2ClientContext clientContext = new
DefaultOAuth2ClientContext();
    OAuth2RestTemplate restTemplate = new
OAuth2RestTemplate(resourceDetails, clientContext);
    restTemplate.setMessageConverters(Arrays.asList(new
MappingJackson2HttpMessageConverter()));
    Random r = new Random();
    Order order = new Order();
    order.setCustomerId((long) r.nextInt(3) + 1);
    order.setProductIds(Arrays.asList(new Long[] { (long) r.nextInt(10) +
1, (long) r.nextInt(10) + 1 }));
    order = restTemplate.postForObject("http://localhost:8090", order,
Order.class);
    if (order.getStatus() != OrderStatus.REJECTED) {
        restTemplate.put("http://localhost:8090/{id}", null,
order.getId());
    }
}
```

Enabling SSO on the API gateway

You may enable the single sign-on feature on the API gateway just by annotating the main class with `@EnableOAuth2Sso`. Indeed, that is the best choice for your microservices architecture to force Zuul to generate or get the access token for the currently authenticated user:

```
@SpringBootApplication
@EnableOAuth2Sso
@EnableZuulProxy
public class GatewayApplication {

    public static void main(String[] args) {
        new
SpringApplicationBuilder(GatewayApplication.class).web(true).run(args);
    }

}
```

By including `@EnableOAuth2Sso`, you trigger an auto-configuration available for a ZuulFilter. The filter is responsible for extracting an access token from the currently authenticated user, and then putting it into the request header forwarded to the microservices hidden behind the gateway. If `@EnableResourceServer` is activated for those services, they will receive the expected token in the `Authorization` HTTP header. The authorization behavior downstream of an `@EnableZuulProxy` may be controlled by declaring `proxy.auth.*` properties.

When using a gateway in your architecture, you may hide an authorization server behind it. In this case, you should provide the additional route in Zuul's configuration settings—for example, `uaa`. Then, all the messages exchanged between OAuth2 clients and the server go through the gateway. Here's the proper configuration in the gateway's `application.yml` file:

```
security:
  oauth2:
    client:
      accessTokenUri: /uaa/oauth/token
      userAuthorizationUri: /uaa/oauth/authorize
      clientId: piotr.minkowski
      clientSecret: 123456
    resource:
      userInfoUri: http://localhost:9999/user

zuul:
  routes:
```

```
account-service:
  path: /account/**
customer-service:
  path: /customer/**
order-service:
  path: /order/**
product-service:
  path: /product/**
uaa:
  sensitiveHeaders:
  path: /uaa/**
  url: http://localhost:9999
add-proxy-headers: true
```

Summary

There wouldn't have been anything wrong if I had included a security section in every single chapter from part two of this book. But I have decided to create a dedicated chapter on this subject in order to show you a step-by-step process of how to secure the key elements of a microservices-based architecture. The topics related to security are usually more advanced than other topics, so I took a bit more time to explain some of the basic concepts around the field. I have shown you samples illustrating a two-way SSL authentication, encryption/decryption of sensitive data, Spring Security authentication, and OAuth2 authorization with JWT tokens. I will leave it to you to decide which of them should be used in your system architecture to provide your desired level of security.

After reading this chapter, you should be able to set up both the basic and the more advanced security configurations for your application. You should also be able to secure every component of your system's architecture. Of course, we have discussed only some of the possible solutions and frameworks. For example, you don't have to only rely on Spring as an authorization server provider. We may use third-party tools, such as Keycloak, which can act as an authorization and authentication server in a microservices-based system. It can also easily be integrated with Spring Boot applications. It provides support for all the most popular protocols, such as OAuth2, OpenId Connect, and SAML. So, in fact, Keycloak is a very powerful tool, and should be treated as an alternative to the Spring Authorization Server, especially for large, corporate systems and other more advanced use cases.

In the next chapter we will discuss the different strategies of microservices testing.

13
Testing Java Microservices

While developing a new application, we should never forget about automated tests. These are especially important if we are thinking about microservices-based architecture. Testing microservices requires a different approach than the tests created for monolithic applications. As far as monoliths are concerned, the main focus is on unit testing and integration tests, together with the database layer. In the case of microservices, the most important thing is to provide coverage for each of the communications at the finest possible granularity. Although each microservice is independently developed and released, a change in one of them can affect all of the others that are interacting with that service. The communication between them is realized through messages. Usually, these are messages that are sent via REST or AMQP protocols.

Topics we will cover in this chapter include the following:

- Spring support for automated testing
- Differences between a component and integration testing for Spring Boot microservices
- Implementing contract tests using Pact
- Implementing contract tests using Spring Cloud Contract
- Implementing performance tests using Gatling

Testing strategies

There are five different microservices testing strategies. The first three of them are the same as for monolithic applications:

- **Unit tests**: With unit tests, we test the smallest pieces of code, for example, a single method or component, and mock every call of other methods and components. There are many popular frameworks that support unit tests in Java, such as JUnit, TestNG, and Mockito (for mocking). The main task of this type of testing is to confirm that the implementation meets requirements. Unit testing can be a powerful tool, especially when combined with test-driven development.

- **Integration tests**: Using only unit testing doesn't guarantee that you will verify the behavior of the whole system. Integration tests take the modules and try to test them together. This approach gives you an opportunity to exercise communication paths within the subsystem. We are testing the interaction and communication between components based on their interfaces with external services mocked-up. In a microservices-based system, integration tests can be used in order to include other microservices, data sources, or caches.

- **End-to-end tests**: End-to-end tests are also known as **functional tests**. The main goal of these tests is to verify whether the system meets the external requirements. It means that we should design test scenarios that test all the microservices taking part in that process. The design of a good end-to-end test is not a trivial task. Since we need to test the whole system, it is very important to place a particular emphasis on the test's scenario design.

- **Contract tests**: Contract tests are used to ensure that the explicit and implicit contract of a microservice work as expected. A contract is always formed when a consumer integrates with the interface of a component in order to use it. Usually, in microservice-based systems, there are many consumers of a single component. Each of them usually requires a different contract that meets its demands. Following these assumptions, every consumer is responsible for a source component's interface behavior.

- **Component tests**: After we have completed unit testing of all the objects and methods within a microservice, we should test the whole microservice in isolation. In order to run the tests in isolation, we need to mock or stub the calls of the other microservices. An external data store should be replaced with an equivalent in-memory data store, which also provides significant test performance improvements.

The differences between contract and component tests are obvious. The following diagram illustrates those differences in our sample `order-service` microservice:

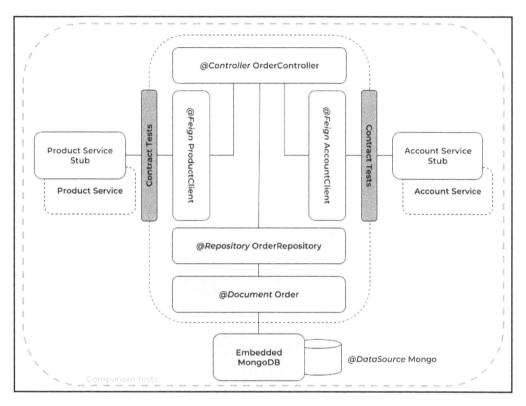

Now, there is a question of whether we really need two additional strategies for testing a microservices-based system. Through the proper unit and integration tests, we may be confident in the correctness of the implementation of the individual components that form part of the microservice. However, without more specific test strategies for microservices, we cannot be sure how they work together in order to meet our business requirements. Therefore, component and contract tests have been added. This is a really important change in order to help us understand the differences between component, contract, and integration tests. Since component tests are performed in isolation from the outside world, integration tests are responsible for verifying interactions with that world. That's why we should provide stubs for an integration test in contrast with a components test. Contract tests, much like integration tests, emphasize interactions between microservices, but they treat them as a black box and verify only the format of the responses.

Once you provide functional tests for your microservices, you should also think about performance testing. We can distinguish the following strategies of performance testing:

- **Load tests**: These are used to determine a system's behavior under the normal and anticipated load conditions. The main idea here is to identify some weaknesses, such as response time latencies, aberrant outages, or too many retries if network timeouts are not set properly.
- **Stress tests**: These check the upper limits of your system to examine how it behaves under an extremely heavy load. In addition to load testing, it also checks out memory leaks, security issues, and data corruption. It may be using the same tools as for load testing.

The following diagram illustrates the logical order of performing all of the test strategies on your system. We are starting from the simplest unit testing, which verifies small pieces of software, and going through the next stages to finally finish with stress testing that pushes the whole system to the limit:

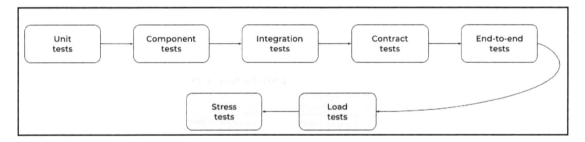

Testing Spring Boot applications

As you might have read in the previous section, there are some different strategies and approaches to the tests in your application. I have briefly mentioned all of them, so now we may proceed to the practical aspects. Spring Boot provides a set of utilities that help in the implementation of automated tests. In order to enable these features in the project, you have to include the `spring-boot-starter-test` starter to the dependencies. It imports not only the `spring-test` and `spring-boot-test` artifacts, but also some other useful test libraries, such as JUnit, Mockito, and AssertJ:

```
<dependency>
    <groupId>org.springframework.boot</groupId>
    <artifactId>spring-boot-starter-test</artifactId>
    <scope>test</scope>
</dependency>
```

Building the sample application

Before we start to work on automated tests, we need to prepare a sample business logic for testing purposes. We may use the same example system from the previous chapters, but it has to be modified a little. Until now, we have never used an external data source for storing and collecting test data. In this chapter, it would be helpful to do this in order to illustrate how the different strategies approach the issue of persistence testing. Now, each service has its own database although, generally, it doesn't really matter which database is chosen. There is a large choice of solutions supported by Spring Boot, including both relational and NoSQL databases. I have decided to use Mongo. Let us remind ourselves of the architecture of the sample system. The current model shown in the following diagram takes into account the assumptions described previously regarding dedicated databases per service:

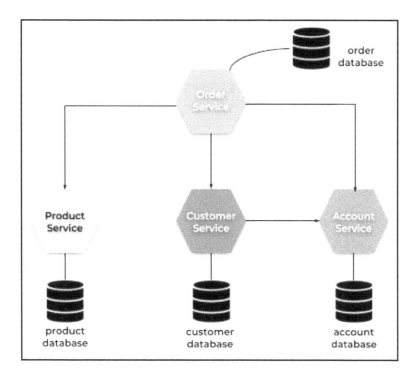

Integration with the database

In order to enable Mongo support for our Spring Boot application, include the `spring-boot-starter-data-mongo` starter to the dependencies. This project provides some interesting features to simplify integration with MongoDB. Among these features, it is worth mentioning particular rich object mapping, `MongoTemplate`, and of course support for the repository writing style, well-known from other Spring Data projects. Here's the required dependency declaration in `pom.xml`:

```
<dependency>
 <groupId>org.springframework.boot</groupId>
 <artifactId>spring-boot-starter-data-mongodb</artifactId>
</dependency>
```

The instance of MongoDB may be easily started using its Docker image. Run the following command to launch the Docker container that exposes the Mongo database on port `27017`:

```
docker run --name mongo -p 27017:27017 -d mongo
```

In order to connect the application with a previously started data source, we should override some `auto-configured` settings in `application.yml`. This can be achieved with the `spring.data.mongodb.*` properties:

```
spring:
 application:
  name: account-service
 data:
  mongodb:
   host: 192.168.99.100
   port: 27017
   database: micro
   username: micro
   password: micro123
```

I have already mentioned the object mapping feature. Spring Data Mongo provides some annotations that may be used for this. Every object stored in the database should be annotated with `@Document`. The primary key of the target collection is a 12 byte string, which should be indicated in every mapped class with Spring Data `@Id`. Here's the fragment of `Account` object implementation:

```
@Document
public class Account {

    @Id
    private String id;
    private String number;
    private int balance;
    private String customerId;
    // ...

}
```

Unit tests

I have taken a lot of time to describe integration with MongoDB. However, testing persistence is one of the key points of automated tests, so it is very important to configure it properly. Now, we may proceed to the test's implementation. Spring Test provides support for the most typical testing scenarios, such as integration with other services through a REST client or integration with databases. We have a set of libraries available that allows us to easily mock interactions with external services, which is especially important for unit tests.

The following test class is a typical unit test implementation for a Spring Boot application. We have used the JUnit framework, which is the de facto standard for Java. The Mockito library is used here for replacing the real repository and controller with their stubs. Such an approach allows us to easily verify the correctness of every method implemented by the `@Controller` class. The test is performed in isolation from the external components, which is the main assumption of unit testing:

```
@RunWith(SpringRunner.class)
@WebMvcTest(AccountController.class)
public class AccountControllerUnitTest {

    ObjectMapper mapper = new ObjectMapper();

    @Autowired
```

```
    MockMvc mvc;
    @MockBean
    AccountRepository repository;

    @Test
    public void testAdd() throws Exception {
        Account account = new Account("1234567890", 5000, "1");
        when(repository.save(Mockito.any(Account.class))).thenReturn(new
Account("1","1234567890", 5000, "1"));
mvc.perform(post("/").contentType(MediaType.APPLICATION_JSON).content(mappe
r.writeValueAsString(account)))
  .andExpect(status().isOk());
  }

    @Test
    public void testWithdraw() throws Exception {
        Account account = new Account("1", "1234567890", 5000, "1");
        when(repository.findOne("1")).thenReturn(account);
        when(repository.save(Mockito.any(Account.class))).thenAnswer(new
Answer<Account>() {
            @Override
            public Account answer(InvocationOnMock invocation) throws
Throwable {
                Account a = invocation.getArgumentAt(0, Account.class);
                return a;
              }
        });
        mvc.perform(put("/withdraw/1/1000"))
            .andExpect(status().isOk())
.andExpect(content().contentType(MediaType.APPLICATION_JSON_UTF8))
            .andExpect(jsonPath("$.balance", is(4000)));
    }

}
```

The good news, especially within the context of microservices, is that we may easily mock Feign client communication. The following example test class verifies the endpoint from `order-service` used for withdrawing money by calling the endpoint exposed by `account-service`. As you have probably noticed, that endpoint has in turn been tested by the previously introduced test class. Here's the class with unit test implementation for `order-service`:

```
@RunWith(SpringRunner.class)
@WebMvcTest(OrderController.class)
public class OrderControllerTest {

    @Autowired
```

```
    MockMvc mvc;
    @MockBean
    OrderRepository repository;
    @MockBean
    AccountClient accountClient;

    @Test
    public void testAccept() throws Exception {
        Order order = new Order("1", OrderStatus.ACCEPTED, 2000, "1", "1",
null);
        when(repository.findOne("1")).thenReturn(order);
        when(accountClient.withdraw(order.getAccountId(),
order.getPrice())).thenReturn(new Account("1", "123", 0));
        when(repository.save(Mockito.any(Order.class))).thenAnswer(new
Answer<Order>() {
            @Override
            public Order answer(InvocationOnMock invocation) throws
Throwable {
                Order o = invocation.getArgumentAt(0, Order.class);
                return o;
            }
        });

        mvc.perform(put("/1"))
            .andExpect(status().isOk())
.andExpect(content().contentType(MediaType.APPLICATION_JSON_UTF8))
            .andExpect(jsonPath("$.status", is("DONE")));
    }

}
```

Component tests

If you have provided the unit tests for all the key classes and interfaces in the application, you may proceed to the component tests. The main idea of component tests is to instantiate the full microservice in memory using in-memory test doubles and data stores. This allows us to skip the network connections. While for unit tests we were mocking all the database or HTTP clients, here we do not mock anything. We provide an in-memory data source for the database client and we simulate HTTP responses for the REST client.

Running tests with an in-memory database

One of the reasons I chose MongoDB is that it can be easily embedded with a Spring Boot application for testing purposes. To enable an embedded MongoDB for your project, include the following dependency in Maven `pom.xml`:

```
<dependency>
    <groupId>de.flapdoodle.embed</groupId>
    <artifactId>de.flapdoodle.embed.mongo</artifactId>
    <scope>test</scope>
</dependency>
```

Spring Boot provides auto-configuration for an embedded MongoDB, so we don't need to do anything else other than setting the local address and port in `application.yml`. Because, by default, we use Mongo running on Docker container, we should declare such a configuration in an additional Spring profile. This specific profile is activated during test case execution by annotating the test class with `@ActiveProfiles`. Here's a fragment of `application.yml`, where we defined two profiles, `dev` and `test`, with different MongoDB connection settings:

```
---
spring:
 profiles: dev
 data:
  mongodb:
   host: 192.168.99.100
   port: 27017
   database: micro
   username: micro
   password: micro123

---
spring:
 profiles: test
 data:
  mongodb:
   host: localhost
   port: 27017
```

If you use databases other than MongoDB, for example, MySQL or Postgres, you may easily replace them with alternative, in-memory, embedded, relational databases, such as H2 or Derby. Spring Boot supports them and provides auto-configuration for the tests that may be activated with `@DataJpaTest`. Instead of using `@SpringBootTest`, you can also use the `@DataMongoTest` annotation for embedded MongoDB. As well as an in-memory, embedded MongoDB, this will configure a `MongoTemplate`, scan for `@Document` classes, and configure Spring Data MongoDB repositories.

Handling HTTP clients and service discovery

The issue regarding testing persistence with an in-memory database is resolved. However, we still need to consider some other aspects of the test, such as simulating HTTP responses from other services or integration with a service discovery. When you implement some tests for microservices, you may choose between two typical approaches to a service discovery. The first of these is to embed the discovery server to the application during the test case execution, and the second is just to disable discovery on the client side. The second option is relatively easy to configure with Spring Cloud. For the Eureka Server, it can be disabled using the `eureka.client.enabled=false` property.

This is only the first part of the exercise. We should also disable discovery for the Ribbon client, which is responsible for load balancing in an interservice communication. If there is more than one target service, we have to label every client with the service name. The value of the last property in the following configuration, `listOfServers`, is strictly related to the framework used for automated test implementation. I'm going to show you the sample based on the Hoverfly Java library, which has already been introduced in Chapter 7, *Advanced Load Balancing and Circuit Breakers*. It was used then for simulating delays in calling target services in order to present how the Ribbon client and Hystrix deal with network timeouts. Here, we will just use it to return prepared responses to make our component tests to touch the network communications. Here's a fragment of the configuration file with the profile responsible for disabling Eureka's discovery and setting the test properties of the Ribbon client. That profile should also be activated for the test class by annotating it with `@ActiveProfiles`:

```
---
spring:
 profiles: no-discovery
eureka:
 client:
  enabled: false
account-service:
 ribbon:
```

```
    eureka:
      enable: false
      listOfServers: account-service:8080
  customer-service:
   ribbon:
    eureka:
      enable: false
      listOfServers: customer-service:8080
  product-service:
   ribbon:
    eureka:
      enable: false
      listOfServers: product-service:8080
```

I wouldn't like to go into the details of Hoverfly usage because it has already been discussed in Chapter 7, *Advanced Load Balancing and Circuit Breakers*. As you probably remember, Hoverfly can be activated for the JUnit test by declaring @ClassRule with HoverflyRule, defining the list of services and endpoints that should be simulated. The name of each service has to be the same as its address defined with the listOfServers property. Here's a definition of the Hoverfly test rule that simulates responses from three different services:

```
@ClassRule
public static HoverflyRule hoverflyRule = HoverflyRule
 .inSimulationMode(dsl(
 service("account-service:8080")
 .put(startsWith("/withdraw/"))
 .willReturn(success("{\"id\":\"1\",\"number\":\"1234567890\",\"balance\":50
00}", "application/json")),
 service("customer-service:8080")
 .get("/withAccounts/1")
 .willReturn(success("{\"id\":\"{{ Request.Path.[1]
}}\",\"name\":\"Test1\",\"type\":\"REGULAR\",\"accounts\":[{\"id\":\"1\",\"
number\":\"1234567890\",\"balance\":5000}]}", "application/json")),
 service("product-service:8080")
 .post("/ids").anyBody()
 .willReturn(success("[{\"id\":\"1\",\"name\":\"Test1\",\"price\":1000}]",
"application/json"))))
 .printSimulationData();
```

Implementing sample tests

To conclude everything that has been said in the last two sections, we will now prepare component tests using an in-memory, embedded MongoDB, Hoverfly (to simulate HTTP responses), and disabled service discovery. The correct configuration settings prepared especially for our testing purposes are available under profiles `test` and `no-discovery`. Every component test is initialized by the `TestRestTemplate`, which calls `order-service` HTTP endpoints. The test result verification may be performed based on the HTTP response or data stored in the embedded MongoDB. Here's a sample implementation of component tests for `order-service`:

```
@RunWith(SpringRunner.class)
@SpringBootTest(webEnvironment = WebEnvironment.RANDOM_PORT)
@FixMethodOrder(MethodSorters.NAME_ASCENDING)
@ActiveProfiles({"test", "no-discovery"})
public class OrderComponentTest {

    @Autowired
    TestRestTemplate restTemplate;
    @Autowired
    OrderRepository orderRepository;
    // ...
    @Test
    public void testAccept() {
        Order order = new Order(null, OrderStatus.ACCEPTED, 1000, "1", "1",
Collections.singletonList("1"));
        order = orderRepository.save(order);
        restTemplate.put("/{id}", null, order.getId());
        order = orderRepository.findOne(order.getId());
        Assert.assertEquals(OrderStatus.DONE, order.getStatus());
    }

    @Test
    public void testPrepare() {
        Order order = new Order(null, OrderStatus.NEW, 1000, "1", "1",
Collections.singletonList("1"));
        order = restTemplate.postForObject("/", order, Order.class);
        Assert.assertNotNull(order);
        Assert.assertEquals(OrderStatus.ACCEPTED, order.getStatus());
        Assert.assertEquals(940, order.getPrice());
    }

}
```

Integration tests

After creating unit and component tests, we have verified all the functionalities inside the microservices. However, we still need to test the interaction with other services, external data stores, and caches. In microservices-based architecture integration, tests are treated differently than they are in monolithic applications. Because all the relationships between internal modules have been tested through the component tests, we have tested only those modules that interact with external components.

Categorizing tests

It also makes sense to separate integration tests in the CI pipeline so that external outages don't block or break the build of the project. You should consider categorizing your tests by annotating them with `@Category`. You may create the interface especially for integration tests, for example, `IntegrationTest`:

```
public interface IntegrationTest  { }
```

Then, you can mark your test with that interface using the `@Category` annotation:

```
@Category(IntegrationTest.class)
public class OrderIntegrationTest { ... }
```

Finally, you can configure Maven to run only the selected type of tests, for example, with `maven-failsafe-plugin`:

```
<plugin>
  <artifactId>maven-failsafe-plugin</artifactId>
  <dependencies>
    <dependency>
      <groupId>org.apache.maven.surefire</groupId>
      <artifactId>surefire-junit47</artifactId>
    </dependency>
  </dependencies>
  <configuration>
    <groups>pl.piomin.services.order.IntegrationTest</groups>
  </configuration>
  <executions>
    <execution>
      <goals>
        <goal>integration-test</goal>
      </goals>
      <configuration>
        <includes>
```

```
        <include>**/*.class</include>
      </includes>
    </configuration>
  </execution>
 </executions>
</plugin>
```

Capturing HTTP traffic

Categorization is one of the ways of dealing with problems in communication with external microservices during automated tests. Another popular approach to that issue involves recording outgoing requests and incoming responses in order to use them in the future without establishing a connection to the external services.

In the previous examples, we have only used Hoverfly in simulation mode. However, it can also be run in capture mode, which means that requests will be made to the real service as normal, but they will be intercepted, recorded, and stored in the file by Hoverfly. The file that stores the captured traffic in JSON format may then be used in simulation mode. You can create a Hoverfly Rule in your JUnit test class, which is started in capture mode if the simulation file does not exist and in simulate mode if it does exist. It is always stored inside the `src/test/resources/hoverfly` directory.

This is a simple way of breaking dependencies to the external service. For example, if you know that there were no changes there, it is not necessary to interact with the real service. If such a service were to be modified, you can remove the JSON simulation file and thereby switch to capture mode. If your test fails, it means that the modification affected your service and you have to perform some fixes before moving back to capture mode.

Here's a sample integration test located inside `order-service`. It adds a new account and then calls a method for withdrawing money from that account. Thanks to using the `inCaptureOrSimulationMode` method, the real service is invoked only if the `account.json` file does not exist or you change the input data passed to the services in the test:

```
@RunWith(SpringRunner.class)
@SpringBootTest
@ActiveProfiles("dev")
@Category(IntegrationTest.class)
public class OrderIntegrationTest {

    @Autowired
    AccountClient accountClient;
    @Autowired
```

```
    CustomerClient customerClient;
    @Autowired
    ProductClient productClient;
    @Autowired
    OrderRepository orderRepository;

    @ClassRule
    public static HoverflyRule hoverflyRule =
HoverflyRule.inCaptureOrSimulationMode("account.json").printSimulationData(
);

    @Test
    public void testAccount() {
        Account account = accountClient.add(new Account(null, "123",
5000));
        account = accountClient.withdraw(account.getId(), 1000);
        Assert.notNull(account);
        Assert.equals(account.getBalance(), 4000);
    }


}
```

Contract tests

There are some interesting tools especially dedicated to contract testing. We will discuss this concept by looking at two of the most popular tools—Pact and Spring Cloud Contract.

Using Pact

As we have already mentioned, the main concept around contract tests is to define a contract between the consumer and provider, and then verify it independently for each service. Since the responsibility for creating and maintaining a contract lies mainly on the consumer side, this type of test is usually referred to as a consumer-driven test. The division into a consumer and provider side is clearly visible in Pact JVM. It provides two separated libraries, the first prefixed by `pact-jvm-consumer` and the second prefixed by `pact-jvm-provider`. Of course, the contract is created by the consumer in agreement with the provider, which has been illustrated in the following diagram:

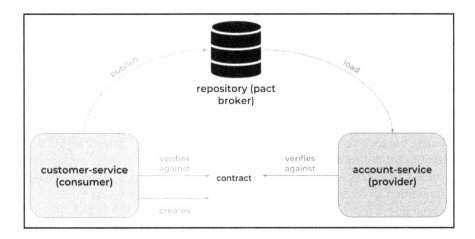

Pact is, in fact, a collection of frameworks that provide support for consumer-driven contract testing. These implementations are available for different languages and frameworks. Fortunately, Pact may be used together with JUnit and Spring Boot. Let's consider one of the integrations implemented in our sample system, namely the one between customer-service and account-service. The microservice named customer-service uses the Feign client for communication with account-service. The Feign client definition on the consumer side de facto represents our contract:

```
@FeignClient(name = "account-service")
public interface AccountClient {

    @GetMapping("/customer/{customerId}")
    List<Account> findByCustomer(@PathVariable("customerId") String customerId);

}
```

Consumer side

To enable Pact with JUnit support on the consumer side, include the following dependency to your project:

```
<dependency>
    <groupId>au.com.dius</groupId>
    <artifactId>pact-jvm-consumer-junit_2.12</artifactId>
    <version>3.5.12</version>
    <scope>test</scope>
</dependency>
```

Now the only thing we have to do is to create the JUnit test class. We may implement it as a standard Spring Boot test by annotating it with `@SpringBootTest` and running it using Spring Runner. To perform the created test successfully, we first need to disable the discovery client and ensure that the Ribbon client will communicate with the stub of the `account-service` represented by `@Rule PactProviderRuleMk2`. The key point of the test is the `callAccountClient` method, which is annotated with `@Pact` and returns a `RequestResponsePact`. It defines the format of the request and the content of the response. During the test case execution, Pact automatically generates the JSON representation of that definition, which is available in the `target/pacts/addressClient-customerServiceProvider.json` file. Finally, the method implemented in the Feign client is invoked and the response returned by Pact `@Rule` is verified in the test method annotated with `@PactVerification`. Here's a sample implementation of a consumer-side contract test for `customer-service`:

```
@RunWith(SpringRunner.class)
@SpringBootTest(properties = {
  "account-service.ribbon.listOfServers: localhost:8092",
  "account-service.ribbon.eureka.enabled: false",
  "eureka.client.enabled: false",
})
public class CustomerConsumerContractTest {

    @Rule
    public PactProviderRuleMk2 stubProvider = new
PactProviderRuleMk2("customerServiceProvider", "localhost", 8092, this);
    @Autowired
    private AccountClient accountClient;

    @Pact(state = "list-of-3-accounts", provider =
"customerServiceProvider", consumer = "accountClient")
    public RequestResponsePact callAccountClient(PactDslWithProvider
builder) {
        return builder.given("list-of-3-accounts").uponReceiving("test-
account-service")
.path("/customer/1").method("GET").willRespondWith().status(200)
.body("[{\"id\":\"1\",\"number\":\"123\",\"balance\":5000},{\"id\":\"2\",\"
number\":\"124\",\"balance\":5000},{\"id\":\"3\",\"number\":\"125\",\"balan
ce\":5000}]", "application/json").toPact();
    }

    @Test
    @PactVerification(fragment = "callAccountClient")
    public void verifyAddressCollectionPact() {
        List<Account> accounts = accountClient.findByCustomer("1");
        Assert.assertEquals(3, accounts.size());
```

```
    }

  }
```

The JSON test result file generated in the `target/pacts` directory has to be available on the provider side. The simplest possible solution assumes that it can just access the generated file using the `@PactFolder` annotation. Of course, it requires the provider to have access to the `target/pacts` directory. Although it would work for our sample since its source code is stored in the same Git repository, it is not our target solution. Fortunately, we may publish the Pact test result in the network using Pact Broker. Pact Broker is a repository server that provides an HTTP API for publication and consumption of Pact files. We may start Pact Broker locally using its Docker image. It requires a Postgres database as a backend store, so we also start the container with Postgres. Here are the required Docker commands:

```
docker run -d --name postgres -p 5432:5432 -e POSTGRES_USER=oauth -e
POSTGRES_PASSWORD=oauth123 -e POSTGRES_DB=oauth postgres
docker run -d --name pact-broker --link postgres:postgres -e
PACT_BROKER_DATABASE_USERNAME=oauth -e
PACT_BROKER_DATABASE_PASSWORD=oauth123 -e
PACT_BROKER_DATABASE_HOST=postgres -e PACT_BROKER_DATABASE_NAME=oauth -p
9080:80 dius/pact_broker
```

After running Pact Broker on Docker, we have to publish our test report there. We may easily perform this using the Maven plugin `pact-jvm-provider-maven_2.12`. If you run the `mvn clean install pack:publish` command, all the files placed in the `/target/pacts` directory will be sent to the broker's HTTP API:

```
<plugin>
    <groupId>au.com.dius</groupId>
    <artifactId>pact-jvm-provider-maven_2.12</artifactId>
    <version>3.5.12</version>
    <configuration>
        <pactBrokerUrl>http://192.168.99.100:9080</pactBrokerUrl>
    </configuration>
</plugin>
```

The full list of published Pacts can be displayed using the web console available at `http://192.168.99.100:9080`. It also provides the information about the last verification date and the details of every Pact in the list, as shown in the following screenshot:

Producer side

Assuming the consumer has created a Pact and published it on the broker, we may proceed to implement a verification test on the provider side. To enable Pact with JUnit support on the provider side, include the `pact-jvm-provider-junit` dependency to your project. There is also another framework available, `pact-jvm-provider-spring`. This library allows you to run contract tests against a provider using Spring and JUnit. The list of required dependencies is visible on the following fragment of Maven `pom.xml`:

```
<dependency>
    <groupId>au.com.dius</groupId>
    <artifactId>pact-jvm-provider-junit_2.12</artifactId>
    <version>3.5.12</version>
    <scope>test</scope>
</dependency>
<dependency>
    <groupId>au.com.dius</groupId>
    <artifactId>pact-jvm-provider-spring_2.12</artifactId>
    <version>3.5.12</version>
    <scope>test</scope>
</dependency>
```

Thanks to the dedicated library for Spring, we may use `SpringRestPactRunner` instead of the default `PactRunner`. This, in turn, allows you to use the Spring test annotations, such as `@MockBean`. In the following JUnit test, we mock the `AccountRepository` bean. It returns three objects expected by the test on the consumer side. The test automatically starts the Spring Boot application and calls the `/customer/{customerId}` endpoint. There are also two other important things. By using the `@Provider` and `@State` annotations, we need to set the same names as were set for the test on the consumer side inside the `@Pact` annotation. Finally, by declaring `@PactBroker` on the test class, we provide the connection settings to the Pact's repository. Here's sample test using Pact, that verifies contract published by `customer-service`:

```
@RunWith(SpringRestPactRunner.class)
@Provider("customerServiceProvider")
@PactBroker(host = "192.168.99.100", port = "9080")
@SpringBootTest(webEnvironment =
SpringBootTest.WebEnvironment.DEFINED_PORT, properties = {
"eureka.client.enabled: false" })
public class AccountProviderContractTest {

    @MockBean
    private AccountRepository repository;
    @TestTarget
    public final Target target = new HttpTarget(8091);

    @State("list-of-3-accounts")
    public void toDefaultState() {
        List<Account> accounts = new ArrayList<>();
        accounts.add(new Account("1", "123", 5000, "1"));
        accounts.add(new Account("2", "124", 5000, "1"));
        accounts.add(new Account("3", "125", 5000, "1"));
        when(repository.findByCustomerId("1")).thenReturn(accounts);
    }

}
```

Using Spring Cloud Contract

Spring Cloud Contract presents a slightly different approach to contract testing than Pack. While in Pack the consumer is responsible for publishing the contract, in Spring Cloud Contract the initiator of this action is the provider. The contracts are stored in a Maven repository as JARs, containing the stubs automatically generated based on the contract definition file. These definitions may be created using the Groovy DSL syntax. Each of them consists of two main parts: the request and the response specification. On the basis of these files, Spring Cloud Contract generates JSON stub definitions, which are used by WireMock for integration testing on the client side. In contrast to Pact, which is used as the tool supporting consumer-driven contracts testing for REST APIs, it has been designed especially for testing JVM-based microservices. It consists of three subprojects:

- Spring Cloud Contract Verifier
- Spring Cloud Contract Stub Runner
- Spring Cloud Contract WireMock

Let's analyze how they should be used in our contract tests based on the same example that was previously described in the section about the Pact framework.

 WireMock is a simulator for HTTP-based APIs. Some might consider it a service virtualization tool or a mock server. It is able to get up and running quickly by capturing traffic to and from an existing API.

Defining contracts and generating stubs

As I have already mentioned in contrast to Pact, in Spring Cloud Contract, the provider (server side) is responsible for publishing the contract specification. Therefore, we will begin the implementation from `account-service`, which serves the endpoint invoked by `customer-service`. But before proceeding to the implementation, take a look at the following diagram. It illustrates the main components taking part in our testing process. The source code of the sample application is available in the same GitHub repository as the previous samples, but on a different branch contract:

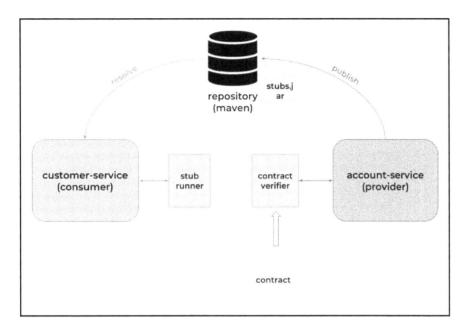

To enable Spring Cloud Contract functionalities for the provider-side application, first you have to include Spring Cloud Contract Verifier to your project dependencies:

```
<dependency>
    <groupId>org.springframework.cloud</groupId>
    <artifactId>spring-cloud-starter-contract-verifier</artifactId>
    <scope>test</scope>
</dependency>
```

The next step is to add the Spring Cloud Contract Verifier Maven plugin, which generates and runs your contract tests. It also produces and installs stubs in the local Maven repository. The only parameter you have to define for it is the package where the base classes extended by the generated test classes are located:

```
<plugin>
    <groupId>org.springframework.cloud</groupId>
    <artifactId>spring-cloud-contract-maven-plugin</artifactId>
    <version>1.2.0.RELEASE</version>
    <extensions>true</extensions>
    <configuration>
<packageWithBaseClasses>pl.piomin.services.account</packageWithBaseClasses>
    </configuration>
</plugin>
```

Now, we have to create a base class for the contract tests. It should be placed within the `pl.piomin.services.account` package. In the following base class, we set up a Spring Boot application with `@SpringBootTest` and then mock away the `AccountRepository`. We also use `RestAssured` to mock Spring MVC and send requests only to our controller. Thanks to all these mocks, the test does not interact with any external components, such as a database or an HTTP endpoint, and tests only the contract:

```
@RunWith(SpringRunner.class)
@SpringBootTest(classes = {AccountApplication.class})
public abstract class AccountProviderTestBase {

    @Autowired
    private WebApplicationContext context;
    @MockBean
    private AccountRepository repository;

    @Before
    public void setup() {
        RestAssuredMockMvc.webAppContextSetup(context);
        List<Account> accounts = new ArrayList<>();
        accounts.add(new Account("1", "123", 5000, "1"));
        accounts.add(new Account("2", "124", 5000, "1"));
        accounts.add(new Account("3", "125", 5000, "1"));
        when(repository.findByCustomerId("1")).thenReturn(accounts);
    }

}
```

We have provided all the configuration and base classes needed for running tests with Spring Cloud Contract. Therefore, we may proceed to the most important part, defining the contract using the Spring Cloud Contract Groovy DSL. All the specifications of the contracts should be located in the `/src/test/resources/contracts` directory. The specific location under this directory, which contains stub definitions, is treated as a base test class name. Each stub definition represents a single contract test. Based on this rule, `spring-cloud-contract-maven-plugin` automatically finds the contract and assigns it to the base test class. In the example we are currently discussing, I have placed my stub definition in the `/src/test/resources/contracts/accountService` directory. So the generated test class name is `AccountServiceTest`, and it also extends the `AccountServiceBase` class.

Here's the sample contract specification that returns a list of accounts belonging to the customer. This contract is not very trivial, so some things need to be explained. You can use regular expressions to write your requests in Contract DSL. You can also provide different values for every property depending on the communication side (consumer or producer). Contract DSL also gives you the ability to reference a request in your response by using the fromRequest method. The following contract returns a list of three accounts, taking the customerId field from the request path and the id field, consisting of five digits:

```
org.springframework.cloud.contract.spec.Contract.make {
  request {
   method 'GET'
   url value(consumer(regex('/customer/[0-9]{3}')), producer('/customer/1'))
  }
  response {
   status 200
   body([
     [
       id: $(regex('[0-9]{5}')),
       number: '123',
       balance: 5000,
       customerId: fromRequest().path(1)
     ], [
       id: $(regex('[0-9]{5}')),
       number: '124',
       balance: 5000,
       customerId: fromRequest().path(1)
     ], [
       id: $(regex('[0-9]{5}')),
       number: '125',
       balance: 5000,
       customerId: fromRequest().path(1)
     ]
   ])
   headers {
    contentType(applicationJson())
   }
  }
}
```

Test classes are generated under the `target/generated-test-sources` directory during the test phase of the Maven build. Here's the class generated from the contract specification described earlier:

```
public class AccountServiceTest extends AccountServiceBase {

    @Test
    public void validate_customerContract() throws Exception {

        // given:
        MockMvcRequestSpecification request = given();

        // when:
        ResponseOptions response = given().spec(request)
 .get("/customer/1");

        // then:
        assertThat(response.statusCode()).isEqualTo(200);
        assertThat(response.header("Content-
Type")).matches("application/json.*");

        // and:
        DocumentContext parsedJson =
JsonPath.parse(response.getBody().asString());
assertThatJson(parsedJson).array().contains("['number']").isEqualTo("123");
assertThatJson(parsedJson).array().contains("['balance']").isEqualTo(5000);
assertThatJson(parsedJson).array().contains("['number']").isEqualTo("124");
assertThatJson(parsedJson).array().contains("['customerId']").isEqualTo("1"
);
assertThatJson(parsedJson).array().contains("['id']").matches("[0-9]{5}");
    }

}
```

Verifying a contract on the consumer side

Assuming we have successfully built and run tests on the provider side, the stubs will have been generated and then published in our local Maven repository. To be able to use them during the consumer application test, we should include Spring Cloud Contract Stub Runner to the project dependencies:

```
<dependency>
    <groupId>org.springframework.cloud</groupId>
    <artifactId>spring-cloud-starter-contract-stub-runner</artifactId>
    <scope>test</scope>
```

```
</dependency>
```

Then we should annotate our test class with `@AutoConfigureStubRunner`. It takes two input parameters—`ids` and `workOffline`. The `Ids` field is a concatenation of the `artifactId`, `groupId`, version number, `stubs` qualifier, and port number, and generally points out to the JAR which stubs are published by the provider. The `workOffline` flag indicates where the repository with the stubs is located. By default, the consumer tries to download artifacts automatically from Nexus or Artifactory. If you would like to force Spring Cloud Contract Stub Runner to download stubs only from the local Maven repository, you can switch the value of the `workOffline` parameter to `true`.

Here's a JUnit test class that uses the Feign client to invoke the endpoint from the stub published by the provider side. Spring Cloud Contract looks for the newest version of the `pl.piomin.services:account-service` artifact. It has been indicated by passing the + sign as a version of the stub inside the `@AutoConfigureStubRunner` annotation. If you would like to use the concrete version of that artifact, you may set the current version from your `pom.xml` file instead of +, for example, `@AutoConfigureStubRunner(ids = {"pl.piomin.services:account-service:1.0-SNAPSHOT:stubs:8091"})`:

```
@RunWith(SpringRunner.class)
@SpringBootTest(properties = {
  "eureka.client.enabled: false"
})
@AutoConfigureStubRunner(ids = {"pl.piomin.services:account-
service:+:stubs:8091"}, workOffline = true)
public class AccountContractTest {

    @Autowired
    private AccountClient accountClient;

    @Test
    public void verifyAccounts() {
        List<Account> accounts = accountClient.findByCustomer("1");
        Assert.assertEquals(3, accounts.size());
    }

}
```

The only thing left is to build the whole project using the `mvn clean install` command in order to verify that tests are running successfully. However, we should remember that the tests created before cover only integration between `customer-service` and `account-service`. In our sample system, there are some other integrations between microservices that should be verified. I'll show you one more example, which tests the whole system. It tests methods exposed `order-service`, which communicates with all the other microservices. For this, we are going to use another interesting feature of Spring Cloud Contract scenarios.

Scenarios

Defining scenarios with Spring Cloud Contract is not difficult. The only thing you have to do is to provide the proper naming convention while creating a contract. This convention assumes that every contract's name that is a part of the scenario is prefixed by an order number and an underscore. All the contracts included in a single scenario have to be located in the same directory. Spring Cloud Contract scenarios are based on WireMock's scenarios. Here's a directory structure with contracts defined for the needs of scenario that creates and accepts an order:

```
src\main\resources\contracts
 orderService\
   1_createOrder.groovy
   2_acceptOrder.groovy
```

The following is the test's source code generated for this scenario:

```
@FixMethodOrder(MethodSorters.NAME_ASCENDING)
public class OrderScenarioTest extends OrderScenarioBase {

    @Test
    public void validate_1_createOrder() throws Exception {
        // ...
    }

    @Test
    public void validate_2_acceptOrder() throws Exception {
        // ...
    }

}
```

Now, let's imagine that we have a lot of microservices, and most of them communicate with one or more other microservices. So, even if you test a single contract, you can't be sure that all other contracts during interservice communication work as expected. However, with Spring Cloud Contract, you may easily include all required stubs to your test class. That gives you the ability to verify all the contracts in the defined scenarios. This is required to include both `spring-cloud-starter-contract-verifier` and `spring-cloud-starter-contract-stub-runner` dependencies to the project. The following class definition acts as a base for the Spring Cloud Contract test class and includes stubs generated by other microservices. The stub generated for `order-service` endpoints may be used by any other external service that needs to verify the contract with `order-service`. A test such as the following code will verify not only the contract between this service and `order-service`, but also the contract between `order-service` and other services used by that service:

```
@RunWith(SpringRunner.class)
@SpringBootTest(properties = {
    "eureka.client.enabled: false"
})
@AutoConfigureStubRunner(ids = {
        "pl.piomin.services:account-service:+:stubs:8091",
        "pl.piomin.services:customer-service:+:stubs:8092",
        "pl.piomin.services:product-service:+:stubs:8093"
}, workOffline = true)
public class OrderScenarioBase {

    @Autowired
    private WebApplicationContext context;
    @MockBean
    private OrderRepository repository;
    @Before
    public void setup() {
        RestAssuredMockMvc.webAppContextSetup(context);
when(repository.countByCustomerId(Matchers.anyString())).thenReturn(0);
        when(repository.save(Mockito.any(Order.class))).thenAnswer(new
Answer<Order>() {
            @Override
            public Order answer(InvocationOnMock invocation) throws
Throwable {
                Order o = invocation.getArgumentAt(0, Order.class);
                o.setId("12345");
                return o;
            }
        });
    }
```

```
}
```

Performance testing

We still have one last type of automated test to discuss. It has already been mentioned at the beginning of the chapter. I am, of course, talking about performance tests. There are some really interesting tools and frameworks that help you to create and run this kind of test. There is a large choice of instruments, especially if we are talking about HTTP API tests. I wouldn't like to discuss all of them, but I will talk about one framework that might be helpful. It's Gatling. Let's take a closer look at it.

Gatling

Gatling is an open source performance testing tool written in Scala. It allows you to develop the tests in an easily readable and writable **domain-specific language** (**DSL**). It stands out from the competition by generating comprehensive, graphical load reports illustrating all the metrics collected during a test case. There are plugins available for integrating Gatling with Gradle, Maven, and Jenkins.

Enabling Gatling

To enable the Gatling framework for a project, we should include the `io.gatling.highcharts:gatling-charts-highcharts` artifact in the dependencies.

Defining the test scenario

Every Gatling test suite should extend the `Simulation` class. In every test class, we may declare a list of scenarios using the Gatling Scala DSL. We usually declare the number of simultaneous threads that can call HTTP endpoints and the whole number of requests sent per single thread. In the Gatling nomenclature, the number of threads is determined by the number of users set using the `atOnceUsers` method. The test class should be placed in the `src/test/scala` directory.

Assuming that we would like to test two endpoints that are exposed by `order-service` running 20 clients, where each of them sends 500 requests sequentially, we would have 20,000 requests sent in total. By sending them all in a short period of time, we would be able to test the performance of our application.

The following test scenario is written in Scala. Let's take a closer look at it. Before running this test, I created some accounts and products by calling the HTTP API, exposed by `account-service` and `product-service`. Because they are connected to an external database, IDs are automatically generated. In order to provide some test data, I have copied them into the test class. Both the lists with the account and product IDs are passed to the test scenario as feeds. Then, during every iteration, the required values are randomly picked from the lists. Our test scenario is named `AddAndConfirmOrder`. It consists of two `exec` methods. The first of them creates a new order by calling the POST `/order` HTTP method. The order's ID is automatically generated by the service, so it should be saved as an attribute. Then it can be used in the next `exec` method, which confirms the order by calling the PUT `/order/{id}` endpoint. The only thing that is validated after the test is the HTTP status:

```scala
class OrderApiGatlingSimulationTest extends Simulation {

    val rCustomer = Iterator.continually(Map("customer" ->
List("5aa8f5deb44f3f188896f56f", "5aa8f5ecb44f3f188896f570",
"5aa8f5fbb44f3f188896f571",
"5aa8f620b44f3f188896f572").lift(Random.nextInt(4)).get))
    val rProduct = Iterator.continually(Map("product" ->
List("5aa8fad2b44f3f18f8856ac9","5aa8fad8b44f3f18f8856aca","5aa8fadeb44f3f1
8f8856acb","5aa8fae3b44f3f18f8856acc","5aa8fae7b44f3f18f8856acd","5aa8faedb
44f3f18f8856ace","5aa8faf2b44f3f18f8856acf").lift(Random.nextInt(7)).get))

    val scn =
scenario("AddAndConfirmOrder").feed(rCustomer).feed(rProduct).repeat(500,
"n") {
        exec(
            http("AddOrder-API")
                .post("http://localhost:8090/order")
                .header("Content-Type", "application/json")
.body(StringBody("""{"productIds":["${product}"],"customerId":"${customer}"
,"status":"NEW"}"""))
                .check(status.is(200), jsonPath("$.id").saveAs("orderId"))
        )
        .
        exec(
            http("ConfirmOrder-API")
                .put("http://localhost:8090/order/${orderId}")
                .header("Content-Type", "application/json")
```

```
                        .check(status.is(200))
            )
        }

        setUp(scn.inject(atOnceUsers(20))).maxDuration(FiniteDuration.apply(10,
    "minutes"))

    }
```

Running a test scenario

There are a few different ways of running a Gatling performance test on your machine. One of them is through one of the available through Gradle plugins, which provide support for running tests during the building of a project. You may also use Maven plugins or just try to run it from your IDE. If you build your project with Gradle, you can also define simple tasks that just run tests by launching the io.gatling.app.Gatling main class. Here's a definition of such a task in the gradle.build file:

```
task loadTest(type: JavaExec) {
    dependsOn testClasses
    description = "Load Test With Gatling"
    group = "Load Test"
    classpath = sourceSets.test.runtimeClasspath
    jvmArgs = [
        "-
Dgatling.core.directory.binaries=${sourceSets.test.output.classesDir.toStri
ng()}"
    ]
    main = "io.gatling.app.Gatling"
    args = [
        "--simulation",
"pl.piomin.services.gatling.OrderApiGatlingSimulationTest",
        "--results-folder", "${buildDir}/gatling-results",
        "--binaries-folder", sourceSets.test.output.classesDir.toString(),
        "--bodies-folder",
sourceSets.test.resources.srcDirs.toList().first().toString() +
"/gatling/bodies",
    ]
}
```

Now you can run that task just by calling the `gradle loadTest` command. Of course, you need to have all the sample microservices, MongoDB, and `discovery-service` started before running those tests. By default, Gatling will print all the requests sent, the received responses, and the final test result, with time statistics and the number of success and failure API calls. If you need more detailed information, you should refer to the files generated after the test, which are available under the `build/gatling-results` directory. You might find that the HTML files there provide visualization in the form of diagrams and graphs. The first of them (shown in the following diagram) shows a summary with the total number of generated requests and the maximum response time broken down by percentiles. For example, you may see that the maximum response time in 95% of responses for the `AddOrder` API is 835 ms:

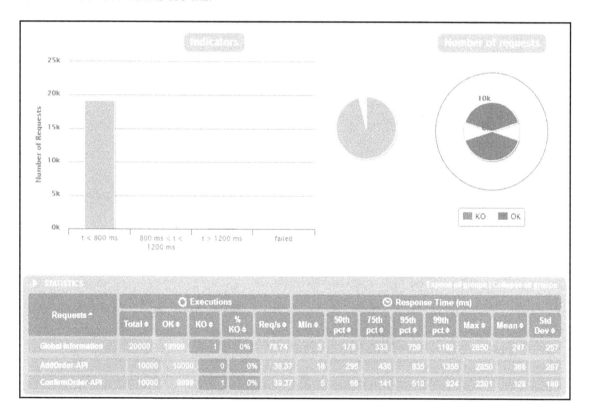

There are also some other interesting statistics visualized. Let's pay particular attention to the following two reports. The first of them shows a graph displaying the percentage of requests grouped by the average response time, while the second shows the timeline with the average response time by percentile:

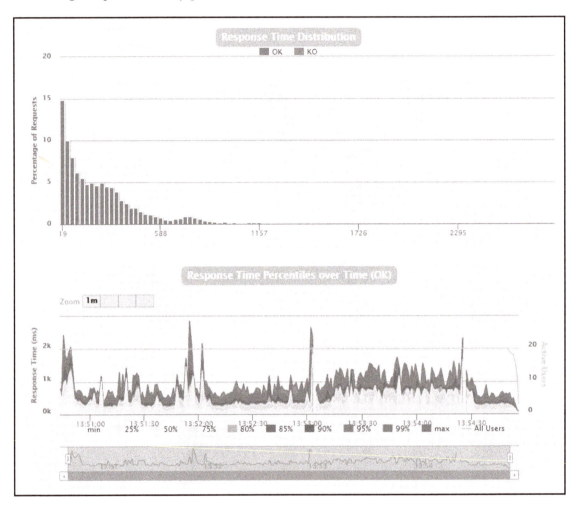

Summary

In this chapter, I have introduced some frameworks that can help you effectively test your REST-based applications written in Java. Each of these solutions has been assigned to a particular type of test. I focused on tests strictly related to microservices, such as contract and component tests. The main goal of this chapter was to compare the two most popular frameworks used for contract testing, namely Pact and Spring Cloud Contract. Despite appearances, there are some significant differences between them. I tried to show you the most important similarities and differences based on the same sample applications that we looked at in previous chapters.

Microservices are strictly related to automation. Remember that migration from monolith to microservices gives you an opportunity to refactor your code, and, moreover, to improve the quality and code coverage of your automated tests. Frameworks such as Mockito, Spring Test, Spring Cloud Contract, and Pact, when used together, give you a really powerful solution to develop tests for REST-based Java microservices. Automated tests are a significant part of the CI/CD process, which will be discussed in the next chapter.

14
Docker Support

We have already discussed the basics of microservices architecture and Spring Cloud projects in the first part of this book. In the second part, we looked at the most common elements of that architecture and we discussed how to implement them using Spring Cloud. So far, we have talked about some important topics related to microservice migration, such as centralized logging, distributed tracing, security, and automated testing. Now, as we are armed with that knowledge, we may proceed to the final part of the book, where we will discuss the real power of microservices as a cloud-native development approach. The ability to isolate applications from each other using containerization tools, implementing continuous deployment in the software delivery process and the ability to easily scale an application are things that all contribute to the rapidly growing popularity of microservices.

As you will probably remember from earlier chapters, we have used Docker images for running third-party tools and solutions on the local machine. With that in mind, I would like to introduce you to the main concepts of Docker, such as its basic commands and use cases. This information will help you to run the samples presented in previous chapters. We will then discuss how to build images with our example Spring Boot application, as well as how to run them inside the containers on the local machine. We will use simple Docker commands for that, as well as more advanced tools such as the Jenkins server, which helps you to perform full, continuous delivery and enables a Continuous Integration process in your organization. Finally, we will introduce one of the most popular tools used for the automation of deploying, scaling, and managing containerized applications: Kubernetes. All of our examples will be run locally on a single-node Kubernetes cluster via Minikube.

The topics we will cover in this chapter are as follows:

- Most useful Docker commands
- Building Docker containers with Spring Boot microservices
- Running Spring Cloud components on Docker
- Continuous Integration/Continuous Delivery with Jenkins and Docker
- Deploying and running microservices on Minikube

Introducing Docker

Docker is a tool that helps you to create, deploy, and run applications by using containers. It was designed with the view to benefit both developers and system administrators in accordance with the DevOps philosophy. Docker helps to improve the software delivery process by solving some important concerns related with it. One of those concerns is the idea of immutable delivery, which is related to something called **it works for me**. It is especially important that a developer uses the same image for their tests as the one that is used in production when working in Docker. The only difference that should be seen is during configuration. Software delivery in an immutable delivery pattern seems to be particularly important for a microservices-based system as there are many applications deployed independently. Thanks to Docker, developers can now focus on writing code without worrying about the target OS (where the application would be launched). The operation can, therefore, use the same interface for deploying, starting, and maintaining all the applications.

There are also many other reasons for Docker's growing popularity. After all, the containerization idea is nothing new in the Information Technology world. Linux containers were introduced many years ago and have been a part of the kernel since 2008. However, Docker has introduced several new things and solutions that other technologies haven't. Firstly, it provides a simple interface that allows you to easily package an application with dependencies to a single container before running it across different versions and implementations of Linux kernel. The container may be run locally or remotely on any Docker-enabled server, and every container starts in seconds. We can also easily run every command on it without going inside a container. In addition, the sharing and distribution mechanisms of Docker images allows developers to commit their changes and push and pull images in the same way they share source code, for example, using Git. Currently, almost all of the most popular software tools are published on Docker Hub as an image, some we have successfully used for running the tools required for our sample applications.

There are some essential definitions and elements that Docker architecture is composed of; the most important is a container. Containers run on a single machine and share the OS kernel with that machine. They contain everything you need to run specific software on your machine code: runtime, system tools, system libraries, and settings. Containers are created from the instructions found within a Docker image. Images are like a kind of recipe or template that defines the steps for installing and running necessary software on a container. Containers can also be compared to virtual machines as they have similar resource isolation and allocation benefits. However, they virtualize the operating system instead of the hardware, making them more portable and efficient than VMs. The following diagram illustrates the architectural differences between a Docker container and a virtual machine:

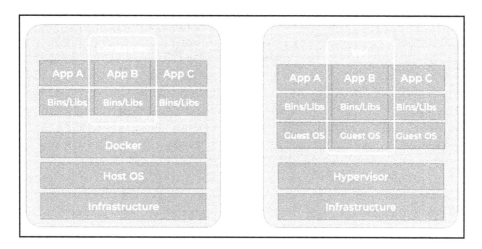

All containers are launched on a physical or virtual machine that is called a **Docker host**. Docker hosts, in turn, run a Docker daemon, which listens for the commands sent by the Docker client through a Docker API. Docker clients may be command-line tools or other software such as Kinematic. Besides running a daemon, a Docker host is responsible for storing cached images and containers created from those images. Every image is built from a set of layers. Each layer contains only the incremental differences from the parent layer. Such an image is not small and needs to be stored elsewhere. This place is called the **Docker registry**. You may create your own private repository or use the existing public repository available on the web. The most popular repository is Docker Hub, which contains almost all of the required images.

Installing Docker

Docker installation instructions for Linux are specific to each distribution (`https://docs.docker.com/install/#supported-platforms`). However, sometimes you have to run a Docker daemon after installation, which you can do by calling the following command:

```
dockerd --host=unix:///var/run/docker.sock --host=tcp://0.0.0.0:2375
```

In this section, we will focus on instructions for the Windows platform. Generally, you have two available options when installing Docker Community Edition (CE) on Windows or Mac. The fastest and easiest way is by using Docker for Windows, which is available at `https://www.docker.com/docker-windows`. This is a native Windows application that provides an easy-to-use development environment for building, shipping, and running containerized applications. This is definitely the best option to utilize, because it uses Windows-native Hyper-V virtualization and networking. There is, however, one disadvantage—it is available only for Microsoft Windows 10 Professional or Enterprise 64-bit. Earlier versions of Windows should use Docker Toolbox, which can be downloaded here at, `https://docs.docker.com/toolbox/toolbox_install_windows/`. This includes the Docker platform, the command-line with Docker Machine, Docker Compose, Kitematic, and VirtualBox. Note that you can't run Docker Engine natively on Windows using Docker Toolbox because it uses Linux-specific kernel features. Instead, you must use the Docker Machine command (`docker-machine`), which creates a Linux VM on the local machine and runs it using Virtual Box. This VM may be accessed by your machine using a virtual address that is, by default, `192.168.99.100`. All previously discussed examples were integrating with the Docker tools available at that IP address.

Commonly used Docker commands

After installing Docker Toolbox on Windows you should run Docker Quickstart Terminal. It does everything that is needed, including creating and starting Docker Machine and providing the command line interface. If you type a Docker command without any parameters, you should now be able to see the full list of available Docker client commands with descriptions. These are the types of commands we will look at:

- Running and stopping a container
- List and remove container
- Pull and push images
- Building an image
- Networking

Running and stopping a container

The first Docker command that is usually run after installation is `docker run`. As you may remember, this command is one of the most commonly used in previous examples. This command does two things: it pulls and downloads the image definition from the registry, in case it is not cached locally, and starts the container. There are many options that can be set for this command, which you can easily check by running `docker run --help`. Some options have one-letter shortcuts, which are often the most commonly used options. Option `-d` runs a container in the background, while `-i` keeps `stdin` open even if it is not attached. If your container has to expose any ports outside, you can use the activate option `-p` with the definition `<port_outside_container>:<port_inside_container>`. Some images need additional configurations that are usually done through environment variables that can be overridden with the `-e` option. It is also often useful to set a friendly name for the container using the `--name` option in order to run other commands on it with ease. Take a look at the example Docker command visible here. It starts the container with Postgres, creates a database user with a password, and exposes it on port `55432`. Now, the Postgres database is available at the address `192.168.99.100:55432`:

```
$ docker run -d --name pg -e POSTGRES_PASSWORD=123456 -e
POSTGRES_USER=piomin -e POSTGRES_DB=example -p 55432:5432 postgres
```

The container with Postgres persists data. The recommended mechanism for containers that store data accessed by outside applications is via volumes. A volume may be passed to the container with the `-v` option, where the value consists of fields separated by a colon, `:`. The first field is the name of the volume, while the second is the path where the file or directory is mounted in the container. The next interesting option is the ability to limit the maximum RAM allocated for the container using the `-m` option. The following are the commands that create new volumes and mount them to the launched container. The maximum amount of RAM is set to 500 MB. The container is automatically removed after stopping using the activated option `--rm`, shown as follows:

```
$ docker volume create pgdata
$ docker run --rm -it -e -m 500M -v pgdata:/var/lib/postgresql/data -p
55432:5432 postgres
```

Every running container can be stopped using the `docker stop` command. We have already set a name for our container so we can easily use it as a label, shown as follows:

```
$ docker stop pg
```

The entire state of the container is written to the disk, so we may run it again with exactly the same set of data as we did before stopping, for example:

```
$ docker start pg
```

If you only want to restart a container, you can use the following command instead of stopping/starting container:

```
$ docker restart  pg
```

Listing and removing containers

If you have started some containers, you may want to consider displaying a list of all the running containers on your Docker machine. The docker ps command should be used for that. This command displays some basic information about the container, such as a list of exposed ports and the name of the source image. This command prints only the currently started containers. If you would like to see containers that have been stopped or are inactive, use option -a on the Docker command, as follows:

If a container is no longer needed, it can be removed using the docker rm command. Sometimes it is necessary that you remove a running container, which is not allowed by default. To force this option, set the -f option on Docker with the following command:

```
$ docker rm -f pg
```

You should remember that the docker ps command removes only the container. The image from which it has been created is still cached locally. Such images can take up a significant amount of space, ranging from a megabyte to several hundred megabytes. You may remove every image by using the docker rmi command with the image ID or name as a parameter, as follows:

```
$ docker rmi 875263695ab8
```

We haven't created any Docker images yet, but it's not unusual to generate a large amount of unwanted or unnamed images during image creation. These images can be easily recognized, as they are denoted with a name of <none>. In Docker nomenclature, these are called **dangling images** and can be easily removed with the following command. The list of all currently cached images can be displayed with the docker images command, shown as follows:

```
$ docker rmi $(docker images -q -f dangling=true)
```

Pulling and pushing images

We've already discussed Docker Hub. It is the biggest and most popular Docker repository available on the web. It is available at https://hub.docker.com. The Docker client, by default, tries to pull all the images for that repository. There are many certified official images for common software such as Redis, Java, Nginx, or Mongo, but you may also find hundreds of thousands of images created by other people as well. If you use the command docker run , the image is pulled from the repository in case it is not cached locally. You may also run the following command docker pull, which is only responsible for downloading an image:

```
$ docker pull postgres
```

The preceding command downloads the newest version of an image (with the latest tag's name). If you would like to use an older version of a Postgres Docker image, you should append the tag with the specific version's number. The full list of available versions is usually published on the image's site, and is no different in this case. Visit https://hub. docker.com/r/library/postgres/tags/ for a list of the available tags.

```
$ docker pull postgres:9.3
```

Once you have run and validated your image, you should think about saving it remotely. The most appropriate place for it is, of course, Docker Hub. However, sometimes you might want to store images in alternative storage, such as a private repository. Before pushing an image, you have to tag it with your registry username, image name, and its version number. The following command creates a new image from a Postgres source image with the name piomin/postgres and the 1.0 version tag:

```
$ docker tag postgres piomin/postgres:1.0
```

Now if you run the `docker images` command you will see two images with the same ID. The first has the name Postgres and the latest tag, while the second has the name `piomin/postgres` and the tag `1.0`. What is important is that `piomin` is my username on Docker Hub. So, before proceeding any further we should first register the image there. After, we should also log in to our Docker client using the `docker login` command. Here, you will be prompted for a username, password, and the email address you used for registration. Finally, you can push a tagged image with the following `docker push` command:

```
$ docker push piomin/postgres:1.0
```

Now all that's left to do is log in to your Docker Hub account using a web browser to check if the pushed image has appeared. If everything worked correctly, you will see a new public repository with your image on-site. The following screenshot shows the image currently pushed to my Docker Hub account:

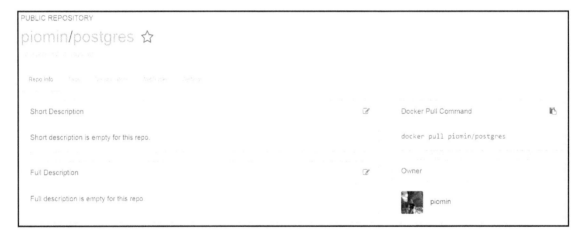

Building an image

In the previous section, we pushed the copy of the Postgres Docker image to a Docker Hub registry. Usually, we push our own images created from the file `Dockerfile`, which defines all the instructions required when installing and configuring software on the container. The details related to the structure of `Dockerfile` will be discussed later. What is important for now, though, is the command used for building a Docker image, `docker build`. This command should be run in the same directory where `Dockerfile` is located. When building a new image it is recommended to set its name and tag using the `-t` option. The following command creates the image `piomin/order-service`, tagged with a `1.0` version. The image may be pushed to your Docker Hub account in the same way as the previous image was with Postgres, as follows:

```
$ docker build -t piomin/order-service:1.0 .
```

Networking

Networking is an important aspect of Docker architecture since we often have to provide communication between applications running on different containers. A common use case may be a web application that needs access to a database. We're now going to refer to another example that has already been introduced in *Chapter 11*, *Message Driven Microservices*. It is communication between Apache Kafka and ZooKeeper. Kafka requires ZooKeeper because it stores a variety of configuration as a key/value pair in the ZK data tree and uses it across the cluster. As you may remember, we first had to create a custom network and run those two containers there. The following command is used to create a user-defined network on a Docker host:

```
$ docker network create kafka-network
```

After the previous command has finished running, you can check out the list of available networks using the following command. By default, Docker creates three networks for you, so you should see four networks with the names bridge, host, none, and `kafka-network`:

```
$ docker network ls
```

The next step is to pass the network name to the container created with the `docker run` command. It can be achieved through the `--network` parameter, as you can see in the following example. If you set the same network's name for two different containers, they will be started on the same network. Let's analyze what this means in practice. If you were inside one container, you could call it its name instead of using its IP address, which is why we could have set the environment variable `ZOOKEEPER_IP` to ZooKeeper when starting a container with Apache Kafka. Kafka, which starts inside this container, connects the ZooKeeper instance on the default port as follows:

```
$ docker run -d --name zookeeper --network kafka-net zookeeper:3.4
$ docker run -d --name kafka --network kafka-net -e
ZOOKEEPER_IP=zookeeper ches/kafka
```

Creating a Docker image with microservices

We have already discussed the basic Docker commands that are available for running, creating, and managing containers. It's now time to create and build our first Docker image that starts the sample microservice that we introduced in the previous chapter. For that, we should move back to the repository available at the address `https://github.com/piomin/sample-spring-cloud-comm.git` and then switch to the branch `feign_with_discovery` on `https://github.com/piomin/sample-spring-cloud-comm/tree/feign_with_discovery`. There, you will find a `Dockerfile` for every single microservice, gateway, and discovery. Before discussing these examples however we should refer to the `Dockerfile` reference to understand the basic commands that we can place there. In fact, `Dockerfile` is not the only way to build Docker images; we're also going to show you how to create an image with a microservice using the Maven plugin.

Dockerfiles

Docker can build images automatically by reading the instructions provided in a `Dockerfile`, a document that contains all the commands that are invoked on the command line to assemble an image. All of those commands have to be preceded by the keywords defined in the `Dockerfile` specification. The following is a list of the most commonly used instructions. They are executed in the order in which they are found in the `Dockerfile`. Here, we can also append some comments that have to be followed by the # character:

Instruction	Description
FROM	This initializes a new build stage and sets the base image for subsequent instructions. In fact, every valid `Dockerfile` has to start with a FROM instruction.
MAINTAINER	This sets author identities of the generated images. This instruction is deprecated, so you may find it in many older images. We should use the LABEL instruction instead of MAINTAINER , as follows:LABEL maintainer="piotr.minkowski@gmail.com".
RUN	This executes Linux commands for configuring and installing the required software in a new layer on top of the current image and then commits the results. It can have two forms:RUN <command> or RUN ["executable", "param1", "param2"].
ENTRYPOINT	This configures a final script that is used when bootstrapping the container that will run as an executable. It overrides all elements specified using CMD and has two forms: ENTRYPOINT ["executable", "param1", "param2"] and ENTRYPOINT the command param1 param2. It is worth noticing that only the last ENTRYPOINT instruction in the `Dockerfile` will have an affect.
CMD	`Dockerfile` can contain only one CMD instruction. This instruction provides the default arguments to ENTRYPOINT using a JSON array format.
ENV	This sets the environment variable for a container in key/value form.
COPY	This copies new files or directories from a given source path to the filesystem inside the container at the path defined by the target path. It has the following form: COPY [--chown=<user>:<group>] <src>... <dest>.

Instruction	Description
ADD	This is an alternative to a COPY instruction. It is allowed to do a little more than COPY, for example, it allows \<src\> to be a URL address.
WORKDIR	This sets the working directory for RUN, CMD, ENTRYPOINT, COPY, and ADD.
EXPOSE	This is responsible for informing Docker that the container listens on the specified network ports at runtime. It does not actually publish the port. The ports are published through the -p option on the docker run command.
VOLUME	This creates a mount point with the specified name. Volumes are the preferred mechanism for persisting data inside Docker containers.
USER	This sets the username and, optionally, the user group used when running the image, as well as for the RUN, CMD, and ENTRYPOINT instructions.

Let's take a look how this works in practice. We should define a Dockerfile for every microservice and place it in the root directory of its Git project. The following is a Dockerfile created for account-service:

```
FROM openjdk:8u151-jdk-slim-stretch
MAINTAINER Piotr Minkowski <piotr.minkowski@gmail.com>
ENV SPRING_PROFILES_ACTIVE zone1
ENV EUREKA_DEFAULT_ZONE http://localhost:8761/eureka/
ADD target/account-service-1.0-SNAPSHOT.jar app.jar
ENTRYPOINT ["java", "-Xmx160m", "-jar", "-
Dspring.profiles.active=${SPRING_PROFILES_ACTIVE}", "-
Deureka.client.serviceUrl.defaultZone=${EUREKA_DEFAULT_ZONE}",
"/app.jar"]
EXPOSE 8091
```

The preceding example is not very complicated. It only adds the microservice-generated fat JAR file to the Docker container and uses the java -jar command as ENTRYPOINT. Even so, let's analyze it step-by-step. Our example Dockerfile performs the following instructions:

- The image extends an existing OpenJDK image that is an official, open-source implementation of the Java Platform Standard Edition. OpenJDK images come in many flavors. The main difference between available images' variants is in their size. The image tagged with 8u151-jdk-slim-stretch provides JDK 8 and includes all the libraries needed to run the Spring Boot microservice. It is also much smaller than a basic image with this version of Java (8u151-jdk).

- Here, we defined two environment variables that can be overridden during runtime that have the -e option of the docker run command. The first is the active Spring profile name, which is by default initialized with a zone1 value. The second is the discovery server's address, which is by default equal to http://localhost:8761/eureka/.
- The fat JAR file contains all the required dependencies together with an application's binaries. So, we have to put a generated JAR file inside the container using the ADD instruction.
- We configure our container to run as an executable Java application. The defined ENTRYPOINT is equivalent to running the following command on a local machine:

```
java -Xmx160m -jar -Dspring.profiles.active=zone1 -
Deureka.client.serviceUrl.defaultZone=http://localhost:8761/eureka/
app.jar
```

- Using the EXPOSE instruction we have informed Docker that it may expose our application's HTTP API, which is available inside the container on port 8091.

Running containerized microservices

Assuming we have prepared a valid Dockerfile for each service, the next step is to build the whole Maven project with the mvn clean install command, before building a Docker image for every service.

When building a Docker image, you should always be in the root directory of every microservice source code. The first container that has to be run in our microservices-based system is a discovery server. Its Docker image has been named piomin/discovery-service. Before running Docker's build command, go to the module discovery-service. This Dockerfile is a little simpler than other microservices, because there is no environment variables to set inside the container, shown as follows:

```
FROM openjdk:8u151-jdk-slim-stretch
MAINTAINER Piotr Minkowski <piotr.minkowski@gmail.com>
ADD target/discovery-service-1.0-SNAPSHOT.jar app.jar
ENTRYPOINT ["java", "-Xmx144m", "-jar", "/app.jar"]
EXPOSE 8761
```

There are only five steps to perform here, which you can see in the logs generated during the target image's build, just after running the `docker build` command. If everything works correctly, you should see the progress of all five steps as defined in `Dockerfile` and the following final messages telling you that the image has been successfully built and tagged:

```
$ docker build -t piomin/discovery-service:1.0 .
Sending build context to Docker daemon 39.9MB
Step 1/5 : FROM openjdk:8u151-jdk-slim-stretch
8u151-jdk-slim-stretch: Pulling from library/openjdk
8176e34d5d92: Pull complete
2208661344b7: Pull complete
99f28966f0b2: Pull complete
e991b55a8065: Pull complete
aee568884a84: Pull complete
18b6b371c215: Pull complete
Digest:
sha256:bd394fdc76e8aa73adba2a7547fcb6cde3281f70d6b3cae6fa62ef1fbde327e3
Status: Downloaded newer image for openjdk:8u151-jdk-slim-stretch
 ---> 52de5d98a41d
Step 2/5 : MAINTAINER Piotr Minkowski <piotr.minkowski@gmail.com>
 ---> Running in 78fc78cc21f0
 ---> 0eba7a369e43
Removing intermediate container 78fc78cc21f0
Step 3/5 : ADD target/discovery-service-1.0-SNAPSHOT.jar app.jar
 ---> 1c6a2e04c4dc
Removing intermediate container 98138425b5a0
Step 4/5 : ENTRYPOINT java -Xmx144m -jar /app.jar
 ---> Running in 7369ba693689
 ---> c246470366e4
Removing intermediate container 7369ba693689
Step 5/5 : EXPOSE 8761
 ---> Running in 74493ae54220
 ---> 06af6a3c2d41
Removing intermediate container 74493ae54220
Successfully built 06af6a3c2d41
Successfully tagged piomin/discovery-service:1.0
```

Once we have successfully built an image, we should run it. We recommend creating a network where all the containers with our microservices will be launched. To launch a container inside a newly created network, we have to pass its name to the `docker run` command using the `--network` parameter. In order to check if a container has been successfully started, run the `docker logs` command. This command prints all the lines logged by the application to the console, as follows:

```
$ docker network create sample-spring-cloud-network
$ docker run -d --name discovery -p 8761:8761 --network sample-spring-
cloud-network piomin/discovery-service:1.0
de2fac673806e134faedee3c0addaa31f2bbadcffbdff42a53f8e4ee44ca0674
$ docker logs -f discovery
```

The next step is to build and run the containers with our four microservices—`account-service`, `customer-service`, `order-service`, and `product-service`. The procedure is the same for each service. For example, if you would like to build `account-service`, first go to that directory within the example project's source code. The `build` command is the same here as it is for the discovery service; the only difference is in the image name, as shown in the following snippet:

```
$ docker build -t piomin/account-service:1.0 .
```

The command to run the Docker image is a little more complicated for `discovery-service`. In this case, we have to pass the address of the Eureka server to the starting container. Because this container is running in the same network as the discovery service container, we may use its name instead of its IP address or any other identifier. Optionally, we can also set the container's memory limit by using the `-m` parameter, for example, to 256 MB. Finally, we can see the logs generated by the application running on the container by using the `docker logs` command as follows:

```
$ docker run -d --name account -p 8091:8091 -e
EUREKA_DEFAULT_ZONE=http://discovery:8761/eureka -m 256M --network
sample-spring-cloud-network piomin/account-service:1.0
$ docker logs -f account
```

The same steps as described previously should be repeated for all other microservices. The final result is the five running containers that can be displayed using the `docker ps` command, as shown in the following screenshot:

All the microservices are registered in the Eureka server. The Eureka dashboard is available at the address `http://192.168.99.100:8761/`, as shown in the following screenshot:

Instances currently registered with Eureka			
Application	**AMIs**	**Availability Zones**	**Status**
ACCOUNT-SERVICE	n/a (1)	(1)	UP (1) - 8020c04e6bf0:account-service:8091
CUSTOMER-SERVICE	n/a (1)	(1)	UP (1) - dae7e9221c1d:customer-service:8092
ORDER-SERVICE	n/a (1)	(1)	UP (1) - 91a7423f9d8b:order-service:8090
PRODUCT-SERVICE	n/a (1)	(1)	UP (1) - c313d0a426bc:product-service:8093

There is one more interesting Docker command that we mention here: `docker stats`. This command prints some statistics related to the started container, such as memory or CPU usage. If you use the `--format` parameter of that command you can customize the way it prints the statistics; for example, you can print the container name rather than its ID. Before running that command you may perform some tests in order to check that everything is working as it should. It's worth checking whether the communication between microservices that was started on the containers has finished successfully. You may also want to try to call the endpoint `GET /withAccounts/{id}` from `customer-service`, which calls an endpoint exposed by `account-service`. We run the following command:

```
docker stats --format "table
{{.Name}}\t{{.Container}}\t{{.CPUPerc}}\t{{.MemUsage}}"
```

The following screenshot is visible:

NAME	CONTAINER	CPU %	MEM USAGE / LIMIT
order	f2c679a1c866	0.14%	208.9MiB / 256MiB
product	83f1761de51f	0.22%	199.6MiB / 256MiB
customer	59e747bdd022	0.23%	210.2MiB / 256MiB
account	28cc8ffcc5f7	0.15%	209.8MiB / 256MiB
discovery	de2fac673806	1.31%	255.3MiB / 1.955GiB

Building an image using the Maven plugin

As we've mentioned previously, Dockerfile is not the only way of creating and building containers. There are some other approaches available, for example, by using Maven plugin. We have many available plugins dedicated to building images, which are used with mvn commands. One of the more popular among them is com.spotify:docker-maven-plugin. This has the equivalent tags in its configuration that can be used instead of Dockerfile instructions. The configuration of the plugin inside pom.xml for account-service is as follows:

```
<plugin>
 <groupId>com.spotify</groupId>
 <artifactId>docker-maven-plugin</artifactId>
 <version>1.0.0</version>
 <configuration>
 <imageName>piomin/${project.artifactId}</imageName>
 <imageTags>${project.version}</imageTags>
 <baseImage>openjdk:8u151-jdk-slim-stretch</baseImage>
 <entryPoint>["java", "-Xmx160m", "-jar", "-
Dspring.profiles.active=${SPRING_PROFILES_ACTIVE}", "-
Deureka.client.serviceUrl.defaultZone=${EUREKA_DEFAULT_ZONE}",
"/${project.build.finalName}.jar"] </entryPoint>
 <env>
  <SPRING_PROFILES_ACTIVE>zone1</SPRING_PROFILES_ACTIVE>
<EUREKA_DEFAULT_ZONE>http://localhost:8761/eureka/</EUREKA_DEFAULT_ZONE
>
 </env>
 <exposes>8091</exposes>
 <maintainer>piotr.minkowski@gmail.com</maintainer>
 <dockerHost>https://192.168.99.100:2376</dockerHost>
<dockerCertPath>C:\Users\Piotr\.docker\machine\machines\default</docker
CertPath>
 <resources>
  <resource>
   <directory>${project.build.directory}</directory>
   <include>${project.build.finalName}.jar</include>
  </resource>
 </resources>
 </configuration>
</plugin>
```

This plugin can be invoked during Maven's `build` command. If you would like to build a Docker image just after building the application, use the following Maven command:

```
$ mvn clean install docker:build
```

Alternatively, you can also set the `dockerDirectory` tag in order to perform a build based on `Dockerfile`. No matter which method you choose, the effect is the same. Any new image that is built with an application will be available on your Docker machine. When using `docker-maven-plugin`, you can force the automated image to push to the repository by setting `pushImage` to `true`, shown as follows:

```
<plugin>
 <groupId>com.spotify</groupId>
 <artifactId>docker-maven-plugin</artifactId>
 <version>1.0.0</version>
 <configuration>
  <imageName>piomin/${project.artifactId}</imageName>
  <imageTags>${project.version}</imageTags>
  <pushImage>true</pushImage>
  <dockerDirectory>src/main/docker</dockerDirectory>
  <dockerHost>https://192.168.99.100:2376</dockerHost>
<dockerCertPath>C:\Users\Piotr\.docker\machine\machines\default</docker
CertPath>
  <resources>
   <resource>
    <directory>${project.build.directory}</directory>
    <include>${project.build.finalName}.jar</include>
   </resource>
  </resources>
 </configuration>
</plugin>
```

Advanced Docker images

Until now, we have built rather simple Docker images. However, it is sometimes necessary to create a more advanced image. We will need such an image for the purpose of Continuous Delivery presentation. This Docker image will be run as a Jenkins slave and would be connected to the Jenkins master, which is started as a Docker container. We have not found such an image on Docker Hub, so we created in by ourselves. Here, the image has to contain Git, Maven, JDK8, and Docker. These are all the tools required for building our example microservices using the Jenkins slave. I will give you a brief summary of the basics related to Continuous Delivery using the Jenkins server in a later section of this chapter. For now, we will focus on just building the required image. The following is the full definition of the image provided inside `Dockerfile`:

```
FROM docker:18-dind
MAINTAINER Piotr Minkowski <piotr.minkowski@gmail.com>
ENV JENKINS_MASTER http://localhost:8080
ENV JENKINS_SLAVE_NAME dind-node
ENV JENKINS_SLAVE_SECRET ""
ENV JENKINS_HOME /home/jenkins
ENV JENKINS_REMOTING_VERSION 3.17
ENV DOCKER_HOST tcp://0.0.0.0:2375

RUN apk --update add curl tar git bash openjdk8 sudo

ARG MAVEN_VERSION=3.5.2
ARG USER_HOME_DIR="/root"
ARG
SHA=707b1f6e390a65bde4af4cdaf2a24d45fc19a6ded00fff02e91626e3e42ceaff
ARG
BASE_URL=https://apache.osuosl.org/maven/maven-3/${MAVEN_VERSION}/binar
ies
RUN mkdir -p /usr/share/maven /usr/share/maven/ref \
 && curl -fsSL -o /tmp/apache-maven.tar.gz ${BASE_URL}/apache-maven-
${MAVEN_VERSION}-bin.tar.gz \
 && echo "${SHA} /tmp/apache-maven.tar.gz" | sha256sum -c - \
 && tar -xzf /tmp/apache-maven.tar.gz -C /usr/share/maven --strip-
components=1 \
 && rm -f /tmp/apache-maven.tar.gz \
 && ln -s /usr/share/maven/bin/mvn /usr/bin/mvn
ENV MAVEN_HOME /usr/share/maven
ENV MAVEN_CONFIG "$USER_HOME_DIR/.m2"

RUN adduser -D -h $JENKINS_HOME -s /bin/sh jenkins jenkins && chmod
a+rwx $JENKINS_HOME
RUN echo "jenkins ALL=(ALL) NOPASSWD: /usr/local/bin/dockerd" >
/etc/sudoers.d/00jenkins && chmod 440 /etc/sudoers.d/00jenkins
```

```
RUN echo "jenkins ALL=(ALL) NOPASSWD: /usr/local/bin/docker" >
/etc/sudoers.d/01jenkins && chmod 440 /etc/sudoers.d/01jenkins
RUN curl --create-dirs -sSLo /usr/share/jenkins/slave.jar
http://repo.jenkins-ci.org/public/org/jenkins-ci/main/remoting/$JENKINS
_REMOTING_VERSION/remoting-$JENKINS_REMOTING_VERSION.jar && chmod 755
/usr/share/jenkins && chmod 644 /usr/share/jenkins/slave.jar

COPY entrypoint.sh /usr/local/bin/entrypoint
VOLUME $JENKINS_HOME
WORKDIR $JENKINS_HOME
USER jenkins
ENTRYPOINT ["/usr/local/bin/entrypoint"]
```

Let's analyze what's happened. Here, we have extended the Docker base image. This is a pretty smart solution, because that image now provides Docker inside Docker. Although running Docker inside Docker is generally not recommended, there are some desirable use cases, such as Continuous Delivery with Docker. Besides Docker, there is other software installed on the image using the RUN instruction, such as Git, JDK, Maven, or Curl. We have also added an OS user, which has sudoers permission in the dockerd script, which is responsible for running the Docker daemon on the machine. This is not the only process that has to be started in the running container; launching JAR with the Jenkins slave is also required. Those two commands are executed inside entrypoint.sh, which is set as an ENTRYPOINT of the image. The full source code of this Docker image is available on GitHub at https://github.com/piomin/jenkins-slave-dind-jnlp.git. You can omit building it from source code and just download a ready image from my Docker Hub account by using the following command:

```
docker pull piomin/jenkins-slave-dind-jnlp
```

Here's the script entrypoint.sh inside Docker image that starts Docker deamon and Jenkins slave:

```
#!/bin/sh
set -e
echo "starting dockerd..."
sudo dockerd --host=unix:///var/run/docker.sock --
host=tcp://0.0.0.0:2375 --storage-driver=vfs &
echo "starting jnlp slave..."
exec java -jar /usr/share/jenkins/slave.jar \
  -jnlpUrl $JENKINS_URL/computer/$JENKINS_SLAVE_NAME/slave-agent.jnlp \
  -secret $JENKINS_SLAVE_SECRET
```

Continuous Delivery

One of the key benefits of migrating to microservice-based architecture is the ability to deliver software quickly. This should be the main motivation for implementing continuous delivery or a continuous deployment process in your organization. In short, the continuous delivery process is an approach that tries to automate all the stages of software delivery such as building, testing a code, and releasing an application. There are many tools that empower that process. One of them is Jenkins, an open source automation server written in Java. Docker is something that can take your **Continuous Integration** (**CI**) or **Continuous Delivery** (**CD**) processes to a higher level. Immutable delivery, for example, is one of the most important advantages of Docker.

Integrating Jenkins with Docker

The main goal here is to design and run the continuous delivery process locally using Jenkins and Docker. There are four elements that have a part in this process. The first of them is already prepared: the source code repository of our microservices, which is available on GitHub. The second element, Jenkins, needs to be run and configured. Jenkins is a key element of our continuous delivery system. It has to download the application's source code from the GitHub repository, build it, and then place the resulting JAR file in Docker image, push that image to Docker Hub, and finally run the container with a microservice. All of the tasks within this process are directly performed on a Jenkins master but on its slave node. Both Jenkins and its slave are launched as Docker containers. The architecture of this solution is illustrated as follows:

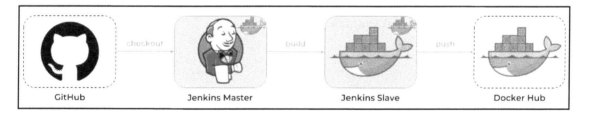

It's worth mentioning that Jenkins is built on the basis of the concept of plugins. The core is too simple an engine for automated builds. The real power of Jenkins is in its plugins, and there are hundreds of them in the Update Center. For now, we will only discuss a few opportunities available to us thanks to the Jenkins server. We will need the following plugins installed to be able to build and run our microservices in Docker containers:

- **Pipeline**: This is a suite of plugins that lets you create automation using Groovy scripts following the idea **Pipeline as code** (https://wiki.jenkins.io/display/JENKINS/Pipeline+Plugin)
- **Docker Pipeline**: This allows you to build Docker containers in pipelines (https://wiki.jenkins.io/display/JENKINS/Docker+Pipeline+Plugin)
- **Git**: This integrates Git with Jenkins (https://wiki.jenkins.io/display/JENKINS/Git+Plugin)
- **Maven integration**: This provides some useful commands when building an application with Maven and Jenkins (https://plugins.jenkins.io/maven-plugin)

The required plugins can be configured using the UI dashboard, either after startup or via **Manage Jenkins** | **Manage Plugins**. To run Jenkins locally, we will use its Docker image. The following commands create the network called `jenkins` and start the Jenkins master container, exposing the UI dashboard on port `38080`. Notice that when you start the Jenkins container and use its web console for the first time you need to set it up using the initial generated password. You can easily retrieve this password from Jenkins logs by invoking the `docker logs jenkins` command as follows:

```
$ docker network create jenkins
$ docker run -d --name jenkins -p 38080:8080 -p 50000:50000 --network
jenkins jenkins/jenkins:lts
```

Once we have successfully configured the Jenkins master with its required plugins, we need to add new slaves' nodes. To do this, you should go to the section **Manage Jenkins | Manage Nodes** and then select **New Node**. In the displayed form, you have to set `/home/jenkins` as a remote root directory, and the launch agent via Java Web Start as the launch method. Now you may start the Docker container with a Jenkins slave, as previously discussed. Note that you will have to override two environment variables indicating the slave's name and secret. The `name` parameter is set during node creation, while the secret is automatically generated by the server. You can take a look at the node's details page for more information, as shown in the following screenshot:

The following is the Docker command that starts a container with the Jenkins slave with Docker in Docker:

```
$ docker run --privileged -d --name slave --network jenkins -e
JENKINS_SLAVE_SECRET=5664fe146104b89a1d2c78920fd9c5eebac3bd7344432e0668
e366e2d3432d3e -e JENKINS_SLAVE_NAME=dind-node-1 -e
JENKINS_URL=http://jenkins:38080 piomin/jenkins-slave-dind-jnlp
```

This short introduction to the configuration of Jenkins should help you to repeat the discussed continuous delivery process on your own machine. Remember that we have only looked at a few aspects related to Jenkins, including settings, which will allow you to set up a CI or CD environment for your own microservices-based system. If you are interested in pursuing this topic in greater depth, you should refer to the documentation available at `https://jenkins.io/doc`.

Building pipelines

In older versions of Jenkins server, the basic unit of work was a job. Currently, its main feature is the ability to define pipelines as code. This change is related to more modern trends in IT architecture that consider application delivery as critical as the application that's being delivered. Since all the components of the application stack are already automated and represented as code in the version control system, the same benefits can be leveraged for CI or CD pipelines.

The Jenkins Pipeline provides a set of tools designed for modeling simple and more advanced delivery pipelines as code. The definition of such a pipeline is typically written into a text file called a `Jenkinsfile`. It supports the domain-specific language with additional, specific steps available through the *Shared Libraries* feature. Pipeline supports two syntaxes: Declarative (introduced in Pipeline 2.5) and Scripted Pipeline. No matter which syntax is used, it will be logically divided into stages and steps. Steps are the most fundamental part of a pipeline as they tell Jenkins what to do. Stages logically group a couple of steps, which are then displayed on the pipeline's result screen. The following code is an example of a scripted pipeline and defines a build process for `account-service`. Similar definitions have to be created for other microservices. All of these definitions are located in the `root` directory of every application's source code as `Jenkinsfile`:

```
node('dind-node-1') {
 withMaven(maven:'M3') {
  stage('Checkout') {
   git url: 'https://github.com/piomin/sample-spring-cloud-comm.git',
credentialsId: 'github-piomin',   branch: 'master'
  }

  stage('Build') {
   dir('account-service') {
    sh 'mvn clean install'
   }
   def pom = readMavenPom file:'pom.xml'
   print pom.version
   env.version = pom.version
   currentBuild.description = "Release: ${env.version}"
  }

  stage('Image') {
   dir ('account-service') {
    def app = docker.build "piomin/account-service:${env.version}"
    app.push()
   }
  }

  stage ('Run') {
   docker.image("piomin/account-service:${env.version}").run('-p
8091:8091 -d --name account --network sample-spring-cloud-network')
  }

 }
}
```

The previous definition is divided into four stages. In the first, `Checkout`, we clone the Git repository with the source code of all the example applications. In the second stage, `Build`, we build an application from the `account-service` module and then read the whole Maven project's version number from `root`'s `pom.xml`. In the `Image` stage we build an image from `Dockerfile` and push it to the Docker repository. Finally, we run a container with the `account-service` application inside the `Run` stage. All the described stages are executed on `dind-node-1` following the definition of a node element, which is a root for all the other elements in the pipeline definition.

Now we can proceed to defining the pipeline in Jenkins' web console. Select **New Item**, then check the Pipeline item type and enter its name. After confirmation you should be redirected to the pipeline's configuration page. The only thing you have to do once there is to provide the location of `Jenkinsfile` in the Git repository and then set the SCM authentication credentials as shown in the following screenshot:

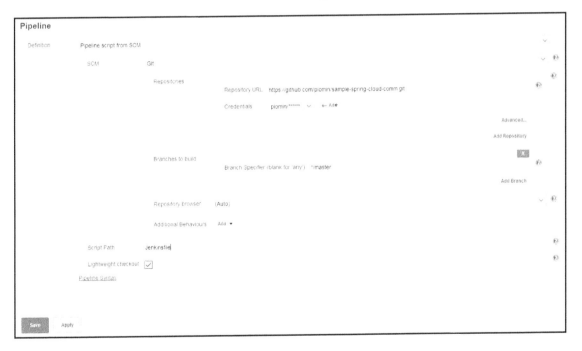

After saving the changes, the configuration of the pipeline is ready. In order to start the build, click the **Build Now** button. There are two things that should be clarified at this stage. In the production mode you can use the `webhook` mechanism, which is provided by the most popular Git host vendors, including GitHub, BitBucket, and GitLab. This mechanism automatically triggers your build on Jenkins after pushing the changes to the repository. In order to demonstrate this, we would have to run the version control system locally with Docker, for example using GitLab. There is also another simplified way of testing. The containerized application is run directly on Jenkins' Docker in Docker slave; under normal circumstances, we would launch on the separated remote machine dedicated only to the deployment of applications. The following screenshot is Jenkins' web console illustrating the build process, divided into different stages, for `product-service`:

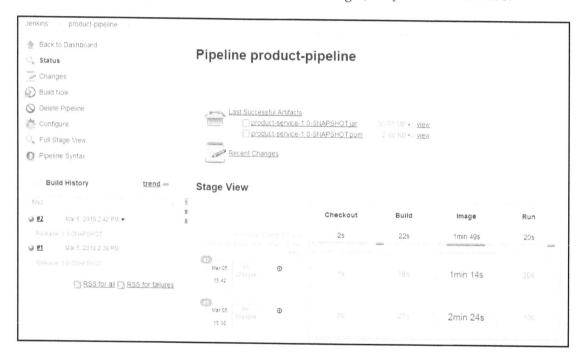

We should now create one pipeline per microservice. The list of all the created pipelines is as follows:

Working with Kubernetes

We have already launched our example microservices on Docker containers. We have even used CI and CD automated pipelines in order to run them on the local machine. You may, however, be asking an important question. How can we organize our environment on a larger scale and in production mode where we have to run multiple containers across multiple machines? Well, this is exactly what we have to do when implementing microservices in accordance with the idea of cloud native development. It turns out that many challenges still remain in this instance. Assuming that we have many microservices launched in multiple instances, there will be plenty of containers to manage. Doing things such as starting the correct containers at the correct time, handling storage considerations, scaling up or down, and dealing with failures manually would be a nightmare. Fortunately, there are some platforms available that help in clustering and orchestrating Docker containers at scale. Currently, the leader in this field is Kubernetes.

Kubernetes is an open-source platform for managing containerized workloads and services. It can act as a container platform, as a microservices platform, as a cloud platform, and a lot more. It automates such actions as running containers across different machines, scaling up and down, distributing load between containers, and keeping storage consistency between multiple instances of an application. It also has a number of additional features, including service discovery, load balancing, configuration management, service naming, and rolling updates. Not all of these features would be useful for us however as many similar features are provided by Spring Cloud.

It is worth mentioning that Kubernetes is not the only container management tool out there. There is also Docker Swarm, the native tool provided within Docker. However, since Docker has announced native support for Kubernetes, it seems to be a natural choice. There are several important concepts and components regarding Kubernetes that we should know before we move on to any practical examples.

Concepts and components

The first term you will probably have to deal with when using Kubernetes is pod, which is a basic building block in Kubernetes. A pod represents a running process in the cluster. It can consist of one or more containers that are guaranteed to be co-located on the host machine and will share the same resources. One container per pod is the most common Kubernetes use case. Each pod has a unique IP address within the cluster but all containers deployed inside the same pod can communicate with others via `localhost`.

Another common component is a service. A service logically groups a set of pods and defines a policy of access to it; it is sometimes called a microservice. By default, a service is exposed inside a cluster but it can also be exposed onto an external IP address. We can expose a service using one of the four available behaviors: `ClusterIP`, `NodePort`, `LoadBalancer`, and `ExternalName`. The default option is `ClusterIP`. This exposes the service on a cluster-internal IP, which makes it reachable only from within the cluster. `NodePort` exposes the service on each Node's IP at a static port, and automatically create `ClusterIP` for exposing service inside a cluster. In turn, `LoadBalancer` exposes the service externally using a cloud provider's load balancer, and `ExternalName` maps the service to the contents of the `externalName` field. We should also take a few moments to discuss Kubernetes's replication controller. This handles replication and scaling by running a specified number of copies of a pod across the cluster. It is also responsible for replacing pods if the underlying node fails. Every controller in Kubernetes is a separate process run by `kube-controller-manager`. You can also find node controller, endpoints controller, and service account and token controllers in Kubernetes.

Kubernetes uses an `etcd` key/value store as a backing store for all cluster data. Inside every node of the cluster is an agent called **kubelet**, which is responsible for ensuring that containers are running in a pod. Every command sent to Kubernetes by a user is processed by Kubernetes API exposed by `kubeapi-server`.

Of course, this is a really simplified explanation of Kubernetes's architecture. There are more components and tools available that have to be configured properly in order to run highly available Kubernetes clusters successfully. This is not a trivial task to perform, and it requires a significant amount of knowledge about this platform. Fortunately, there is a tool out there that makes it easy to run a Kubernetes cluster locally—Minikube.

Running Kubernetes locally via Minikube

Minikube is a tool that makes it easy to run Kubernetes locally. It runs a single-node Kubernetes cluster inside a VM on the local machine. It is definitely the most suitable choice in development mode. Of course, Minikube does not support all of the features provided by Kubernetes; only the most important ones, including DNS, NodePorts, Config Map, Dashboard, and Ingress.

To run Minikube on Windows, we need to have a virtualization tool installed. However, if you have already run Docker, you will have probably installed Oracle VM VirtualBox. In this case, you don't have to do anything other than download and install the latest release of Minikube, which you can check at `https://github.com/kubernetes/minikube/releases`, and `kubectl.exe`, as described at `https://storage.googleapis.com/kubernetes-release/release/stable.txt`. Both files `minikube.exe` and `kubectl.exe` should be included in the `PATH` environment variable. In addition, Minikube provides its own installer, `minikube-installer.exe`, which will automatically add `minikube.exe` to your path. You may then start Minikube from your command line by running the following command:

```
$ minikube start
```

The preceding command initializes a `kubectl` context called `minikube`. It contains the configuration that allows you to communicate with the Minikube cluster. You can now use `kubectl` commands in order to maintain your local cluster created by Minikube and deploy your containers there. An alternative solution to a command-line interface is Kubernetes dashboard. Kubernetes dashboard can be enabled for your node by calling `minikube` dashboard. You can create, update, or delete deployment using this dashboard, as well as list and view a configuration of all pods, services, ingresses, and replication controllers. It is possible to easily stop and remove a local cluster by invoking the following commands:

```
$ minikube stop
$ minikube delete
```

Deploying an application

Every configuration existing on a Kubernetes cluster is represented by Kubernetes objects. These objects can be managed through the Kubernetes API and should be expressed in a YAML format. You may use that API directly, but will probably decide to leverage the `kubectl` command-line interface to make all the necessary calls for you. The description of a newly created object in Kubernetes has to provide specification that describes its desired state, as well as some basic information about the object. The following are some required fields in the YAML configuration file that should always be set:

- `apiVersion`: This indicates the version of the Kubernetes API used to create an object. An API always requires the JSON format in a request but `kubectl` automatically converts YAML input into JSON.
- `kind`: This sets the kind of object to create. There are some predefined types available such as Deployment, Service, Ingress, or ConfigMap.
- `metadata`: This allows you to identify the object by name, UID or, optional namespace.
- `spec`: This is the proper definition of an object. The precise format of a specification depends on an object's kind and contains nested fields specific to that object.

Usually, when creating new objects on Kubernetes, its `kind` is deployment. In the `Deployment` YAML file, shown as follows, there are two important fields set. The first of, `replicas`, specifies the number of desired pods. In practice, this means that we run two instances of the containerized application. The second, `spec.template.spec.containers.image`, sets the name and version of the Docker image that will be launched inside a pod. The container will be exposed on port `8090`, on which `order-service` listens for HTTP connections:

```
apiVersion: apps/v1
kind: Deployment
metadata:
  name: order-service
spec:
  replicas: 2
  selector:
    matchLabels:
      app: order-service
  template:
    metadata:
      labels:
        app: order-service
```

```
    spec:
      containers:
      - name: order-service
        image: piomin/order-service:1.0
        env:
        - name: EUREKA_DEFAULT_ZONE
          value: http://discovery-service:8761/eureka
        ports:
        - containerPort: 8090
          protocol: TCP
```

Assuming the preceding code is stored in the file `order-deployment.yaml`, we can now deploy our containerized application on Kubernetes using imperative management as follows:

```
$ kubectl create -f order-deployment.yaml
```

Alternatively, you can perform the same action based on the declarative management approach, illustrated as follows:

```
$ kubectl apply -f order-deployment.yaml
```

We now have to create the same deployment file for all the microservices and `discovery-service`. The subject of `discovery-service` is a very curious matter. We have the option to use built-in Kubernetes discovery based on pods and services, but our main goal here is to deploy and run Spring Cloud components on that platform. So, before deploying any microservices, we should first deploy, run, and expose Eureka on Kubernetes. The following is a deployment file of `discovery-service` that can also can be applied to Kubernetes by calling the `kubectl apply` command:

```
apiVersion: apps/v1
kind: Deployment
metadata:
 name: discovery-service
 labels:
  run: discovery-service
spec:
 replicas: 1
 selector:
  matchLabels:
    app: discovery-service
 template:
  metadata:
   labels:
    app: discovery-service
  spec:
```

```
containers:
- name: discovery-service
  image: piomin/discovery-service:1.0
ports:
- containerPort: 8761
  protocol: TCP
```

If you create a Deployment, Kubernetes automatically creates pods for you. Their number is equal to the value set in the `replicas` field. A pod is not able to expose the API provided by the application deployed on the container, it just represents a running process on your cluster. To access the API provided by the microservices running inside pods, we have to define a service. Let's remind ourselves what a service is. A service is an abstraction that defines a logical set of pods and a policy by which to access them. The set of pods targeted by a service is usually determined by a label selector. There are four types of service available in Kubernetes. The simplest and default one is `ClusterIP`, which exposes a service internally. If you would like to access a service from outside the cluster, you should define the type `NodePort`. This option has been set out in the following example YAML file; now, all the microservices can communicate with Eureka using its Kubernetes service name:

```
apiVersion: v1
kind: Service
metadata:
 name: discovery-service
  labels:
    app: discovery-service
spec:
 type: NodePort
 ports:
    - protocol: TCP
      port: 8761
      targetPort: 8761
 selector:
    app: discovery-service
```

In fact, all of our microservices deployed on Minikube should be available outside the cluster, as we would like to access the API exposed by them. To do this, you need to provide the similar YAML configuration to that in the preceding example, changing only the service's name, labels and port.

There is only one last component that should be present in our architecture: API Gateway. We could deploy a container with the Zuul proxy, however we need to introduce the popular Kubernetes object, Ingress. This component is responsible for managing external access to services that are typically exposed via HTTP. Ingress provides load balancing, SSL termination, and name-based virtual hosting. The Ingress configuration YAML file is shown as follows; note that all the services can be accessed on the same port, 80, on different URL paths:

```
apiVersion: extensions/v1beta1
kind: Ingress
metadata:
 name: gateway-ingress
spec:
 backend:
  serviceName: default-http-backend
  servicePort: 80
 rules:
 - host: microservices.example.pl
   http:
   paths:
   - path: /account
     backend:
       serviceName: account-service
       servicePort: 8091
   - path: /customer
     backend:
       serviceName: customer-service
       servicePort: 8092
   - path: /order
     backend:
       serviceName: order-service
       servicePort: 8090
   - path: /product
     backend:
       serviceName: product-service
       servicePort: 8093
```

Maintaining a cluster

Maintaining a Kubernetes cluster is rather complex. In this section, we will show you how to use some basic commands and the UI dashboard in order to view the object currently existing on the cluster. Let's first list the elements that have been created for the purpose of running our example microservices-based system. First, we display a list of deployments by running the command `kubectl get deployments`, which should result in the following:

One deployment can create a number of pods. You can check the list of pods by calling the `kubectl get pods` command as follows:

The same list can be viewed using the UI dashboard. You can view these details by clicking on the selected row, or check out the container logs by clicking the icon available on the right-hand side of each row, as shown in the following screenshot:

The full list of available services can be displayed using the command `kubectl get services`. There are some interesting fields here, including one that indicates an IP address on which a service is available inside a cluster (**CLUSTER-IP**), and a pair of ports (**PORT(S)**) on which services are exposed internally and externally. We can also call the HTTP API exposed on `account-service` at the address `http://192.168.99.100:31099`, or the Eureka UI dashboard at the address `http://192.168.99.100:31931`, as follows:

```
C:\Users\minkowp>kubectl get services
NAME                TYPE        CLUSTER-IP      EXTERNAL-IP   PORT(S)           AGE
account-service     NodePort    10.111.189.70   <none>        8091:31099/TCP    3h
discovery-service   NodePort    10.98.219.32    <none>        8761:31931/TCP    3h
kubernetes          ClusterIP   10.96.0.1       <none>        443/TCP           4h
order-service       NodePort    10.98.218.69    <none>        8090:30837/TCP    3h
product-service     NodePort    10.98.83.89     <none>        8093:30565/TCP    2h
```

Similar to previous objects, services can also be displayed using the Kubernetes dashboard, as shown in the following screenshot:

Summary

In this chapter, we discussed a lot of topics not obviously related to Spring Cloud, but the tools explained in this chapter will allow you to take advantage of migrating to microservices-based architecture. When using Docker, Kubernetes, or tools for CI or CD, there is an obvious advantage to cloud-native development with Spring Cloud. Of course, all of the presented examples have been launched on the local machine, but you can refer to these to imagine how that process could be designed in a production environment across a cluster of remote machines.

In this chapter, we wanted to show you how simple and quick it can be to move from running Spring microservices manually on the local machine to a fully-automated process that builds the application from source code, creates and runs a Docker image with your application, and deploys it on a cluster consisting of multiple machines. It is not easy to describe all of the features provided by such complex tools as Docker, Kubernetes, or Jenkins in a single chapter. Instead, the main purpose here was to give you a look at the bigger picture of how to design and maintain a modern architecture based on concepts such as containerization, automated deploying, scaling, and a private, on-premise cloud.

We're now getting very close to the end of the book. We have already discussed most of the planned topics related to the Spring Cloud framework. In the next chapter, we will show you how to use two of the most popular cloud platforms available on the web, allowing you to continuously deliver Spring Cloud applications.

15
Spring Microservices on Cloud Platforms

Pivotal defines Spring Cloud as a framework that accelerates cloud-native application development. Today, when we talk about cloud-native applications, the first thing that comes to mind is the ability to deliver software quickly. To meet these demands, we should be able to quickly build new applications and design architectures that are scalable, portable, and prepared to be frequently updated. The tools that provide the mechanisms for containerization and orchestration help us in setting up and maintaining such an architecture. In fact, tools such as Docker or Kubernetes, which we have looked at in previous chapters, allow us to create our own private cloud and run Spring Cloud microservices on it. Although an application does not have to be deployed on a public cloud, it contains all of the most important characteristics of cloud software.

Deploying your Spring application on a public cloud is just a possibility, not a necessity. However, there are some really interesting cloud platforms that allow you to easily run microservices and expose them on the web in just a few minutes. One of those platforms is **Pivotal Cloud Foundry** (**PCF**); its advantage over other platforms is its native support for Spring Cloud services, including discovery with Eureka, Config Server, and circuit breaker with Hystrix. You can also easily set up a full microservices environment just by enabling brokered services provided by Pivotal.

Another cloud platform that we should mention is Heroku. In contrast to PCF, it does not favor any programming framework. Heroku is a fully-managed, multi-language platform that allows you to quickly deliver software. It can build and run applications automatically once you have pushed changes in the source code stored on the GitHub repository. It also offers many add-on services that can be provisioned and scaled with a single command.

The topics covered in this chapter are as follows:

- Introduction to Pivotal Web Services platform
- Deploying and managing applications on Pivotal Cloud Foundry using CLI, the Maven plugin, and the UI dashboard
- Using Spring Cloud Foundry libraries to prepare an application to work properly on the platform
- Deploying Spring Cloud microservices on the Heroku platform
- Managing brokered services

Pivotal Cloud Foundry

Although the Pivotal platform can run applications written in many languages, including Java, .NET, Ruby, JavaScript, Python, PHP, and Go, it has the best support for Spring Cloud Services and Netflix OSS tools. It makes perfect sense because they are the ones who developed Spring Cloud. Take a look at the following diagram, which is also available on Pivotal's official website. The following diagram illustrates the microservices-based architecture provided by the Pivotal Cloud platform. You can use Spring Cloud on Cloud Foundry to quickly leverage common microservice patterns, including distributed configuration management, service discovery, dynamic routing, load balancing, and fault tolerance:

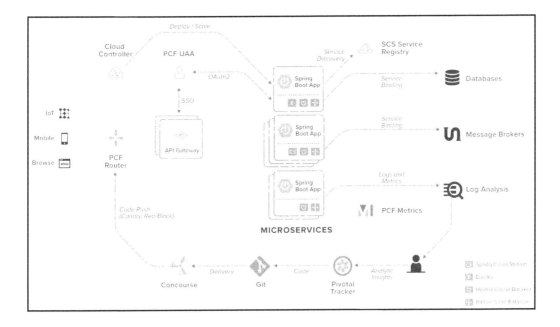

Usage models

You can use the Pivotal platform in three different models. Models are distinguished based on the host, which is where the applications are deployed. The following is a list of the available solutions:

- **PCF Dev**: This instance of the Pivotal platform can be run locally on a single virtual machine. It is designed for experimental and developmental needs. It does not offer all possible features and services. For example, there are only some built-in services, such as Redis, MySQL, and RabbitMQ. However, PCF Dev also supports **Spring Cloud Services** (**SCS**), as well as all the languages supported in the full version of PCF. It is worth noting that if you want to run PCF Dev locally with SCS, you need more than 6 GB of RAM available.

- **Pivotal Web Services**: This is a cloud-native platform available online at `https:/ /run.pivotal.io/`. It's like Pivotal Cloud Foundry with hosted, pay-by-the-hour pricing. It does not offer all the features and services available in Pivotal Cloud Foundry. For example, we may only enable services offered by SaaS partners of Pivotal. Pivotal Web Services is best suited for startups or individual teams. We will use this model of Pivotal platform hosting for presentation purposes in upcoming sections of this chapter.

- **Pivotal Cloud Foundry**: This is a full-featured cloud-native platform that runs on any major public IaaS, including AWS, Azure, and Google Cloud Platform, or on a private cloud based on OpenStack or VMware vSphere. It's a commercial solution for large enterprise environments.

Preparing the application

Since Pivotal Web Services has native support for Spring Cloud applications, the deployment process is very straightforward. However, it does require specific dependencies and configuration on the application side—especially if your microservices have to integrate with built-in services provided by Pivotal platforms such as Service Registry, Config Server, or Circuit Breaker. Besides standard dependency management for Spring Cloud, we should also include `spring-cloud-services-dependencies` in `pom.xml` with the newest version working with the `Edgware.SR2` release train, shown as follows:

```
<dependencyManagement>
    <dependencies>
        <dependency>
            <groupId>org.springframework.cloud</groupId>
            <artifactId>spring-cloud-dependencies</artifactId>
            <version>Edgware.SR2</version>
            <type>pom</type>
            <scope>import</scope>
        </dependency>
        <dependency>
            <groupId>io.pivotal.spring.cloud</groupId>
            <artifactId>spring-cloud-services-dependencies</artifactId>
            <version>1.6.1.RELEASE</version>
            <type>pom</type>
            <scope>import</scope>
        </dependency>
    </dependencies>
</dependencyManagement>
```

Depending on the chosen services for integration you may want to include the following artifacts in your project. We decided to use all of the Spring Cloud features provided by the Pivotal platform, so our microservices fetch properties for a configuration server, register themselves in Eureka, and wrap inter-service communication with Hystrix commands. Here are the dependencies required for enabling discovery client, config client, and circuit breaker for an application deployed on the Pivotal platform:

```
<dependency>
    <groupId>io.pivotal.spring.cloud</groupId>
    <artifactId>spring-cloud-services-starter-circuit-breaker</artifactId>
</dependency>
<dependency>
    <groupId>io.pivotal.spring.cloud</groupId>
    <artifactId>spring-cloud-services-starter-config-client</artifactId>
</dependency>
<dependency>
    <groupId>io.pivotal.spring.cloud</groupId>
    <artifactId>spring-cloud-services-starter-service-registry</artifactId>
</dependency>
```

We will provide one more integration for our sample microservices. All of them will store data in MongoDB, which is also available as a service on the Pivotal platform. To achieve it, we should first include starter `spring-boot-starter-data-mongodb` in the project dependencies:

```
<dependency>
  <groupId>org.springframework.boot</groupId>
  <artifactId>spring-boot-starter-data-mongodb</artifactId>
</dependency>
```

A MongoDB address should be provided in configuration settings using the `spring.data.mongodb.uri` property. In order to allow an application to connect with MongoDB, we have to create a Pivotal's service mLab and then bind it to the application. By default, metadata related to the bound services are exposed to the application as the environment variable `$VCAP_SERVICES`. The main motivation for such an approach is that Cloud Foundry has been designed to be a polyglot, meaning that any language and platform can be supported as a buildpack. All Cloud Foundry properties may be injected using the `vcap` prefix. If you would like to access Pivotal's service, you should use the `vcap.services` prefix and then pass the service's name shown as follows:

```
spring:
  data:
    mongodb:
      uri: ${vcap.services.mlab.credentials.uri}
```

In fact, this is all that needs to be done on the application side to make them work properly with the components created on the Pivotal platform. Now we just have to enable Spring Cloud features in the same way as we did for a standard microservice written in Spring, as shown in the following example:

```
@SpringBootApplication
@EnableDiscoveryClient
@EnableFeignClients
@EnableCircuitBreaker
public class OrderApplication {

    public static void main(String[] args) {
        SpringApplication.run(OrderApplication.class, args);
    }

}
```

Deploying the application

Applications can be managed on the **Pivotal Web Service** (**PWS**) platform in three different ways. The first is through a web console available at `https://console.run.pivotal.io`. We may monitor, scale, restart deployed applications, enable and disable services, define new quotas, and change account settings in this way. However, it is not possible to do this using a web console—in other words, an initial application deployment. It may be performed using a **CLI** (**command-line interface**). You can download the required installer from the `pivotal.io` website. After installation, you should be able to invoke the Cloud Foundry CLI on your machine by typing `cf`, for example, `cf help`.

Using CLI

CLI provides a set of commands that allows you to manage your applications, brokered services, spaces, domains, and other components on Cloud Foundry. Let me show you the most important commands you should know to be able to run your application on PWS:

1. In order to deploy the application, you must first navigate to its directory. You should then sign in to PWS using the `cf login` command as follows:

   ```
   $ cf login -a https://api.run.pivotal.io
   ```

2. The next step is to push the application to PWS with the `cf push` command, passing the service's name:

```
$ cf push account-service -p target/account-service-1.0.0-
SNAPSHOT.jar
```

3. Alternatively, you can provide `manifest.yml` in the application's root directory with all the required deployment settings. In that case, all you need is to run the `cf push` command without any additional parameters, as follows:

```
---
applications:
- name: account-service
  memory: 300M
  random-route: true
  path: target/account-service-1.0-SNAPSHOT.jar
```

4. Deployment with the configuration settings provided in `manifest.yml` as shown in the preceding example will fail. To see why, run the command `cf logs`. The reason is an insufficient memory limit for heap:

```
$ cf logs account-service --recent
```

By default, the platform allocates 240 MB for the code cache, 140 MB for metaspace, and 1 MB for every thread, with an assumption that there is a maximum of 200 threads for the Tomcat connector. It is easy to calculate that, with these settings, every application needs around 650 MB of allocated memory. We may change these settings by calling the `cf set-env` command and passing the `JAVA_OPTS` parameter, as you can see in the following sample. Such a memory limit would not be enough in production mode but would be okay for testing purposes. To ensure that these changes take affect, use the `cf restage` command as follows:

```
$ cf set-env account-service JAVA_OPTS "-Xmx150M -Xss250K -
XX:ReservedCodeCacheSize=70M -XX:MaxMetaspaceSize=90M"
$ cf restage account-service
```

Allocated memory is important, especially if there is only 2 GB RAM available for a free account. With the default memory settings applied, we can only deploy two applications on the Pivotal platform, as each of them takes up 1 GB of RAM. Although we have fixed the problems described previously, our application still does not work properly.

Binding to services

During boot, the applications were not able to connect with the required services. The problem occurs because services are not bound by default to the applications. You can display all of the services created in your space by running the command `cf services`, and bind each of them to a given microservice by invoking the command `cf bind-service`. In the following example command's executions, we have bound Eureka, configuration server, and MongoDB to `account-service`. Finally, we can run `cf restage` once more and everything should work fine, shown as follows:

```
$ cf bind-service account-service discovery-service
$ cf bind-service account-service config-service
$ cf bind-service account-service sample-db
```

Using the Maven plugin

As we have mentioned before, CLI and the web console are not the only ways to manage your application on the Pivotal platform. The Cloud Foundry team has implemented the Maven plugin in order to facilitate and speed up application deployment. What's interesting is that the same plugin can be used to manage pushes and updates to any Cloud Foundry instance, not only those provided by Pivotal.

When using Cloud Foundry's Maven plugin you can easily integrate cloud deployments into their Maven projects' life cycles. This allows you to push, remove, and update projects in Cloud Foundry. If you would like to push your project together with Maven, just run the following command:

```
$ mvn clean install cf:push
```

Generally, the commands provided by the Maven plugin are pretty similar to the commands offered by CLI. For example, you can display a list of applications by executing the command `mvn cf:apps`. In order to delete an application, run the following command:

```
$ mvn cf:delete -Dcf.appname=product-service
```

If you would like to upload some changes to the existing application, use the `cf:update` command as follows:

```
$ mvn clean install cf:update
```

Before running any commands, we have to configure the plugin properly. First, it is required to pass Cloud Foundry login credentials. It is recommended to store them separately in Maven's `settings.xml`. A typical entry inside a server tag might look like the following:

```
<settings>
    ...
    <servers>
        <server>
            <id>cloud-foundry-credentials</id>
            <username>piotr.minkowski@play.pl</username>
            <password>123456</password>
        </server>
    </servers>
    ...
</settings>
```

Using the Maven plugin instead of CLI commands has one important advantage: you can configure all the necessary configuration settings in one place and can apply them using a single command during application build. The full configuration of the plugin is shown in the following snippet. Besides some basic settings including space, memory, and a number of instances, it's also possible to change memory limits with the `JAVA_OPTS` environment variable and by binding the required services to the application. After running the `cf:push` command, `product-service` is ready to use at the address `https://product-service-piomin.cfapps.io/`:

```
<plugin>
    <groupId>org.cloudfoundry</groupId>
    <artifactId>cf-maven-plugin</artifactId>
    <version>1.1.3</version>
    <configuration>
        <target>http://api.run.pivotal.io</target>
        <org>piotr.minkowski</org>
        <space>development</space>
        <appname>${project.artifactId}</appname>
        <memory>300</memory>
        <instances>1</instances>
        <server>cloud-foundry-credentials</server>
        <url>https://product-service-piomin.cfapps.io/</url>
        <env>
            <JAVA_OPTS>-Xmx150M -Xss250K -XX:ReservedCodeCacheSize=70M -
XX:MaxMetaspaceSize=90M</JAVA_OPTS>
        </env>
        <services>
            <service>
                <name>sample-db</name>
```

```
            <label>mlab</label>
            <plan>sandbox</plan>
        </service>
        <service>
            <name>discovery-service</name>
            <label>p-service-registry</label>
            <plan>standard</plan>
        </service>
        <service>
            <name>config-service</name>
            <label>p-config-server</label>
            <plan>standard</plan>
        </service>
    </services>
  </configuration>
</plugin>
```

Maintenance

Assuming all of the applications forming our example microservices-based system have been successfully deployed, we can easily manage and monitor them using the Pivotal Web Services dashboard, or even just CLI commands. The free trial provided by the Pivotal platform gives us a lot of possibilities and tools for maintaining applications, so let's discover some of its most interesting features.

Accessing deployment details

We can list all of the deployed applications by running the command `cf apps` or by navigating to the main site of our space in the web console. You can see that list in the following screenshot. Each row of the table represents a single application. Besides its name, there is also information about its status, the number of instances, allocated memory, deployment time, and a URL at which a service is available outside the platform. If you didn't specify a URL address during application deployment, it is automatically generated:

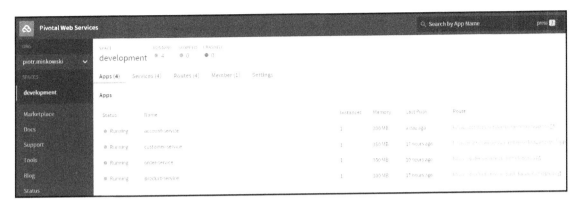

You can click each row in order to discover details about the application. Similar information can be accessed using the CLI commands `cf app <app-name>` or `cf app order-service`. The following screenshot shows the main panel of an application's detailed view that contains the history of events, summary, as well as memory, disk, and CPU usage of every instance. In this panel, you may scale an application by clicking the **Scale** button. There are also several other tabs available. By switching to one of them, you can check out all bounded services (**Services**), external URLs assigned (**Rules**), display logs (**Logs**), and incoming requests history (**Trace**):

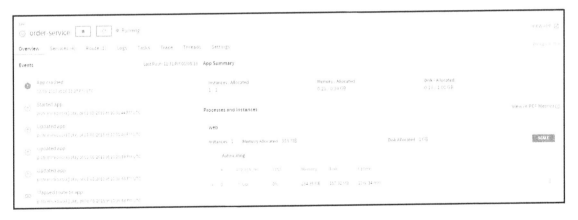

Of course, you can always use the CLI to collect the same details as shown in the previous example. If you execute the command `cf logs <app-name>`, you would be attached to `stdout` , which is generated by the application. You can also display the list of activated Pivotal managed services with the list of bound applications, as shown in the following screenshot:

Managing application life cycles

Another really helpful feature provided by Pivotal Web Services is the ability to manage an application's life cycle. In other words, we can easily stop, start, and restart an application with just one click. Before executing the requested command, you will be prompted for confirmation, as shown in the following screenshot:

The same result can be achieved by running one of the following CLI commands:

```
$ cf stop <app-name>
$ cf restart <app-name>
$ cf start <app-name>
```

Scaling

One of the most important reasons for using cloud solutions is the ability to scale your applications easily. The Pivotal platform deals with these issues in a very intuitive way. Firstly, you may decide how many instances of an application are started at each stage of deployment. For example, if you decided to use `manifest.yml` and deploy it with the `cf push` command, the number of created instances will be determined by field instances, as shown in the following code snippet:

```
---
applications:
- name: account-service
  memory: 300M
  instances: 2
  host: account-service-piomin
  domain: cfapps.io
  path: target/account-service-1.0-SNAPSHOT.jar
```

The number of running instances, as well as memory and CPU limits, can be modified on the started application. In fact, there are two available approaches to scaling. You can either manually set how many instances should be launched or enable autoscaling, where you only need to define a criteria based on a selected metric's thresholds. Autoscaling on the Pivotal platform is realized by a tool called **PCF App Autoscaler**. We can choose from the following five available rules, and they are as follows:

- CPU utilization
- Memory utilization
- HTTP latency
- HTTP throughput
- RabbitMQ depth

You can define more than one active rule. Each of these rules has a minimum value per every single metric for scaling down and a maximum value for scaling up. Autoscale settings for `customer-service` are shown in the following screenshot. Here, we decided to apply HTTP throughput and HTTP latency rules. If latency for 99% of traffic is lower than `20` ms, one instance of an application should be disabled in case there is more than one instance. Analogously, if a latency is greater than `200` ms, the platform should attach one more instance:

We can also control the number of running instances manually. Autoscaling has many advantages but a manual approach gives you more control over that process. Thanks to limited memory for each application, there is still space for other instances. The most overloaded application in our example system is `account-service`, because it is called during an order's creation as well as order's confirmation. So, let's add one more instance of that microservice. To do so, go to the `account-service` details panel and click on **Scale** under **Processes and Instances**. You should then increase the number of instances and apply the necessary changes; you should then see two instances of `account-service` available, as shown in the following screenshot:

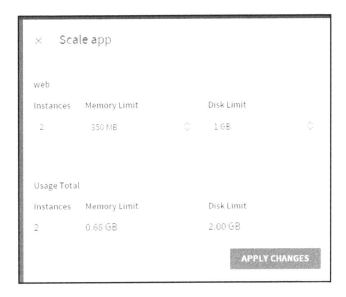

Provisioning brokered services

We have already looked at how to bind an application to a service using the `cf bind-service` command and the Maven plugin. However, we should now look at how to enable and configure our service. You can easily display a list of all the available services and then enable them using Pivotal's dashboard; this can be found under **Marketplace**.

The provisioning of a brokered service with Pivotal Web Services is very easy. After installation, some services are already available to use without any additional configuration. All we have to do is to bind them to selected applications and properly pass their network addresses in the application's settings. Every application can be easily bound to a service using the UI dashboard. First, navigate to the main page of the service. There, you will see a list of the currently bound applications. You can bind a new application to the service by clicking **BIND APP** and then choosing one from the list displayed, as shown in the following screenshot:

You don't have to do anything more than enable the registry service in the marketplace and bind it to the application in order to enable the discovery feature on Pivotal Web Services. Of course, you can override some configuration settings on the client-side if needed. A full list of registered applications can be displayed in the Eureka dashboard under **Manage** in the main configuration panel of the service. There are two running instances of account-service because we scaled it up in the previous section; the other microservices however have only one running instance, shown as follows:

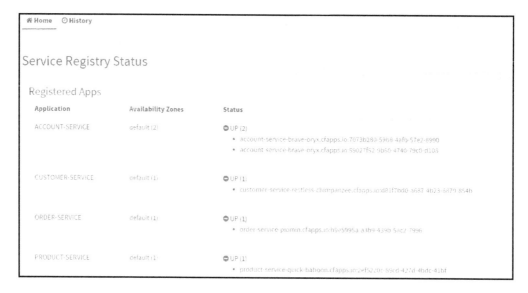

In contrast to a discovery service, a configuration server needs to include additional settings. As before, you should navigate to its main panel and then select **Manage**. Here, you will be redirected to the configuration form. The configuration parameters have to be provided there as a JSON object. The `count` parameter specifies the number of nodes needed for provision, upgrade options if an instance can be upgraded, and `force` forces that upgrade even if the instance is already the latest available version. Other configuration parameters are dependent on a type of backend used to store property sources. As you may remember from `Chapter 5`, *Distributed Configuration with Spring Cloud Config*, the most popular solution for Spring Cloud Config Server is based on the Git repository. We have created an example repository on GitHub, where all the required sources have been committed. The following are the parameters in a JSON format that should be provided for a Config Server on Pivotal Web Services:

```
{
    "count": 1,
    "git": {
        "password": "****",
        "uri":
"https://github.com/piomin/sample-spring-cloud-pcf-config.git",
        "username": "piomin"
    }
}
```

The last brokered service used by the example application provided hosted an instance of MongoDB. After navigating to **Manage** on the main panel of that service, you should be redirected to `https://mlab.com/home`, where you will be able to use the database's node.

The Heroku platform

Heroku is one of the oldest cloud platforms created using the **PaaS** (**Platform as a Service**) model. In comparison to Pivotal Cloud Foundry, Heroku doesn't have built-in support for Spring Cloud applications. It complicates our model a little because we can't use a platform's services to enable typical microservices components, including service discovery, a configuration server, or a circuit breaker. In spite of this, Heroku contains some really interesting features that are not provided by Pivotal Web Services.

Deployment methods

We can manage our application using the CLI, web console or a dedicated Maven plugin. Deploying Heroku is pretty similar to deploying the Pivotal platform, however, the methods are slightly different. The main approach assumes that you deploy the application by building it from the source code stored in your local Git repository or on GitHub. The build is executed by the Heroku platform automatically after you have pushed some changes in a branch to a repository, or on demand from the newest version of the code in the selected branch. Another interesting way to deploy an application is by pushing your Docker image to Heroku's container registry.

Using the CLI

You can begin by installing **Heroku Command Line Interface** (**CLI**) available at `https://cli-assets.heroku.com/heroku-cli/channels/stable/heroku-cli-x64.exe` (for Windows). In order to deploy and run your application on Heroku using CLI you have to perform the following steps:

1. After installation, you can use the command `Heroku` from your shell. First, log in to Heroku using your credentials, as follows:

   ```
   $ heroku login
   Enter your Heroku credentials:
   Email: piotr.minkowski@play.pl
   Password: ********
   Logged in as piotr.minkowski@play.pl
   ```

2. Next, navigate to the application's `root` directory and create an application on Heroku. After running the following command, not only will the application be created, but a Git remote called `heroku` will as well. This is associated with your local Git repository, shown as follows:

   ```
   $ heroku create
   Creating app... done, aqueous-retreat-66586
   https://aqueous-retreat-66586.herokuapp.com/ |
   https://git.heroku.com/aqueous-retreat-66586.git
   Git remote heroku added
   ```

3. Now you can deploy your application by pushing the code to Heroku's Git remote. Heroku will then do all the work for you, as follows:

   ```
   $ git push heroku master
   ```

4. If the application is started successfully, you will be able to manage it using some basic commands. In accordance with the order presented as follows, you can display logs, change the number of running dynos (in other words, scale the application), assign new add-ons, and list all of the enabled add-ons:

```
$ heroku logs --tail
$ heroku ps:scale web=2
$ heroku addons:create mongolab
$ heroku addons
```

Connecting to the GitHub repository

Personally, I prefer to deploy my applications to Heroku by connecting to the projects using the GitHub repository. There are two possible approaches related to this deployment method: manual and automatic. You can choose either by navigating to the **Deploy** tab on the application's details panel and then connect it to the specified GitHub repository, as you can see in the following screenshot. If you click the **Deploy Branch** button, the building of and the deployment to Heroku would immediately start on the given Git branch. Alternatively, you can also enable automatic deploys on the chosen branch by clicking **Enable Automatic Deploys**. Additionally, you can configure Heroku to wait for a Continuous Integration build result if it is enabled for your GitHub repository; this is a really helpful feature because it allows you to run automated tests on your project and ensure they have passed before it is pushed:

Docker Container Registry

Following the newest trends, Heroku allows you to deploy a containerized application using Docker. In order to be able to do that, you should have Docker and the Heroku CLI installed on your local machine:

1. First, log in to Heroku Cloud by running the command `heroku login`. The next step is to log in to the Container Registry:

   ```
   $ heroku container:login
   ```

2. Next, make sure that your current directory contains `Dockerfile`. If present, you can proceed to building and pushing the image to Heroku's Container Registry by executing the following command:

   ```
   $ heroku container:push web
   ```

3. If you have an existing built image, you may only be interested in tagging and pushing it to Heroku. In order to do that, you need to use Docker's command line by executing the following commands (assuming your application's name is `piomin-order-service`):

   ```
   $ docker tag piomin/order-service registry.heroku.app/piomin-order-service/web
   $ docker push registry.heroku.app/piomin-order-service/web
   ```

After the image has been successfully pushed, the new application should be visible in the Heroku dashboard.

Preparing an application

When deploying an application based on Spring Cloud components to Heroku, we no longer have to perform any extra changes in its source code or add any additional libraries, which we do when running it locally. The only difference here is in the configuration settings, where we should set an address in order to integrate the application with service discovery, databases, or any other add-on that can be enabled for your microservice. The current example, which is the same as the examples provided for Pivotal's deployment, is to store data in MongoDB that is assigned to the application as an mLab service. Additionally, here, each client registers itself on the Eureka server, which is deployed as `piomin-discovery-service`. The following screenshot displays a list of the applications deployed on Heroku for our examples:

I deployed the previous applications on Heroku by connecting them with the GitHub repository. This, in turn, requires you to create a separate repository per microservice. For example, the repository of `order-service` is available at `https://github.com/piomin/sample-heroku-order-service.git`; other microservices may be at under similar addresses. You can easily fork these microservices and deploy them on your Heroku account in order to perform tests.

Now let's take a look at the configuration settings provided for one of our example applications: `account-service`. First, we have to override the auto-configured address of MongoDB using the `MONGODB_URI` environment variable provided by the Heroku platform. There is also a necessity to provide the correct address of a Eureka server, as well as override the hostname and port sent by a discovery client during registration. This is required because, by default, each application will try to register using an internal address that is not available for other applications. Without overriding these values, inter-service communication with the Feign client would be unsuccessful:

```
spring:
  application:
    name: account-service
  data:
    mongodb:
      uri: ${MONGODB_URI}
  eureka:
    instance:
      hostname: ${HEROKU_APP_NAME}.herokuapp.com
      nonSecurePort: 80
    client:
      serviceUrl:
        defaultZone: http://piomin-discovery-service.herokuapp.com/eureka
```

Notice that the environment variable `HEROKU_APP_NAME` is the name of the current application deployed on Heroku, as seen in the preceding snippet. This is not available by default. To enable a variable for your application, for example, `customer-service`, run the following command with the experimental add-on `runtime-dyno-metadata`:

```
$ heroku labs:enable runtime-dyno-metadata -a piomin-customer-service
```

Testing deployments

After deployment, every application is available at an address made up of its name and a platform's domain name, for example, `http://piomin-order-service.herokuapp.com`. You are able to call the Eureka dashboard exposes using the URL, `http://piomin-discovery-service.herokuapp.com/`, which will allow you to check whether our example microservices have been registered. If everything worked correctly, you should see something similar to the following screenshot:

Instances currently registered with Eureka			
Application	AMIs	Availability Zones	Status
ACCOUNT-SERVICE	n/a (1)	(1)	UP (1) - 4786503c-2d95-43d3-a7f0-111186aa0692.prvt.dyno.rt.heroku.com:account-service:19265
CUSTOMER-SERVICE	n/a (1)	(1)	UP (1) - bb2db4a3-2923-4fc4-a4ce-407c2b7d26be.prvt.dyno.rt.heroku.com:customer-service:35135
ORDER-SERVICE	n/a (1)	(1)	UP (1) - 770d1584-9fe4-4536-8835-5d376f365a28.prvt.dyno.rt.heroku.com:order-service:43145
PRODUCT-SERVICE	n/a (1)	(1)	UP (1) - d529d914-9da9-45e0-9b40-c4a0ce4b6364.prvt.dyno.rt.heroku.com:product-service:17541

Each microservice exposes API documentation automatically generated by Swagger2, so you can easily test every endpoint by calling it from the Swagger UI dashboard, available on `/swagger-ui.html`; for example, `http://piomin-order-service.herokuapp.com/swagger-ui.html`. The HTTP API visualization for `order-service` is as follows:

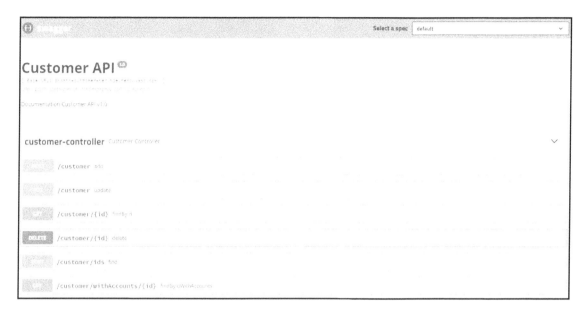

Each microservice stores data in MongoDB. This database can be enabled for your project by adding add-ons provided by Heroku, for example, mLab. As you may remember, we have already used an example of the same service for storing data in applications deployed on the Pivotal platform. Add-ons can be enabled for an application by provisioning it with the selected plan in the **Resources** tab of every application's details panel. Once done, you can manage every plugin by simply clicking on it. For mLab, you will be redirected to the mLab (`mlab.com`) site, where you are able to see a list of all the collections, users, and generated statistics. The following screenshot illustrates the mLab dashboard for our examples:

Summary

We have reached the end of our Spring Cloud microservices journey! Our exercises began with simple deployments on the local machine, but in the last chapter we deployed our microservices in an environment fully-managed by the cloud vendor, which also automatically built, started, and exposed HTTP APIs on specified domains. I personally think that it is amazing how easily we can run, scale, and expose data outside an application using any of the most popular programming languages or third-party tools, such as a database or a message broker. In fact, each one of us can now implement and launch a production-ready application to the web within a few hours without worrying about the software that has to be installed.

This chapter has shown you how easily you can run Spring Cloud microservices on different platforms. The given examples illustrate the real power of cloud-native applications. No matter whether you launch an application locally on your laptop, inside a Docker Container, using Kubernetes, or on an online cloud platform such as Heroku or Pivotal Web Services, you don't have to change anything in the application's source code; the modifications have to be performed only in its properties. (Assuming you use Config Server in your architecture, these changes are not invasive.)

In the last two chapters, we looked at some of the most recent trends seen in the IT world. Such topics as CI and CD, containerization with Docker, orchestration using Kubernetes, and cloud platforms are increasingly used by many organizations. In fact, these solutions are partly responsible for the increasing popularity of microservices. Currently, there is one leader in this area of programming—Spring Cloud. There is no other Java framework with as many features, or that can implement so many patterns related to microservices, as Spring Cloud. I hope this book will help you to use this framework effectively when building and honing your microservice-based enterprise system.

Other Books You May Enjoy

If you enjoyed this book, you may be interested in these other books by Packt:

Spring: Microservices with Spring Boot
Ranga Rao Karanam

ISBN: 978-1-78913-258-8

- Use Spring Initializr to create a basic spring project
- Build a basic microservice with Spring Boot
- Implement caching and exception handling
- Secure your microservice with Spring security and OAuth2
- Deploy microservices using self-contained HTTP server
- Monitor your microservices with Spring Boot actuator
- Learn to develop more effectively with developer tools

Spring Security - Third Edition

Mick Knutson, Robert Winch, Peter Mularien

ISBN: 978-1-78712-951-1

- Understand common security vulnerabilities and how to resolve them
- Learn to perform initial penetration testing to uncover common security vulnerabilities
- Implement authentication and authorization
- Learn to utilize existing corporate infrastructure such as LDAP, Active Directory, Kerberos, CAS, OpenID, and OAuth
- Integrate with popular frameworks such as Spring, Spring-Boot, Spring-Data, JSF, Vaaden, jQuery, and AngularJS.
- Gain deep understanding of the security challenges with RESTful webservices and microservice architectures
- Integrate Spring with other security infrastructure components like LDAP, Apache Directory server and SAML

Leave a review - let other readers know what you think

Please share your thoughts on this book with others by leaving a review on the site that you bought it from. If you purchased the book from Amazon, please leave us an honest review on this book's Amazon page. This is vital so that other potential readers can see and use your unbiased opinion to make purchasing decisions, we can understand what our customers think about our products, and our authors can see your feedback on the title that they have worked with Packt to create. It will only take a few minutes of your time, but is valuable to other potential customers, our authors, and Packt. Thank you!

Index

www.ingramcontent.com/pod-product-compliance
Lightning Source LLC
Chambersburg PA
CBHW060648060326
40690CB00020B/4558